TUPELO

TUPELO

*The True Story of a Northern Clergyman's
Escape from a Confederate Prison*

John Hill Aughey
Edited by Paul Dennis Sporer

BYLANY PRESS

ANZA PUBLISHING, Chester, NY 10918
Blyany Press is an imprint of Anza Publishing
Copyright © 2005 by Anza Publishing

This work is a new edition of *Tupelo* by Rev. John H. Aughey, originally
published in 1905 by Rhodes & McClure.

Library of Congress Cataloging-in-Publication Data
Aughey, John H. (John Hill), 1828–1911.
    Tupelo / John Hill Aughey ; editor, Paul D. Sporer.
        p.   cm.
    Includes index.
    ISBN 1–932490–25–6 (hardcover: alk. paper)
    ISBN 1–932490–03–5 (softcover: alk. paper)
    1. Aughey, John H. (John Hill), 1828–1911.
    2. Unionists (United States Civil War)—Confederate States of
    America—Biography.
    3. Political prisoners—Mississippi—Tupelo—Biography.
    4. Escapes—Mississippi—Tupelo—History—19th century.
    5. United States—History—Civil War, 1861–1865—Personal
    narratives.
    6. Slavery—Political aspects—Southern States—History—19th
    century.
    7. Secession—Southern States.
    8. Southern States—Politics and government—1775–1865.
    9. Tupelo (Miss.)—Biography.
I. Sporer, Paul D. II. Title.

E458.7.A9 2004
973.7'114'0975—dc22   2004015362

Visit AnzaPublishing.com for more information on outstanding authors
and titles. Please support our efforts to restore great literature to a place
of prominence in our culture.

ISBN 1–932490–25–6 (hardcover)
ISBN 1–932490–03–5 (softcover)

∞ This book is printed on acid-free paper.

Contents

Editor's Preface

Repression of dissent in the pre-Civil War South is an issue that is rarely discussed. Although it is known that Southerners and their government officials did not generally tolerate criticism of the prevailing concepts of slavery and states' rights, we have less reliable information as to the extent and methods of censorship. Furthermore, in order to obtain a full understanding of the culture that led to the Civil War, we need to challenge many "facts" of dubious authenticity, especially in respect to the moral and ethical codes of the "genteel" South.

Tupelo, by John Hill Aughey, is a brilliant first person, truthful account, of a Northern clergyman imprisoned and condemned to execution by the brutal officials of the South for his outspoken anti-Secession and pro-Union beliefs. He makes a miraculous escape, to report the details of his ordeal in, what was to become, a highly praised autobiography. Indeed, this book paints a grim picture of political fanaticism, where human rights and justice are sacrificed in the name of patriotism.

Although he has harsh words for his captors, Aughey portrays other Southerners with sympathy. He realized that some residents of the slave states had to conceal their anti-government opinions, lest they too be persecuted, and he urged Northerners not to censure them for their silence. He was especially eager to protect the reputation of his fellow ministers, saying that many had protested slavery and secession before the oppression came, and that at the right time they would again be heard, when constitutional law was restored.

Aughey originally wrote of his personal experiences in a book called *The Iron Furnace of Secession*, published in 1863. He greatly expanded on this work, and it was issued in a new edition entitled *Tupelo* in 1888. In 1905, Rhodes & McClure published a further version of it, which is the one we have used here. We wanted to preserve the exciting narrative, and to focus on Aughey's complex and deeply-felt emotions towards his captors, Southern officials, and clergymen. Thus, the work has been shortened by removing certain digressions. For easier cross-reference to the numerous persons and situations mentioned, we have added an index.

PAUL DENNIS SPORER

Chapter One

At the breaking out of the present rebellion, I was engaged in the work of an Evangelist in the counties of Choctaw and Attala in Central Mississippi. My congregations were large, and my duties onerous. Being constantly employed in ministerial labors, I had no time to intermeddle with politics, leaving all such questions to statesmen, giving the complex issues of the day only sufficient attention to enable me to vote intelligently. Thus was I engaged when the great political campaign of 1860 commenced — a campaign conducted with greater virulence and asperity than any I have ever witnessed. During my casual detention at a store, Colonel Drane arrived according to appointment, to address the people of Choctaw. He was a member of one of my congregations, and as he had long been a leading statesman in Mississippi, having for many years presided over the state senate, I expected to hear a speech of marked ability, unfolding the true issues before the people, with all the dignity, suavity, and earnestness of a gentleman and patriot; but I found his whole speech to be a tirade of abuse of the North, commingled with the bold avowal of treasonable sentiments. The Colonel thus addressed the people:

"MY FELLOW-CITIZENS — I appear before you to urge anew resistance against the encroachments and aggressions of the Yankees. If the Black Republicans carry their ticket, and Old Abe is elected, our right to carry our slaves into the territories will be denied us; and who dare say that he would be a base, craven submissionist, when our God-given and constitutional right to carry slavery into the common domain is wickedly taken from the South. The Yankees cheated us out of Kansas by their infernal Emigrant Aid Societies. They cheated us out of California, which our blood and treasure purchased, for the South sent ten men to one that was sent by the North to the Mexican war, and thus we have no foothold on the Pacific coast; and even now we pay five dollars for the support of the general Government where the North pays one. We help to pay bounties to the Yankee fishermen in New England; indeed we are always paying, paying, paying, and yet the North is always crying, give, give, give. The South has indeed made the North rich, and what thanks do we receive? Our rights are trampled on, our slaves are spirited by thousands over their underground railroad to Canada, our citizens are insulted while traveling in the North, and their servants are tampered with, and by false representations, and often by mob violence, forced from them. Douglas, knowing the power of Emigrant Aid Societies, proposes squatter sovereignty, with the positive certainty that the scum of Europe and the mudsills of Yankeedom can be shipped in, in numbers sufficient to control the destiny of the embryo state. Since the admission of Texas in 1845, there has not been a single foot of slave territory secured to the South, while the North has added to their list the extensive states of California, Minnesota, and Oregon, and Kansas is as good as theirs; while, if Lincoln is elected, the Wilmot proviso will be extended over all the common territories, debarring the South forever from her right to share the public domain.

"The hypocrites of the North tell us that slave-holding is sinful. Well, suppose it is. Upon us and our children let the guilt of this sin rest; we are willing to bear it, and it is none of their business. We are a more moral people than they are. Who originated Mormonism, Millerism, Spirit-rappings, Abolitionism, Free-lovism, and all other abominable 'isms' which curse the world. The reply is, the North. Their puritanical fanaticism and hypocrisy is patent to all. Talk to us of the sin of slavery, when the only difference between us is that our slaves are black and theirs white. They treat their white slaves, the Irish and Dutch, in a cruel manner, giving them just enough to purchase coarse clothing, and when they become sick they are turned off to starve, as they do by hundreds every year. A female servant in the North must have a testimonial of good character before she will be employed; those with whom she is laboring will not give her this so long as they desire her services; she therefore cannot leave them, whatever may be her treatment, so that she is as much compelled to remain with her employer as the slave with his master.

"Their servants hate them; our's love us. My niggers would fight for me and my family. They have been treated well, and they know it. And I don't treat my slaves any better than my neighbors. If ever there comes a war between the North and the South, let us do as Abraham did—arm our trained servants and go forth with them to battle. They hate the Yankees as intensely as we do, and nothing could please our slaves better than to fight them. Ah, the perfidious Yankees. I cordially hate a Yankee. We have all suffered much at their hands; they will not keep faith with us. Have they complied with the provisions of the Fugitive Slave Law? The thousands and ten of thousands of slaves aided in their escape to Canada is a sufficient answer. We have lost millions and are losing millions every year, by the operation of the underground railroad. How deep the perfidy of a people, thus to violate every article of compromise we have made with them! The Yankees are an inferior race, descended from the old Puritan stock, who enacted the Blue Laws. They are desirous of compelling us to submit to laws more iniquitous than ever were the Blue Laws. I have traveled in the North, and have seen the depth of their depravity. Now, my fellow-citizens, what shall we do to resist Northern aggression? Why simply this: If Lincoln or Douglas is elected (as to the Bell-Everett ticket, it stands no sort of chance), let us secede. This remedy will be effectual. I am in favor of no more compromises. Let us have Breckenridge, or immediate, complete, and eternal separation."

The speaker then retired amid the cheers of his audience.

Soon after this there came a day of rejoicing to many in Mississippi. The booming of cannon, the joyous greeting, the soul-stirring music, indicated that no ordinary intelligence had been received. The lightnings had brought the tidings that Abraham Lincoln was President-elect of the United States, and the South was wild with excitement. Those who had been long desirous of a pretext for secession now boldly advocated their sentiments, and joyfully hailed the election of Mr. Lincoln as affording that pretext. The conservative men were filled with gloom. They regarded the election of Mr. Lincoln by the majority of the people of the United States in a constitutional way as affording no cause for secession. Secession they regarded as fraught with all the evils of Pandora's box, and that war, famine, pestilence, and moral and physical desolation would follow in its train. A call was made by Governor Pettus for a convention to assemble early in January, at Jackson, to determine what course Mississippi should pursue, whether her policy should be submission or secession. Candidates, Union and Secession, were nominated for the convention in every county. The speeches of two whom I heard will serve as a specimen of the arguments used pro and con. Captain Love, of Choctaw, thus addressed the people:

"MY FELLOW CITIZENS—I appear before you to advocate the Union—the union of the states under whose favoring auspices we have long prospered. No nation so great, so prosperous, so happy, or so much respected by earth's thousand kingdoms as the Great Republic, by which name the United States is known from the rivers to the ends of the earth. Our flag, the star-spangled banner, is respected on every sea, and affords protection to the citizens of every state, whether amid the pyramids of Egypt, the jungles of Asia, or the mighty cities of Europe. Our Republican Constitution, framed by the wisdom of our Revolutionary fathers, is as free from imperfection as any document drawn up by uninspired men. God presided over the councils of that eminent convention which framed our glorious Constitution. They asked wisdom from on high, and their prayers were answered. Free speech, a free press, and freedom to worship God as our conscience dictates, under our own vine and fig tree, none daring to molest or make us afraid, are some of the blessings which our Constitution guarantees; and these prerogatives which we enjoy are features which bless and distinguish us from the other nations of the earth. Freedom of speech is unknown amongst them; among them a censorship of the press and a national church are established.

"Our country by its physical features seems fitted for but one nation. What ceaseless troubles would be caused by having the source of our rivers in one country and the mouth in another. There are no natural boundaries to divide us into separate nations. We are all descended from the same common parentage, we all speak the same language, and we have really no conflicting interests, the statements of our opponents to the contrary notwithstanding. Our opponents advocate separate state secession. Would not Mississippi cut a sorry figure among the nations of the earth? With no harbor, she would be dependent on a foreign nation for an outlet. Custom-house duties would be ruinous, and the republic of Mississippi would find herself compelled to return to the Union. Mississippi, you remember, repudiated a large foreign debt some years ago; if she became an independent nation, her creditors would influence their government to demand payment, which could not be refused by the weak, defenseless, navyless, armyless, moneyless, repudiating republic of Mississippi. To pay this debt, with the accumulated interest, would ruin the new republic, and bankruptcy would stare us in the face.

"It is true, Abraham Lincoln is elected President of the United States. My plan is to wait till Mr. Lincoln does something unconstitutional. Then let the South unanimously seek redress in a constitutional manner. The conservatives of the North will join us. If no redress is made, let us present our ultimatum. If this, too, is rejected, I for one will not advocate submission; and by the co-operation of all the slave states, we will, in the event of the perpetration of wrong, and a refusal to redress our grievances, be much abler to secure our rights, or to defend them at the cannon's mouth and the point of the bayonet. The Supreme Court favors the South. In the Dred Scott case the Supreme Court decided that the negro was not a citizen, and that the slave was a chattel as we regard him. The majority of Congress on joint ballot is still with the South. Although we have something to fear from the views of the President elect and the Chicago platform, let us wait till some overt act, trespassing upon our rights, is committed and all redress denied; then, and not till then, will I advocate extreme measures.

"Let our opponents remember that secession and civil war are synonymous. Who ever heard of a government breaking to pieces without an arduous struggle for its preservation? I admit the right of revolution when a people's rights cannot otherwise be maintained, but deny the right of secession. We are told that it is a reserved right. The constitution declares that all rights not specified in it are reserved to the people of the respective states; but who ever heard of the right of total destruction of the government being a reserved right in any constitution? The fallacy is evident at a glance. Nine millions of people can afford to wait for some overt act. Let us not follow the precipitate course which the ultra politicians indicate. Let W.L. Yancey urge his treasonable policy of firing the Southern heart and precipitating a revolution, but let us follow no such wicked advice. Let us follow the things which make for peace.

"We are often told that the North will not return fugitive slaves. Will secession remedy this grievance? Will secession give us any more slave territory? No free government ever makes a treaty for the rendition of fugitive slaves—thus recognizing the rights of the citizens of a foreign nation to a species of property which it denies to its own citizens. Even little Mexico will not do it. Mexico and Canada return no fugitives. In the event of secession the United States would return no fugitives, and our peculiar institution would, along our vast border, become very insecure; we would hold our slaves by a very slight tenure. Instead of extending the great Southern institution it would be contracting daily. Our slaves would be held to service at their own option throughout the whole border, and our gulf states would soon become border states; and the great insecurity of this species of property would work, before twenty years, the extinction of slavery, and, in consequence, the ruin of the South. Are we prepared for such a result? Are we prepared for civil war? Are we prepared for all the evils attendant upon a fratricidal contest—for bloodshed, famine, and political and moral desolation? I reply, we are not; therefore let us look before we leap, and avoiding the heresy of secession—

" 'Rather bear the ills we have,
Than fly to others that we know not of.' "

A secession speaker was introduced, and thus addressed the people:

"LADIES AND GENTLEMEN—Fellow citizens, I am a secessionist out and out; voted for Jeff Davis for Governor in 1850, when the same issue was before the people; and I have always felt a grudge against the free state of Tishomingo for giving H.S. Foote, the Union candidate, a majority so great as to elect him, and thus retain the state in this accursed Union ten years longer. Who would be a craven-hearted, cowardly, villainous submissionist? Lincoln, the abominable, white-livered abolitionist, is President-elect of the United States; shall he be permitted to take his seat on Southern soil? No, never! I will volunteer as one of thirty thousand to butcher the villain if ever he sets foot on slave territory. Secession or submission! What patriot would hesitate for a moment which to choose? No true son of Mississippi would brook the idea of submission to the rule of the baboon, Abe Lincoln—a fifth-rate lawyer, a broken-down hack of a politician, a fanatic, an abolitionist. I, for one, would prefer an hour of virtuous liberty to a whole eternity of bondage under Northern, Yankee, wooden-nutmeg rule. The halter is the only argument that should be used against the submissionists, and I predict that it will soon, very soon, be in force.

"We have glorious news from Tallahatchie. Seven tory-submissionists were hanged there in one day, and the so-called Union candidates, having the wholesome dread of hemp before their eyes, are not canvassing the county; therefore the heretical dogma of submission, under any circumstances, disgraces not their county. Compromise! let us have no such word in our vocabulary. Compromise with the Yankees, after the election of Lincoln, is treason against the South; and still its syren voice is listened to by the demagogue submissionists. We should never have made any compromise, for in every case we surrendered rights for the sake of peace. No concession of the scared Yankees will now prevent secession. They now understand that the South is in earnest, and in their alarm they are proposing to yield us much; but the die is cast, the Rubicon is crossed, and our determination shall ever be, no union with the flat-headed nigger-stealing, fanatical Yankees.

"We are now threatened with internecine war. The Yankees are an inferior race; they are cowardly in the extreme. They are descended from the Puritan stock, who never bore rule in any nation. We, the descendants of the Cavaliers, are the Patricians, they the Plebeians. The Cavaliers have always been the rulers, the Puritans have ruled. The dastardly Yankees will never fight us; but if they, in their presumption and audacity, venture to attack us, let the war come—I repeat it—let it come! The conflagration of their burning cities, the desolation of their country, and the slaughter of their inhabitants, will strike the nations of the earth dumb with astonishment, and serve as a warning to future ages, that the slaveholding Cavaliers of the sunny South are terrible in their vengeance. I am in favor of immediate, independent, and eternal separation from the vile Union which has so long oppressed us. After separation, I am in favor of non-intercourse with the United States so long as time endures. We will raise the tariff, to the point of prohibition, on all Yankee manufactures, including wooden-nutmegs, wooden clocks, quack nostrums.

We will drive back to their own inhospitable clime every Yankee who dares to pollute our shores with his cloven feet. Go he must, and if necessary, with the blood-hounds on his track. The scum of Europe and mudsills of Yankeedom shall never be permitted to advance a step south of 36° 30'. South of that latitude is ours—westward to the Pacific. With my heart of hearts I hate a Yankee, and I will make my children swear eternal hatred to the whole Yankee race. A mongrel breed—Irish, Dutch, Puritans, Jews, free niggers, etc.—they scarce deserve the notice of the descendants of the Huguenots, the old Castilians, and the Cavaliers. Cursed be the day when the South consented to this iniquitous league—the Federal Union—which has long dimmed her nascent glory.

"In battle, one southron is equivalent to ten northern hirelings; but I regard it a waste of time to speak of Yankees—they deserve not our attention. It matters not to us what they think of secession, and we would not trespass upon your time and patience, were it not for the tame, tory submissionists with which our country is cursed. A fearful retribution is in waiting for the whole crew, if the war which they predict, should come. Were they then to advocate the same views, I would not give a fourpence for their lives. We would hang them quicker than old Heath would hang a tory. Our Revolutionary fathers set us a good example in their dealings with the tories. They sent them to the shades infernal from the branches of the nearest tree. The North has sent teachers and preachers amongst us, who have insidiously infused the leaven of Abolitionism into the minds of their students and parishioners; and this submissionist policy is a lower development of the doctrine of Wendell Phillips, Gerrit Smith, Horace Greeley, and others of that ilk. We have a genial clime, a soil of uncommon fertility. We have free institutions, freedom for the white man, bondage for the black man, as nature and nature's God designed. We have fair women and brave men. The lines have truly fallen to us in pleasant places. We have indeed a goodly heritage. The only evil we can complain of is our bondage to the Yankees through the Federal Union. Let us burst these shackles from our limbs, and we will be free indeed.

"Let all who desire complete and eternal emancipation from Yankee thraldom, come to the polls on the—day of December, prepared not to vote the cowardly submissionist ticket, but to vote the secession ticket; and their children, and their children's children, will owe them a debt of gratitude which they can never repay. The day of our separation and vindication of states' rights, will be the happiest day of our lives. Yankee domination will have ceased forever, and the haughty southron will spurn them from all association, both governmental and social. So mote it be!"

This address was received with great éclat.

On the next Sabbath after this meeting, I preached in the Poplar Creek Presbyterian church, in Choctaw, now Montgomery county, from Romans xiii. 1: "Let every soul be subject unto the higher powers. For there is no power but of God: the powers that be, are ordained of God."

Previous to the sermon a prayer was offered, of which the following is the conclusion:

"Almighty God — we would present our country, the United States of America, before thee. When our political horizon is overcast with clouds and darkness, when the strong-hearted are becoming fearful for the permanence of our free institutions, and the prosperity, yea, the very existence of our great Republic, we pray thee, O God, when flesh and heart fail, when no human arm is able to save us from the fearful vortex of disunion and revolution, that thou wouldst interpose and save us. We confess our national sins, for we have, as a nation, sinned grievously. We have been highly favored, we have been greatly prospered, and have taken our place amongst the leading powers of the earth. A gospel-enlightened nation, our sins are therefore more heinous in thy sight. They are sins of deep ingratitude and presumption. We confess that drunkenness has abounded amongst all classes of our citizens. Rulers and ruled have been alike guilty; and because of its wide spreading prevalence, and because our legislators have enacted no sufficient laws for its suppression, it is a national sin. Profanity abounds amongst us; Sabbath-breaking is rife; and we have elevated unworthy men to high positions of honor and trust. We are not, as a people, free from the crime of tyranny and oppression. For these great and aggravated offences, we pray thee to give us repentance and godly sorrow, and then, O God, avert the threatened and imminent judgments which impend over our beloved country. Teach our senators wisdom. Grant them that wisdom which is able to make them wise unto salvation; and grant also that wisdom which is profitable to direct, so that they may steer the ship of state safely through the troubled waters which seem ready to engulf it on every side. Lord, hear us, and answer in mercy, for the sake of Jesus Christ our Lord. Amen and Amen!"

The following is a synopsis of my sermon:

Israel had been greatly favored as a nation. No weapon formed against them prospered, so long as they loved and served the Lord their God. They were blessed in their basket and their store. They were set on high above all the nations of the earth. . . . When all Israel assembled, ostensibly to make Rehoboam king, they were ripe for rebellion. Jeroboam and other wicked men had fomented and cherished the spark of treason, till, on this occasion, it broke out into the flame of open rebellion. The severity of Solomon's rule was the pretext, but it was only a pretext, for during his reign the nation prospered, grew rich and powerful. Jeroboam wished a disruption of the kingdom, that he might bear rule; and although God permitted it as a punishment of Israel's idolatry, yet he frowned upon the wicked men who were instrumental in bringing this great evil upon his chosen people.

"The loyal division took the name of Judah, though composed of the two tribes, Judah and Benjamin. The revolted ten tribes took the name of their leading tribe, Ephraim. Ephraim continued to wax weaker and weaker. Filled with envy against Judah, they often warred against the loyal kingdom, until they themselves were greatly reduced. At last, after various vicissitudes, the ten tribes were carried away, and scattered and lost. We often hear of the lost ten tribes. What became of them is a mystery. Their secession ended in their being blotted out of existence or lost amidst the heathen. God alone knows what did become of them. They resisted the powers that be—the ordinance of God—and received to themselves damnation and annihilation.

"As God dealt with Israel, so will he deal with us. If we are exalted by righteousness, we will prosper; if we, as the ten tribes, resist the ordinance of God, we will perish. At this time many are advocating the course of the ten tribes. Secession is a word of frequent occurrence. It is openly advocated by many. Nullification and rebellion, secession and treason, are convertible terms, and no good citizen will mention them with approval. Secession is resisting the powers that be, and therefore it is a violation of God's command. Where do we obtain the right of secession? Clearly not from the word of God, which enjoins obedience to all that are in authority, to whom we must be subject, not only for wrath, but also for conscience's sake.

"There is no provision made in the Constitution of the United States for secession. The wisest statesmen, who made politics their study, regarded secession as a political heresy, dangerous in its tendencies, and destructive of all government in its practical application. Mississippi, purchased from France with United States gold, fostered by the nurturing care, and made prosperous by the wise administration of the general government, proposes to secede. Her political status would then be anomalous. Would her territory revert to France? Does she propose to refund the purchase money? Would she become a territory under the jurisdiction of the United States Congress?

"Henry Clay, the great statesman, Daniel Webster, the expounder of the constitution, General Jackson, George Washington, and a mighty host, whose names would fill a volume, regarded secession as treason. One of our smallest states, which swarmed with tories in the Revolution, whose descendants still live, invented the doctrine of nullification, the first treasonable step, which soon culminated in the advocacy of secession. Why should we secede, and thus destroy the best, the freest, and most prosperous government on the face of the earth, the government which our patriot fathers fought and bled to secure? What has Mississippi lost by the Union? I have resided seven years in this state, and have an extensive personal acquaintance, and yet I know not a single individual who has lost a slave through northern influence. I have, it is true, known of some ten slaves who have run away, and have not been found. They may have been aided in their escape to Canada by northern and southern citizens, for there are many in the South who have given aid and comfort to the fugitive; but the probability is that they perished in the swamps, or were destroyed by the blood-hounds.

"The complaint is made that the North regards slavery as a moral, social, and political evil, and that many of them denounce, in no measured terms, both slavery and slaveholders. To be thus denounced is regarded as a great grievance. Secession would not remedy this evil. In order to cure it effectually, we must seize and gag all who thus denounce our peculiar institution. We must also muzzle their press. As this is impracticable, it would be well to come to this conclusion: If we are verily guilty of the evils charged upon us, let us set about rectifying those evils; if not, the denunciations of slanderers should not affect us so deeply. If our northern brethren are honest in their convictions of the sin of slavery, as no doubt many of them are, let us listen to their arguments without the dire hostility so frequently manifested. They take the position that slavery is opposed to the inalienable rights of the human race; that it originated in piracy and robbery; that manifold cruelties and barbarities are inflicted upon the defenseless slaves; that they are debarred from intellectual culture by state laws, which send to the penitentiary those who are guilty of instructing them; that they are put upon the block and sold, parent and child, husband and wife being separated, so that they never again see each other's face in the flesh; that the law of chastity cannot be observed, as there are no laws punishing rape on the person of a female slave; that when they escape from the threatened cat-o'nine-tails, or overseer's whip, they are hunted down by blood-hounds and bloodier men; that often they are half starved and half clad, and are furnished with mere hovels to live in; that they are often murdered by cruel overseers, who whip them to death, or overtask them until disease is induced which results in death; that masters practically ignore the marriage relation among slaves, inasmuch as they frequently separate husband and wife, by sale or removal; that they discourage the formation of that relation, preferring that the offspring of their female slaves should be illegitimate, from the mistaken notion that it would be more numerous. They charge, also, that slavery induces in the masters, pride, arrogance, tyranny, laziness, profligacy, and every form of vice.

"The South takes the position that if slavery is sinful, the North is not responsible for that sin; that it is a state institution, and that to interfere with slavery in the states in any way, even by censure, is a violation of the rights of the states. The language of our politicians is, upon us and our children rest the evil! We are willing to take the responsibility, and to risk the penalty! You will find evil and misery enough in the North to excite your philanthropy and employ your beneficence. You have purchased our cotton; you have used our sugar; you have eaten our rice; you have smoked and chewed our tobacco— all of which are the products of slave labor. You have grown rich by traffic in these articles; you have monopolized the carrying trade and borne our slave-produced products to your shores. Your northern ships, manned by northern men, brought from Africa the greater part of the slaves which came to our continent, and they are still smuggling them in. When, finding slavery unprofitable, the northern states passed laws for gradual emancipation, but few obtained their freedom, the majority of them being shipped South and sold, so that but few, comparatively, were manumitted. If the slave trade and slavery are great sins, the North is particeps criminis, and has been from the beginning.

"These bitter accusations are hurled back and forth through the newspapers, and in Congress crimination and recrimination occur every day of the session. Instead of endeavoring to calm the troubled waters, politicians are striving to render them turbid and boisterous. Sectional bitterness and animosity prevail to a fearful extent, but secession is not the proper remedy. To cure one evil by perpetrating a greater renders a double cure necessary. In order to cure a disease, the cause should be known, that we may treat it intelligently and apply a proper remedy. Having observed, during the last eleven years, that sectional strife and bitterness were increasing with fearful rapidity, I have endeavored to stem the torrent, so far as it was possible for individual effort to do so. I deem it the imperative duty of all patriots, of all Christians, to throw oil upon the troubled waters, and thus save the ship of-state from wreck among the vertiginous billows.

"Most of our politicians are demagogues. They care not for the people, so that they accomplish their own selfish and ambitious schemes. Give them power, give them money, and they are satisfied. Deprive them of these, and they are ready to sacrifice the best interests of the nation to secure them. They excite sectional animosity and party strife, and are willing to kindle the flames of civil war to accomplish their unhallowed purposes. They tell us that there is a conflict of interest between the free and slave states, and endeavor to precipitate a revolution, that they may be leaders and obtain positions of trust and profit in the new government which they hope to establish. The people would be dupes indeed to abet these wicked demagogues in their nefarious designs. Let us not break God's command, by resisting the ordinance of God —the powers that be. I am not discussing the right of revolution, which I deem a sacred right. When human rights are invaded, when life is endangered, when liberty is taken away, when we are not left free to pursue our own happiness in our own chosen way—so far as we do not trespass upon the rights of others—we have a right, and it becomes our imperative duty to resist to the bitter end the tyranny which would deprive us and our children of our inalienable rights. Our lives are secure; we have freedom to worship God. Our liberty is sacred; we may pursue happiness to our hearts' content. We do not even charge upon the general Government that it has infringed these rights. Whose life has been endangered, or who has lost his liberty by the action of the Government? If that man lives, in all this fair domain of ours, he has a right to complain. But neither you nor I have ever heard of or seen the individual who has thus suffered. We have therefore clearly no right of revolution.

"Treason is no light offence. God, who rules the nations, and who has established governments, will punish severely those who attempt to overthrow them. Damnation is stated to be the punishment which those who resist the powers that be, will suffer. Who wishes to endure it? I hope none of my charge will incur this penalty by the perpetration of treason. You yourselves can bear me witness that I have not heretofore introduced political issues into the pulpit, but at this time I could not acquit my conscience were I not to warn you against the great sin some of you, I fear, are ready to commit.

"Were I to discuss the policy of a high or low tariff, or descant upon the various merits attached to one or another form of banking, I should be justly obnoxious to censure. Politics and religion, however, are not always separate. When the political issue is made, shall we, or shall we not, grant license to sell intoxicating liquors as a beverage? the minister's duty is plain; he must urge his people to use their influence against granting any such license. The minister must enforce every moral and religious obligation, and point out the path of truth and duty, even though the principles he advocates are by statesmen introduced into the arena of political strife, and made issues by the great parties of the day. I see the sword coming, and would be derelict in duty not to give you faithful warning. I must reveal the whole counsel of God. I have a message from God unto you, which I must deliver, whether you will hear, or whether you will forbear. If the sword come, and you perish, I shall then be guiltless of your blood. As to the great question at issue, my honest conviction is (and I think I have the Spirit of God,) that you should with your whole heart, and soul, and mind, and strength, oppose secession. You should talk against it, you should write against it, you should vote against it, and, if need be, you should fight against it.

"I have now declared what I believe to be your high duty in this emergency. Do not destroy the government which has so long protected you, and which has never in a single instance oppressed you. Pull not down the fair fabric which our patriot fathers reared at vast expense of blood and treasure. Do not, like the blind Samson, pull down the pillars of our glorious edifice, and cause death, desolation, and ruin. Perish the hand that would thus destroy the source of all our political prosperity and happiness. Let the parricide who attempts it receive the just retribution which a loyal people demand, even his execution on a gallows high as Haman's. Let us also set about rectifying the causes which threaten the overthrow of our government. As we are proud, let us pray for the grace of humility. As a state, and as individuals, we too lightly regard its most solemn obligations; let us, therefore, pray for the grace of repentance and godly sorrow, and hereafter in this respect sin no more. As many transgressions have been committed by us, let the time past of our lives suffice us to have wrought the will of the flesh, and now let us break off our sins by righteousness, and our transgressions by turning unto the Lord, and he will avert his threatened judgments, and save us from dissolution, anarchy, and desolation.

"If our souls are filled with hatred against the people of any section of our common country, let us ask from the Great Giver the grace of charity, which suffereth long and is kind, which envieth not which vaunteth not itself, is not puffed up, does not behave itself unseemly, seeketh not her own, is not easily provoked, thinketh no evil; rejoiceth not in iniquity, but rejoiceth in the truth; beareth all things, believeth all things, hopeth all things, endureth all things, and which never faileth; then shall we be in a suitable frame for an amicable adjustment of every difficulty; oil will soon be thrown upon the troubled waters, and peace, harmony, and prosperity would ever attend us; and our children, and our children's children will rejoice in the possession of a beneficent and stable government, securing to them all the natural and inalienable rights of man."

Chapter Two

Soon after this sermon was preached, the election was held. Approaching the polls, I asked for a Union ticket, and was informed that none had been printed, and that it would be advisable to vote the secession ticket. I thought otherwise, and going to a desk, wrote out a Union ticket, and voted it amidst the frowns, murmers, and threats of the judges and bystanders, and, as the result proved, I had the honor of depositing the only vote in favor of the Union which was polled in that precinct. I knew of many who were in favor of the Union, who were intimidated by threats, and by the odium attending it, from voting at all. A majority of the secession candidates were elected. The convention assembled, and on the 9th of January, 1861, Mississippi had the unenviable reputation of being the first to follow her twin sister, South Carolina, into the maelstrom of secession and treason. Being the only states in which the slaves were more numerous than the whites, it became them to lead the van in the slave-holders' rebellion. Before the 4th of March, Florida, Georgia, Louisiana, and Texas had followed in the wake, and were engulfed in the whirlpool of secession.

It was now dangerous to utter a word in favor of the Union. Many suspected of Union sentiments were lynched. An old gentleman in Winston county was arrested for an act committed twenty years before, which was construed as a proof of his abolition proclivities. The old gentleman had several daughters, and his mother-in-law had given him a negro girl. Observing that his daughters were becoming lazy, and were imposing all the labor upon the slave, he sent her back to the donor, with a statement of the cause for returning her. This was now the ground of his arrest, but escaping from their clutches, a precipitate flight alone saved his life.

Self-constituted vigilance committees sprang up all over the country, and a reign of terror began; all who had been Union men, and who had not given in their adhesion to the new order of things by some public proclamation, were supposed to be disaffected. The so-called Confederate States, the new power, organized for the avowed purpose of extending and perpetuating

African slavery, was now in full blast. These soi-disant vigilance committees professed to carry out the will of Jeff. Davis. All who were considered disaffected were regarded as being tinctured with abolitionism. My opposition to the disruption of the Union being notorious, I was summoned to appear before one of these august tribunals to answer the charge of being an abolitionist and a Unionist. My wife was very much alarmed, knowing that were I found guilty of the charge, there was no hope for mercy.

On the evening before the session of the vigilance committee, I walked out in the gloaming for meditation and prayer. When a short distance from my residence, I encountered an old colored man who belonged to a planter named Major F.M. Henderson. The old man, who was known as Uncle Simon Peter, embraced every opportunity of hearing me preach. He approached me with his hat under his arm, and in a very deferential manner. Said he, "Master, I is in great trouble."

"What troubles you, Uncle Peter?"

"Master, I brings a note to you, and I'se 'feared it bodes no good to you. Master and Gus Mecklin and some more folks what I didn't know fixed it up las' night, and de way dey talked dey's ready to 'sassinate you."

"Give me the note, Uncle Peter."

"Here it am."

The paper was unique. A skull and cross-bones illuminated one corner, a coffin and newly-made grave were rudely drawn in another corner, a gallows was conspicuous, a victim whose hands were bound behind his back and a cap drawn over his face, stood upon the trap ready for execution. In bold letters was written, "Such be the doom of all traitors." Within was the following citation:

> "Parson John H. Aughey, your treasonable proclivities are known. You have been reported to us as one of the disaffected whose presence is a standing menace to the perpetuity and prosperity of our newly-organized government—the Confederate States of America. Your name heads the proscribed list. You are ordered to appear on tomorrow afternoon at 2 o'clock before our vigilance committee, in W.H. Simpson's carriage shop, to answer to the charges of treason and abolitionism.
> "BY ORDER OF THE VIGILANTES.   K.K.K. & K.G.C."

Flight was now impossible, and I deemed it the safest plan to appear before the committee. I found it to consist of twelve persons, five of whom I knew, viz., Rev. John Locke, Armstrong, Cartledge, Simpson, and Wilbanks. Parson Locke, the chief speaker, or rather the inquisitor-general, was a Methodist minister, though he had fallen into disrepute among his brethren, and was engaged in a tedious strife with the church which he left in Holmes county. The parson was a real Nimrod. He boasted that in five months he had killed forty-eight raccoons, two hundred squirrels, and ten deer; he had followed the blood-hounds, and assisted in the capture of twelve runaway negroes. W. H. Simpson was a ruling elder in my church. Wilbanks was a clever sort of old gentleman, who had little to say in the matter. Armstrong was a monocular Hardshell-Baptist. Cartledge was an illiterate, conceited individual. The rest were a motley crew, not one of whom, I feel confident, knew a letter in the alphabet. The committee assembled in an old carriage shop. Parson Locke acted as chairman, and conducted the trial, as follows:

"Parson Aughey, you have been reported to us as holding abolition sentiments, and as being disloyal to the Confederate States."

"Who reported me, and where are your witnesses?"

"Anyone has a right to report, and it is optional whether he confronts the accused or not. The proceedings of vigilance committees are somewhat informal."

"Proceed, then, with the trial, in your own way."

"We propose to ask you a few questions, and in your answers you may defend yourself, or admit your guilt. In the first place, did you ever say that you did not believe that God ordained the institution of slavery?"

"I believe that God did not ordain the institution of slavery."

"Did not God command the Israelites to buy slaves from the Canaanitish nations, and to hold them as their property for ever?"

"The Canaanites had filled their cup of iniquity to overflowing, and God commanded the Israelites to exterminate them; this, in violation of God's command, they failed to do. God afterwards permitted the Hebrews to reduce them to a state of servitude; but the punishment visited upon those seven wicked nations by the command of God, does not justify war or the slave trade."

"Did you say that you were opposed to the slavery which existed in the time of Christ?"

"I did, because the system of slavery prevailing in Christ's day was cruel in the extreme; it conferred the power of life and death upon the master, and was attended with innumerable evils. The slave had the same complexion as his master; and by changing his servile garb for the citizen dress, he could not be recognized as a slave. You yourself profess to be opposed to white slavery."

"Did you state that you believed Paul, when sent Onesimus back to Philemon, had no idea that he would be regarded as a slave, and treated as such after his return?"

"I did. My proof is in Philemon, verses 15 and 16, where the apostle asks that Onesimus be received not as a servant, but as a brother beloved?"

"Did you tell Mr. Creath that you knew some negroes who were better, in every respect, than some white men?"

"I said that I knew some negroes who were better classical scholars than any white men I had as yet met in Choctaw county, and that I had known some who were pre-eminent for virtue and holiness. As to natural rights, I made no comparison; nor did I say anything about superiority or inferiority of race. I also stated my belief in the unity of the races."

"Have you any abolition works in your library, and a poem in your scrap-book, entitled 'The Fugitive Slave,' with this couplet as a refrain,

'The hounds are baying on my track;
Christian, will you send me back?'"

"I have not Mrs. Stowe's nor Helper's work; they are contraband in this region, and I could not get them if I wished. I have many works in my library containing sentiments adverse to the institution of slavery. All the works in common use amongst us, on law, physic, and divinity, all the text-books in our schools—in a word, all the works on every subject read and studied by us, were, almost without exception, written by men opposed to the peculiar institution. I am not alone in this matter."

"Parson, I saw Cowper's works in your library, and Cowper says:

'I would not have a slave to fan me when I sleep,
And tremble when I wake, for all the wealth
That sinews bought and sold have ever earned.'"

"You have Wesley's writings, and Wesley says that 'Human slavery is the sum of all villainy.' You have a work which has this couplet:

'Two deep, dark stains, mar all our country's bliss:
Foul slavery one, and one, loathed drunkenness.'

You have the work of an English writer of high repute, who says, 'Forty years ago, some in England doubted whether slavery were a sin, and regarded adultery as a venial offence; but behold the progress of truth! Who now doubts that he who enslaves his fellow-man is guilty of a fearful crime, and that he who violates the seventh commandment is a great sinner in the sight of God?'"

"You are known to be an adept in phonography, and you are reported to be correspondent of an abolition phonographic journal."

"I understand the science of phonography, and I am a correspondent of a phonographic journal, but the journal eschews politics."

Another member of the committee then interrogated me.

"Parson Aughey, what is funnyography?"

"Phonography, sir, is a system of writing by means of a philosophic alphabet, composed of the simplest geometrical signs, in which one mark is used to represent one and invariably the same sound."

"Kin you talk funnyography? and where does them folks live what talks it?"

"Yes, sir, I converse fluently in phonography, and those who speak the language live in Columbia."

"In the Deestrict?"

"No, sir, in the poetical Columbia."

I was next interrogated by another member of the committee.

"Parson Aughey, is phonography a abolition fixin'?"

"No, sir; phonography, abstractly considered, has no political complexion; it may be used to promote either side of any question, sacred or profane, mental, moral, physical, or political."

"Well, you ought to write and talk plain English, what common folks can understand, or we'll have to say of you, what Agrippa said of Paul, 'Much learning hath made thee mad.' Suppose you was to preach in phonography, who'd understand it?—who'd know what was piped or harped? I'll bet high some Yankee invented it to spread his abolition notions underhandedly. I, for one, would be in favor of makin' the parson promise to write and talk no more in phonography. I'll bet phonography is agin slavery, tho' I never hearn tell of it before. I'm agin all secret societies. I'm agin the Odd-fellers, Free-masons, Sons of Temperance, Good Templars, and phonography. I want to know what's writ and what's talked. You can't throw dust in my eyes. Phonography, from what I've found out about it today, is agin the Confederate States, and we ought to be agin it."

Parson Locke then resumed:

"I must stop this digression. Parson Aughey, are you in favor of the South?"

"I am in favor of the South, and have always endeavored to promote the best interests of the South. However, I never deemed it for the best interests of the South to secede. I talked against secession, and voted against secession, because I thought that the best interests of the South would be put in jeopardy by the secession of the Southern States. I was honest in my convictions and acted accordingly. Could the sacrifice of my life have stayed the swelling tide of secession, it would gladly have been made."

"It is said that you have never prayed for the Southern Confederacy."

"I have prayed for the whole world, though it is true that I have never named the Confederate States in prayer."

"Where and by whom were you educated?"

"In my childhood I attended the free schools in New York state and also in Steubenville, O. I was a student of Grove Academy, in Steubenville, O., 1844–5. Rev. J. W. Scott, D.D., was the principal. I was a student of Richmond College, Richmond, Jefferson Co., Ohio, three years. Rev. J. R. W. Sloane, D.D., was the president. Prior to this I studied classics two years with Rev. John Knox, of Springfield, Jefferson Co., O. I am an alumnus of Franklin College, New Athens, Harrison Co., O., was graduated during the presidency of Rev. A. D. Clark, D.D."

"Did you ever attend Oberlin College, O.?" said the presiding officer.

"I never had that honor, sir."

"What were the views of your educators on the slavery question?"

"They all believed that human slavery was a moral, social, and political evil —a cancer on the body politic, to be eradicated as soon as possible by mild means, or by heroic treatment as the exigencies of the case might demand, in order to the preservation of the national life. Since I came South I have taught in Winchester, Ky., Baton Rouge, La., Memphis, Tenn., Holly Springs and Rienzi, Miss., and have been acting pastor of the churches of Waterford and Spring Creek, in the Presbytery of Chickasaw, near Holly Springs, Miss.; and of Bethany Church in North Mississippi Presbytery."

"Are you a Mason or Odd Fellow?" said Parson Locke.

"I object to that question," said Mr. Armstrong, who belonged to a church that refused to fellowship any members of secret societies.

"I will not press the question," said the parson. "You may retire."

As I wended my way home I saw a large concourse in front of the shop, in the garb or rather guise of hunters. They had guns upon their shoulders and pistols in their belts. I recognized the majority of them as Unionists who had come, doubtless, to see that no harm befell me. There were a few virulent secessionists in the post-office, who, as I passed through it to the street, looked fiercely at me, and with horrid blasphemy gave their views as to what fate should befall traitors, tories, submissionists, and unionists. These remarks were intended for my ears.

After I had retired, Parson Locke said: "Mr. Cartledge, what is your opinion? Is Parson Aughey guilty or not guilty of the crimes charged against him in the indictment?"

"Guilty, sir, guilty. I node that afore I come here today. I node it after I hearn him preach that sermon agin secession, an' when I seed him rite out an' vote the Union ticket I dident need no more evidence of his a being guilty of all that is charged agin him, an' more too. Put me down in favor of hangin'."

"Very well said, Mr. Cartledge. An honest, unequivocal, straightforward expression of your convictions. General Bolivar, let us hear from you."

Bolivar was a foundling. The gentleman at whose gate the babe was abandoned gave him to the colored women to raise. He was a great admirer of the South American patriot and liberator, General Simon Bolivar, so he named the waif, Simon Bolivar. The gentleman lived in Boyle Co., Ky., on Rock Creek, near Danville. Bolivar, when grown, married a poor white girl, and they lived in a cave on the banks of that stream. He joined his fortunes to a class of poverty-stricken people who were known as rock angels, from their habitation amid the clefts of the rocks. They procured a precarious livelihood by hunting and fishing, often eking out their meagre supply of life's necessaries by predatory excursions to the sheep-folds and hen-roosts of the neighboring gentry. Bolivar came to Mississippi in the employ of a man who brought a drove of mules for sale, and liking the climate he returned and brought his family.

Bolivar, when addressed, started suddenly as from an apparent revery, and ejecting a quantity of ambier from his filthy mouth, replied: "I agrees with my neighbor Cartledge. Better men nor him hez been hung in this county lately, an' it has done good. I can't see no reason why he shouldent hang, an' that's the way I votes."

"Major Wilbanks, how do you vote in regard to the guilt or innocence of the prisoner?"

"You wish my candid opinion?"

"Yes, we do."

"Well, then, I will give it for what it is worth. I am in favor of a free country, a free press, free speech—free men, a free ballot and fair count."

"You might have added free niggers and completed your free catalogue," said Parson Locke. "Bro. Simpson, please give us your opinion and advice."

"Parson, I am halting between two opinions. I do not approve the views of my pastor, but he has never committed any overt act of treason. We can afford to wait for that. It may be possible should the sentiments of those who have spoken prevail—that civil war would be inaugurated in our midst. The crowd in front of this building is ominous of evil. I have looked out upon them, and I know that many of the men out there have been far more outspoken in the expression of opinions adverse to the Southern Confederacy than him whom we have had before us today, and they are armed to the teeth."

Parson Locke turned pale, and said if Bro. Simpson thought there was any immediate danger of exciting a riot, he would adjourn the session till some time in the near future, when, it was hoped, the excitement would have subsided.

Mr. John Mecklin arose and said, "I am but a spectator, but I would advise you to adjourn at once. Many of our best people think this to be an unwarranted and illegal proceeding. Civil law is still in force, and even if it were superseded by military law that fact would not justify the arbitrary course of this committee, who have acted without any proper or competent authority, civil or military. This man is not under your jurisdiction, and you may have to answer for this day's proceedings."

Parson Locke, who was an arrant coward, replied that he could not fully agree with the last two speakers, but in the interests of peace and harmony he would adjourn this meeting to a time in the near future, when it would be convened at the call of the president.

The committee then hastily adjourned. Parson Locke made his exit by a door in the rear of the building, and, making a circuit through the woods, reached his home without observation.

The crowd was informed that an adjournment had taken place, and that no formal verdict had been rendered. In a short time the crowd had dispersed. Some of the more violent secessionists were greatly exasperated when they learned that the vigilance committee had not rendered a verdict of guilty and ordered my execution. They determined to take the matter into their own hands. I was speedily advised of their threats. My friends provided me with arms, and I resolved to defend myself to the best of my ability. One evening I had gone over to a neighbor's, Mr. Pickens Mecklin's. It was the dark of the moon. As I returned, at a late hour, I heard the trampling of steeds. I concealed myself as they approached me. When they had come quite near, the men dismounted and tied their horses to trees. One said, "Do you think he's at home?" Another, "Well, boys, the tory parson's got to sup with Pluto tonight." Another said, "All I'm afeard of is that some of us will have to sup with him in Pluto's dominions. He's got fight in him, an' no mistake."

I had heard enough. I hastened home. My wife had retired. I quickly armed myself, after barricading the doors. After awhile there came a knock. No notice was taken of it. Soon a voice said, "Halloo!" Within the house all was silent as the grave. I had cocked both barrels of a gun heavily loaded with buckshot. I sat on a chair and aimed at the door, resolved to shoot the first that entered, should they succeed in breaking in the door. Soon there was a noisy demonstration. At length two of the men volunteered to go to the rear of the building, to the woodpile, and get a log to use as a battering-ram to break down the door. In their hot haste they ran against a clothes-line. I had eked the line with a piece of telegraph wire that someone in Vaiden had given me a short time before. Both of these men, John Cook and a Mr. Tower, were prostrated by the recoil, and quite severely injured. Cook was rendered unconscious, and Tower howled like a beaten hound. Several ran to their assistance. At this juncture two volleys of firearms were heard in quick succession. My would-be assassins ran and cried and fled.

A Mr. Denman had just finished digging a well for me. The structure at the surface, to guard against the danger of falling into the well, had not been completed. Some of the fugitives fell into the well, descending with the bucket. How they succeeded in getting out, I know not. Dr. Le Grand told me of one man, who was his patient, who died of the injuries received on that eventful night. How I had been so opportunely delivered was a mystery I could not fathom.

My little daughter said to her mother in the lull of the storm, "Ma, may I pray those verses you taught me?" Upon receiving permission, she arose in bed, knelt upon the pillow, and folding her little hands, said: "The angel of the Lord encampeth round about them that fear him, and he delivereth them. The righteous cry, and the Lord heareth them and delivereth them out of all their troubles. They cry unto the Lord in their trouble, and he bringeth them out of their distresses. Oh, that men would praise the Lord for his goodness and for his wonderful works to the children of men. Deliver us, O our God, out of the hand of the wicked, out of the hand of the unrighteous and cruel men. Oh, God! be not far from us. Oh, God! make haste for our help. For Christ our Redeemer's sake. Amen." Then she lay down, and was soon lost in innocent and unconscious slumber.

In an hour after the flight of these midnight marauders I heard a knock, which I recognized as a preconcerted signal of recognition among Unionists. I went to the back door, whence the knock sounded, and signaled a reply. A low voice then uttered in a distinct tone the sentence, "Liberty and union, now and forever, one and inseparable." I opened the door, half a dozen friends entered. They and others, who remained on duty, had been guarding my house unknown to me. They remained an hour, uttering words of comfort, and gave me the assurance of all the assistance I should need, though at the peril of their lives. After parting salutations, I opened the door, and my friends disappeared in the darkness. We named this the battle of Wyandotte, the name of my home. Probably the first blood of the war was shed in this recontre.

> "War is dread when battle shock and fierce affray
>   Perpetuate a tyrant's name;
>   But guarding freedom's holy fane,

Confided to her valiant keeping,
The sword from scabbard leaping
Flashes a heavenly light."

In the afternoon of the next day Elder John Mecklin and his estimable wife came to visit us, bringing their young son Reemer with them. Mr. Mecklin advised us to say nothing about this attempt upon my life, as reticence in war time was a virtue. The perpetrators of the dastardly attack would conceal their participation in it, even though some of their number should die of their wounds. Excitement must be allayed as much as possible. He feared that this assault would be followed by others, till they had accomplished their nefarious purpose. He said that my public position and avowed sentiments, and the fact that I was of northern birth and education, had concentrated upon me the malice of all those of secession proclivities, but he assured me that my friends would defend me at the risk of their lives. I advised him of my intentions of removing into Attala county, near Nazareth church, which was also in my field of labor. He approved this course, since the excitement here ran very high, but affirmed that there was no place within the seceded states very safe for one whose Unionism was of so pronounced a type.

At this time there was a man named Dr. Smith who resided in Canton, Mississippi. He frequently visited friends in Choctaw county. He was a violent secessionist. Having learned of the failure of the attempt upon my life, he resolved to take charge of the matter himself, and execute summary vengeance upon one who had too long been suffered to live.

I had the charge of three churches—Poplar Creek and French Camp, in Choctaw county, and Nazareth, in Attala county. French Camp was twelve miles from my home, and Nazareth twenty-eight miles distant. Dr. Smith determined to come to French Camp on the Sabbath I preached in that church and kill me there. He ordered his fast trotter, Bucephalus, to be attached to the buggy, and preparing his pistols, he started in hot haste to effect his murderous purpose. He reached French Camp about one o'clock P. M. He learned that after the service I had gone to dine with Major Garrard. This was a mistake; I dined with Col. Hemphill. Dr. Smith dined with Dr. John Hemphill. He made known to Dr. Hemphill the object of his visit. The doctor tried in vain to dissuade him from his purpose. He now determined to follow me to my home and murder me there. He called at Col. Hemphill's and learned that I had dined with the colonel, and had left en route for my home an hour before. I called at Esquire Pilcher's to see his daughter, Miss Belle, who was quite ill of malarial fever. After administering to her spiritual need, I pursued my journey homeward. Dr. Smith had just passed, driving Jehu-like (furiously). I followed rapidly, as a storm seemed imminent. I heard the vehicle in advance and tried to overtake it, as I desired company on this lonely road, but my horse was no match for the doctor's swift steed, so I providentially failed to overtake him.

About three miles from my home Dr. Smith left the main road for one that led to a Methodist chapel. He drove up to the chapel, descended from his buggy and ordered a colored boy to hold his horse. He approached a group of men, and noticing one who was quite well dressed and had a ministerial look and bearing, addressed him thus:

"Are you, sir, a messenger of the Lord of Hosts?"

The gentleman smiled and made no reply. The doctor then presented a pistol and fired. The ball passed through the lungs of his victim. Reason had left her throne. The doctor was a raving maniac. The congregation rushed out of the chapel, took the doctor into custody, and resolved to administer summary vengeance according to the code of Judge Lynch. While they were waiting for a halter for which they had sent, Dr. Smith's brother and other friends arrived. They rescued him with difficulty from the infuriated crowd, conveyed him to his home in Canton, an alienist pronounced him hopelessly insane, and he soon after became an inmate of the insane asylum at Jackson. Deacon Ludlow (pro. kokely), the doctor's victim, lingered for months on the border of the spirit land. The latest information I had indicated a fatal termination. Thus in the providence of God I was once more delivered from the wrath of man.

A rumor found its way into the papers that I had been fatally shot by Dr. Smith, of Canton. A friend residing in Carthage, Leake county, sent me a paper containing this notice:

"Rev. John H. Aughey, a Presbyterian minister, who has been doing evangelistic work in Attala and Choctaw counties, was fatally shot last week by Dr. Smith, of Canton. The doctor was a monomaniac. He believed himself to be commissioned by heaven to exterminate all who were not friendly to the Confederate States of America. He had been informed that Mr. Aughey had expressed disloyal sentiments, and was a leader of the disaffected. He left home with the avowed intention of killing him on sight. The doctor's brother, learning the nature of his mission, followed, but was unable to overtake him till he had committed the fatal deed. The particulars we have not learned. Mr. Aughey had the reputation of being an able minister, and very faithful in the discharge of his ministerial duties. That he was one of the disaffected is true. The extent of his opposition we have not learned. In times of great excitement rash acts are committed which are not warranted or required for the public safety. We regret Mr. Aughey's tragic end, and if justifiable we regret the necessity that required it. He leaves a widow and one child. Requiescat in pace."

Commodore Spiva, a planter and leading member of my church in Attala county, offered myself and family a home as members of his family upon condision that I would superintend the studies of his son and daughter. They had entered upon a course of private study supplementary to the finished education they had received at the college and seminary. We were now domiciled in his spacious mansion on the banks of the meandering Yockanookany. We enjoyed comparative quiet for a time. My students were very much enamored of belles-lettres, and we took delightful rambles in the higher walks of literature. We enjoyed a continuous feast of reason and flow of soul. In my absence my wife became my vicegerent, and their rapid advance was not retarded.

The battle of Manassas had been fought and the boastful spirit of the secessionists was almost unendurable. The whole confederacy did nothing but brag of what had been done and what would be done if the Yankees persisted in their futile attempts to subjugate the South. The South was arming for the war. Joyfully and with alacrity the young chivalric sons of the slave-holding aristocracy responded to the call for volunteers. The young ladies presented company and regimental flags of costly material, deftly embroidered by their own fair fingers with rare and significant designs, to every regiment as it left for the theater of war. Upon their departure to the seat of war, they were given an ovation, barbecues were held, grandiloquent orations were pronounced, in which the superiority of the South over the North in valor, military skill, and chivalric spirit was announced in terms that admitted no contrary opinion. They were assured that when they returned victorious—of which result there was not the least shadow of doubt—and had secured the independence of a glorious slave-holding confederacy, they would be honored living, and when dead their memory would be embalmed in the hearts of a grateful posterity and remembered with veneration, even until the last moment of recorded time. Sax-horn bands discoursed delicious music. "The Bonnie Blue Flag that Boasts a Single Star," "Maryland, my Maryland," and preeminently, "Dixie," were played and sung by band and orchestra and choir. The South had donned her holiday attire, and wine-cup, dance, and song ruled the hour.

"Oh! that the Yankees would come," cried they, "we would welcome them with bloody hands to hospitable graves. One of our companies is equivalent to a regiment of Yankees, and a southern regiment more than a match for ten thousand northern mudsills."

One evening Commodore Spiva met me as I walked museful in a grove. He joined me in a walk, and shortly drew me to a seat beneath a fig tree and thus began:

"Are you aware that your life is in danger?"

"Whence the danger?"

"There are men in our neighborhood that would have made the attempt to assassinate you ere this, but they know you are under my protection. I fear that as you travel about in the discharge of your pastoral duty they may waylay and murder you."

"I am prepared, if attacked, to defend myself."

"Your pistols would avail nothing at long range against men armed with rifles."

"Well, what would you advise?"

"Dr. Hughes will call upon you tomorrow and inform you of the decision arrived at an informal meeting attended by the leading members and supporters of Nazareth Church."

On the next day Dr. Hughes called to inform me that if I wished to live long on the earth I must declare my adhesion unequivocally to the government of our nation, the sovereign state of Mississippi, and also my good-will toward the subordinate Confederate States of America, and my approval of their constitutions.

"Declare my adhesion unequivocally to the government of our nation, the sovereign state of Mississippi, and also my good-will toward the subordinate Confederate States of America, and my approval of their constitutions? Doctor, is there any virtue in such a political creed to promote long life?"

"Yes, we all think so, and we believe the time has come when we cannot longer tolerate any sentiments in conflict with the views of the dominant class in our country. We like you as a man and as a minister, but we deprecate your treasonable opinions, and we cannot much longer, if we would, save you from the vengeance of the soldiers and the vigilantes. I will call tomorrow for your decision."

On the morrow he called, and I told him that I had decided to return to Tishomingo county. He expressed his approval. I removed my household goods to Goodman, a town on the Mississippi Central R. R., ordering their shipment to Iuka. I conveyed my wife and child by private conveyance. We spent one night in Macon, Noxubee Co. Rev. James Pelan had been called to the pastorate of the Presbyterian church of Macon. He was a Unionist. A committee was appointed by the citizens to examine his library. Many of his books were condemned by this committee as containing abolition sentiments. Rev. James Pelan was a man of excellent spirit—a ripe scholar and a worthy christian gentleman. His life was being embittered by his political enemies. Every sermon was misconstrued and tortured into teaching something contrary to the interests of the sovereign state of Mississippi and the Confederate States of America. Threats of lynching were freely made. The Unionists often conveyed secret information of plots against the life of this good man. Often his foes endeavored to impair his reputation by slander and calumny, but these as often recoiled upon their fabricators. Wearied of such a life of turmoil, he resigned his charge and removed to the country, but the malice of his enemies pursued him to his rural retreat. One evening, when walking on the lawn near his home, concealed assassins fired upon him, wounding him severely. For a long time he lingered between life and death, but a naturally strong constitution, together with good nursing, triumphed, and he began to convalesce. But his enemies were on the alert, and ascertaining that he was likely to recover, three devils incarnate came armed to his house. Mr. Pelan was sitting in a chair eating some delicacy that his wife had prepared for him. These demons in human form asked Mrs. Pelan if they could have supper. She replied, "Certainly, I will order my servants to prepare supper for you." She left the room to give the order. These men then arose and one of them said, "All the supper we want is to kill you, you infernal Unionist and abolitionist." Instantly they all three fired upon their wounded and defenseless victim. Mrs. Pelan, hearing the report, rushed in and caught her husband in her arms. In ten minutes he was a corpse. Before losing consciousness the dying martyr said, "Father, forgive them, they know not what they do." He also said, "Farewell, dear wife, I die, but the government still lives and will eventually subvert rebellion, for God is just." His last utterance was, "Lord Jesus, receive my spirit." Rev. James Pelan was of English birth and parentage. His brother, Rev. Wm. Pelan, was pastor of the Presbyterian church in Connorsville, Ind., for twenty years, now of Wells, Faribault Co., Minn.

Thus died one of my co-presbyters and dear friends. When our presbytery —the presbytery of Tombeckbee—convened at Aberdeen, we lodged and roomed together at the female seminary, of which Rev. R. S. Gladney was principal. Rev. R. S. Gladney was a violent secessionist. He had just written a poetical defense of slavery, and was woefully vexed that the blockade had prevented his publishers, the Lippen of Philadelphia, from sending him the books. A young licentiate named Gallaudet was ordained at this session of presbytery to the full work of the gospel ministry. Mr. Gladney rebuked him quite severely in open presbytery because he had given a negative answer to the question, "Will slavery exist during the millennium?" Mr. Gladney affirmed that it would exist during the millennium, and would also exist in a modified form in heaven. The necessity of the marriage relation would terminate with earth, but he thought the southern people would require slaves in heaven in order to promote their highest happiness.

Rev. Gallaudet became pastor of the Presbyterian church in Aberdeen. Being a Unionist, the secessionists bitterly opposed him. At length to save his life he was compelled to abandon his field of labor. He made good his escape to the North. But poor Pelan was not so fortunate. The villain most prominent in his murder was killed in battle just three days after his diabolical crime. The righteous retribution of Divine Providence was not long delayed. Near this Judge Chisholm and his lovely daughter were murdered by the Ku Klux Klan.

We spent one night in Okolona, lodging at a hotel. A friend whom I had long known lived here. His name was Col. Carothers. He was a strong secessionist. He met me just as I had given my horse and buggy into the care of the proprietor of the hotel. He advised me to register under an assumed name, as the vigilantes had my name on their list of proscribed persons, and if recognized my fate would be sealed. He said: "On the morrow a regiment will leave for the seat of war in Virginia, and if your presence should become known they will surely take your life. Colin McIvor was hanged last Monday as a Unionist, although I and several others exerted our utmost influence to save his life. But it was without avail. We pleaded, but in vain, for a respite of two hours that he might make his will and bid his family farewell."

I demurred and declared that I was not ashamed of my name, that I had not done anything to disgrace it. He assured me that I must take his advice or pay the penalty of my temerity with my life. I walked up to the register and made this record: "George Bushrod Washington, wife, and daughter, Mt. Vernon, Va." After supper we entered the ladies parlor. Mrs. Des Lande, a lady boarder at the hotel, called our child to her, took her into her lap and said: "What is your name, my dear?"

"Anna Kate Aughey," she lisped.

"Where do you live?"

"Near Kosciusko, Attala Co., Mississippi."

"Where are you traveling?"

"To grandpa's, Mr. Alexander Paden's, at Iuka. But I think my pa is going to 'scape Norf from the bad people that tried to kill him. I heard him tell ma so. I ask God every day to take care of my dear pa, and ma does too. We are good people and love God; what do they want to shoot my poor pa for?"

The ladies present gave each other significant glances. Soon after Col. Carothers called me out. Said he: "You should not have registered by a name so renowned. It has attracted the attention of all the loungers at the hotel, and your little daughter, Major Linden informs me, has betrayed your secret. You should have registered your nom de guerre as John Smith, of Pontotoc, or some obscure town. Now do you and family retire to your room at once. I will arrange for your safety with Major Linden. He will order an early breakfast, and you can start by daylight or a little before. Drive rapidly to avoid pursuit, if it should be made, and it would be well to start southward and make a circuit as a blind."

We took his advice, and left ere the shades of night had lifted from the magnolia-embowered streets of Okolona. We started in a southern direction, made a circuit of several squares, and left the town via the northern suburbs. My good horse, Bellerophon, assumed a gait that led us to fear no pursuers.

"They will have swift steeds that follow with any prospect of success," said my wife.

Our horse slackened not his speed for several hours, and our babe slept sweetly and calmly. While the guests were at breakfast that morning in Okolona the chief of the vigilantes called to ascertain the antecedents and business in their city of the traveler who had registered as George Bushrod Washington. He learned, to his surprise and regret, that he had left at an early hour. The landlord disclaimed all knowledge of him or of his destination. At a meeting of the vigilantes that morning this matter was brought to their attention, but no definite action was taken for lack of testimony, except that this telegram was sent to Tupelo, "Look sharp for a suspicious character traveling in a buggy with a lady and child. He travels incognito, or rather, under the assumed name of George Bushrod Washington. If he visits Tupelo, arrest him and send us word. He evaded us by leaving in the night. All charges will be paid out of our secret service fund." Similar messages were sent southward to the vigilantes in Columbus, Lowndes county, and Meridian, Lauderdale county.

Upon reaching Marietta, Prentiss county, we met Misses Bettie Greene and Josephine Young, my former pupils at the Rienzi Female College. At their urgent solicitation, we spent the night with their parents. These families were Unionists. They informed us that Messrs. Wroten and Nowlin, Unionists, had been abducted by the vigilantes a month ago, and had not been heard of since. They were either languishing in prison, or had been murdered. Their families were in great distress because of their ominous absence. We reached the residence of Mr. Alexander Paden, my wife's father, the next afternoon, at four o'clock, without further incident of interest, except that when we reached Mackey's creek we met Major Stephen Davenport and Dr. Orton Choate, two virulent seccessionists, who hurrahed for Jeff Davis and the Southern Confederacy. They asked me how that suited me. I replied, "I am in favor of the Union, the Constitution, and the enforcement of the laws." They produced a flask of liquor and drank confusion and death to all Yankees, tories, traitors, submissionists, renegades and abolitionists, North and South. Saying, "We will see you later," they rode off, brandishing their sword-canes and singing "Dixie" in maudlin tones.

Upon our arrival in Tishomingo county I found that the great heart of the county still beat true to the music of the Union. At the last election they were permitted to hold the Union delegates received 1,400 majority. Union sentiments could be expressed with entire safety in many localities. Corinth, Iuka, and Rienzi had been from the commencement of the war camps of instruction for the training of Confederate soldiers. These three towns in the county being thus occupied, Unionists found it necessary, in their vicinity, to be more cautious, as the cavalry made frequent raids throughout the county, arresting and maltreating those suspected of disaffection. Corinth is a very important strategical point, situated in a semi-mountainous country, a branch of the Appalachian range which diverges from the Allegheny mountains and forms the mountains and gold-bearing regions of Georgia and Alabama. Here, also, is the junction of the Memphis and Charleston with the Mobile and Ohio railroads, which form the means of communication between the Atlantic and Gulf seaboards. After the reduction of Forts Henry and Donelson, and the surrender of Nashville, the Confederates made the Memphis and Charleston railroad the base of their operations, their armies extending from Memphis to Chattanooga. Soon, however, they were all concentrated at Corinth, in Tishomingo county.

Tishomingo and Iuka were two Indian chieftains. The town of Iuka was named for one and Tishomingo Co. for the other. After the battle of Shiloh, which was fought on the 6th and 7th of April, 1862, the Federal army advanced to Farmington, four miles north of Corinth, while the Confederates occupied Corinth, their rear extending to Rienzi, twelve miles south on the Mobile& Ohio railroad. Thus there were two vast armies encamped in Tishomingo Co. Being within the Confederate lines, I, in common with many other loyalists, found it difficult to evade the rigorously enforced conscript law. Believing that in a multitude of counselors there is wisdom, we held secret meetings in order to devise the best methods for evading the law. We met at midnight's weird and solemn hour. Often our wives, sisters, and daughters met with us. Our meeting place was some ravine or secluded glen, or by some mountain mere, as far as possible from the from the haunts of the secessionists. All were armed; even the ladies carried concealed revolvers which they knew well how to use. We had countersigns so as to recognize friends and discern enemies. *Taisez vous* was the countersign known by loyalists from the Ohio river to the Gulf of Mexico. The recognition of it was *Oui, Oui*. It was never discovered by the disloyal during the war.

The nefarious crime of treason we were resolved not to commit, but our counsels were somewhat divided. We did not coincide in opinion upon the question whether we should tend the militia musters. Some advocating as a matter of policy the propriety of attending them; others, myself among the number, opposing it for conscience's sake, and for the purpose of avoiding every appearance of evil. Many who would not muster nor be enrolled as conscripts resolved to escape to the Federal lines, and making the attempt in squads, under skillful guides who could course it from point to point through the densest forests, with the unerring instinct of the panther or catamount or aborigines, at length reached the Union army, enlisted under the old flag, and have since done good service as patriot warriors.

The vigilantes became very troublesome. They arrested and murdered Unionists wherever they could be found. Few loyalists dared sleep at home, but seeking out some jungle or copse they improvised a rude arbor or den in which they spent the night, and to which they betook themselves when an alarm was given by their families or friends. Late one evening I saw the beacon fires burning. Mt. Sinai was all ablaze, the flames ascending high. The moon was obscured by dark dismal clouds. Mt. Nebo was lurid. The lambent flames from Pisgah had enveloped a stately pine—long since dead—standing on the lofty summit far above all other trees. Hermon and Horeb were dark as Erebus. Unless these two were illuminated it was but a call to an ordinary meeting. We gave these peaks those names to designate them so that by the fires kindled upon them they might serve as danger signals or call together in solemn assemblage the scattered Unionists. At 10 o'clock P.M. Horeb and Hermon blazed out from their lofty summits. The fierce and spiral flames recalled the pictures of Etna and Vesuvius in the geographies of my school days, where the mighty waves of glittering fire, through some internal convulsion, shot from their craters far upward into the midnight sky. These indicated a special call, either some impending danger was to be guarded against or some Unionist had been wounded or slain. I was just returning from a visit to Josselyn, Amos, Petrie, Aaron, and Morrow, who were in hiding and were awaiting the return of the guides who had gone with a squad to the Federal lines. As soon as I ascertained that Hermon and Horeb were blazing I returned to the lair of these hidden ones, and when from the summit of a hill they had seen the signal fires blazing, they at once started to the place of rendezvous. I did the same after I had secreted my horse in the stable of a friend.

THE MIDNIGHT MEETING, AND
BATTLE IN GOOD SPRINGS GLEN. Dark hills frowned on every side; the waters of a crystal spring bubbled up and in mournful cadence murmured a sad refrain, then swiftly glided away adown the glen; the midnight moon gazed wistfully down from the zenith; fitful clouds and the overarching branches of the lofty forest trees, stately monarchs of the woods, obscured her light. I reached the place of rendezvous just at the noon of night. Quietly approaching from all possible points, human forms appeared, gliding noise-lessly into the narrow arena around the spring. The numbers increasing, this place was tacitly surrendered to the women, the men retreating to the hill-sides adjacent. John Beck received in a whisper from each the countersign, "The Union Forever." He reported ninety-four present, sixty-five men and twenty-nine ladies. I was the presiding officer, supported by two vice presi-dents, Henry Spence and Byron Hall.

Washington Gortney arose and said: "Mr. President—We are here assem-bled to determine what is the best method of evading the conscript law and keeping out of the rebel army. I favor enlisting in the Federal army. We will then be far more efficient in defending our government from subversion by traitors—James Reece, who is seated by yonder linden tree, and I have proved our faith by our works. We are soldiers in the Federal army. We fought at Shiloh and are with the army at Farmington assisting in the siege of Corinth, and soon we hope to capture that stronghold and bring deliverance to the persecuted Unionists in North Mississippi. If you stay here you will be forced into the rebel army, or you will be shot or hung, as too many of our loyal fellow citizens have been. There are already three hundred from this county in the Federal army, and four hundred from Franklin, the county contiguous to this in North Alabama. Leave your families; it will be only for a short time. Corinth will fall and before the Fourth of July this county, and probably the whole state, will be delivered from rebel domination. I will make this motion: Be it resolved, that we believe it to be conducive to the best interests of ourselves personally, and the Union cause, to which we will ever adhere, for all of suitable military age to escape to the Federal army now besieging Cor-inth and to enlist in that army."

Carle Ritter arose and said: "With all my heart I second this motion, and

I hope that it may be adopted with entire unanimity. Our numbers have been more than decimated by rebel violence within the last month, and I firmly believe that this resolution presents the best method of securing our own safety and overthrowing this ungodly rebellion against the best government that ever existed on earth—a rebellion inaugurated by slave-holders in the interests of an institution we detest."

The president called for remarks. Several made brief addresses in favor of its passage. It was then passed with entire unanimity.

At this juncture ominous sounds were heard. Dark forms were seen on the hillside to the south. Soon a line of battle was formed by our foes. We quietly formed in line on the north hillside. They dispatched a messenger who crossed the ravine to inform us that they were friends. John Beck hurried over and found that they had a former countersign, but he saw Bill Robinson and Major Ham at the head of the line. Then we knew that we had been betrayed and must fight for our lives without hope of quarter if defeated. We told them not to approach a step nearer as we knew their character. Major Ham was in command of this force sent to destroy us. He crossed the ravine and informed us that he had been within twenty feet of the president of the meeting, had heard the speeches and resolutions passed, was cognizant of our traitorous designs against the Southern Confederacy, and informed us that we must surrender unconditionally, give up our arms, and be sent as prisoners to Corinth. He would give us ten minutes for consultation. Should we refuse he would not hold himself responsible for the consequences. He feared that we would all be put to death. We replied that we would not surrender but would stand for our lives and do the best we could, if attacked. He retired, deprecating our course. They were startled at our apparent numbers. They were led to believe that there were but few of us, and that our disparity of force compared with theirs would lead us to surrender at once. Had we surrendered not one of us would have left that glen alive. The gathering clouds indicated the near approach of a storm. The lightening flashed, the thunder rolled, the rain commenced to fall in torrents. In the midst of the storm, Ham's men advanced and delivered a volley. James Brown fell dead at my side. Smith Burgess was shot through the left hand. We returned the fire with effect. The women crowded round the spring in terror, all except Sadie Beck and Sallie Ritter, who from behind two trees kept up an incessant fire with navy repeaters. This indecisive contest had continued for an hour. The storm had passed and the moon shone brightly, no cloud intervening. John Beck detached nineteen men, passed down the glen, and making a circuit approached from the summit of the hill in the rear of Ham's men. Our fire slacking somewhat, Ham resolved on a charge across the ravine. As they crossed the ravine we fired rapidly; one man approaching me I emptied all the chambers of my revolver. He did the same with his. I was now without any means of defense. He approached and raised his revolver to strike me with it. I struck first and he fell unconscious at my feet. At that moment I received a blow on my head and fell unconscious on my prostrate foe. The last sounds I heard were the cheers of Beck and his men coming down the hill in the rear of Ham. When consciousness returned I was lying on a bed in a cabin surrounded by forest trees. Two ladies were the only persons present in the cabin, one of whom was seated at my bedside. On the green-sward in front of the door lay a man bound with cords. Gortney and Reece were seated on the ground near him. Gortney had recognized him as the guerilla who had murdered his brother only a week before because of his Unionism, and for this crime declared that he must die. At the moment of my fall Ham and his force, finding themselves assaulted in front and rear, precipitately retreated, leaving the Unionists masters of the field. Six were killed outright, two Unionists and four rebels. The dead were buried in separate graves on the hillside. I pleaded for the life of Bill Hodge, but Gortney was inexorable. I told him that I forgave Hodge for the wound he had inflicted upon me. Gortney and Reece went to procure me some water. After considerable persuasion I secured the consent of the ladies and after receiving a solemn oath from Hodge that he would not reveal the whereabouts of the cabin or anything to our injury I severed the cords that bound him and let him loose. He sprang away nimbly, and was ascending a knoll fifty yards distant when the sharp report of a rifle rang out on the morning, air and I saw Hodge fall. When Gortney reached him he was dead. He and Reece buried him where he fell.

On the evening preceding this the vigilantes had tried and immediately hung George Payson and Rhoderick Murchison. They compelled them to dig their own graves, and then hung them and buried them in the graves they had dug. They had insisted upon being buried. The vigilantes said, "Yes, we'll bury you, but you shall dig your graves."

Payson said that he was a citizen of Bay Minette, Baldwin Co., Ala., and Murchison claimed his residence in Citronelle, Mobile Co., in the same state. He had removed from Multona Springs, Miss., a few months before. They said when arrested that they were en route to Enola, Butler Co., Ky., to visit friends. Upon searching them a letter was found on the person of Payson which read thus:

ALPHARETTA, MILTON CO., GA.,
Jan. 28, 1862.
Dear Geo.:

The Confederate authorities are becoming very cruel. They have incarcerated a number of our neighbors in a filthy prison, and forced several into their army. They say traitors to their Confederacy must die the death of dogs. My brothers, Leonidas and Perceval, have not slept at home for a month. More than fifty Unionists are in hiding. Good guides are difficult to procure. Two are expected from Selma soon, and we trust they will be successful in conducting to the Federal lines a large company. Gillam, Gilson, and Gillette, three Unionists of Seguin, Guadalupe Co., Texas, arrived here yesterday. They had many hairbreadth adventures in reaching this place. They were pursued by hounds, but succeeded in poisoning the dogs. They were compelled to leave Lee Ayler, who started with them, sick at the house of that staunch Unionist, Hornbrook Gradwohl. O, the troublous times we have fallen upon. I hear while I write the howling of the hounds in search of my brothers and other Unionists, led by those terrible vigilantes. But I feel sure that they will not be able to find them, thanks to the swamp, Little Dismal, and their knowledge of all the successful methods of destroying the scent and of evading or killing the dogs. I must close. I have to prepare food for the hidden ones. It will be taken to them tonight. Dear cousin, the loyal people will never be satisfied till the cruel perpetrators of so great outrages upon them are adequately punished. They deserve a severe penalty for the crimes committed to promote the interests of a usurpation organized to destroy the best government this world has ever known, and to perpetuate an institution subversive of the rights of man.

Your affectionate Cousin,
JENNIE SILVERTHORN.

This letter led the vigilantes to infer that Payson and Murchison were endeavoring to escape to the Federal lines. They were convicted and hanged, and buried in the grave they were compelled to dig.

I received three citations to appear on a certain day to be enrolled to attend muster as a conscript. I paid no attention to the citations. At length I received this summons to attend court-martial:

Ma. the 22, 1862.
Parson John H. Awhay:
You havent tended nun of our mustters as a konskrip. Now you is herby summenzd to atend a kort marshal at Jim Mocks. June the furst.
BLOUNT.

When I received this summons I called a meeting of the Unionists. Several had on the same day received similar official notices to attend the court-martial. We spent a whole night in consultation. We were one hundred strong, and I advocated attending in a body, properly armed, and, if necessary, to accept the gage of battle, but McElhinny and Scotland's wives had learned that a large force of cavalry from Corinth would be sent to assist the vigilantes. The majority refused to credit this report till a note was read from Miss May Coe, who was a spy in our interest. We could not doubt the authenticity of her information, corroborative of Mesdames McElhinny and Scotland's report. We then resolved as a dernier resort to make the attempt to reach Farmington, where the Federal army was encamped besieging Corinth. When I reached Rienzi it was evident that the Confederates were evacuating Corinth. On the 1st day of June (the day appointed for the convening of the court-martial) I had the pleasure of once more beholding the star spangled banner, as it was borne in front of General Gordon Granger's command, which led the van of the pursuing army. Thus for the present I escaped death at the hands of the rebels.

General W. S. Rosecrans upon his arrival made his head-quarters at the house of my brother, David H. Aughey, where I had the pleasure of forming his acquaintance, and that of Generals Ammen, Smith, Pope, and others. Tishomingo county was now measurably in possession of the Federal army. Col. Elliott, in his successful raid upon Booneville, passed Jim Mock's, at whose house the court-martial was to convene, scaring him so greatly that he dared not sleep in his house for several weeks. The Union cavalry scoured the country in all directions, and we were rejoicing in the prospect of continuous safety and freedom from outrage.

The rebels in their retreat had burned all the cotton which was accessible to their cavalry on their route. At night the flames of the burning cotton lighted up the horizon for miles around. These baleful pyres with their lurid glare bore sad testimony to the horrors of war. In this wanton destruction of the great southern staple, many families lost their whole staff of bread, and starvation stared them in the face. Many would have perished had it not been for the liberal contributions of the North, for learning of the sufferings of the poor of the South, whose whole supply had been destroyed by pretended friends, they sent provisions and money, and thus many who were left in utter destitution were rescued from perishing by this timely succor. I have often heard the rejoicings and benedictions of the poor, who, abandoned by their supposed friends, were saved with their children from death by the beneficence of those whom they had been taught to regard as enemies—the most bitter, implacable, and unmerciful. Their prayer might well be, "Save us from our friends, whose tender mercies are cruel." I have never known a man to burn his own cotton, and I have heard bitter anathemas and fierce invective hurled at those who thus robbed them, and their denunciations were loud and deep against the government which authorized such cruelty. It is true those who lose their cotton, if secessionists, receive a promise to pay, which all regard as not worth the paper upon which it is written. Ere pay day those who are dependent upon their cotton for the necessaries of life would have passed that bourne whence no traveler returns.

'Tis like the Confederate bonds—at first they were made payable two years after date, and they were printed upon paper so worthless that it would be entirely worn out in six months, and the promise to pay would have become illegible in half that time. The succeeding issues were made payable six months after the ratification of a treaty of peace between the United States and the Confederate States. Though not a prophet, nor a prophet's son, I venture the prediction that those bonds will never become due. The war of elements, the wreck of matter, and the crash of worlds announcing the final consummation of all things will be heard sooner.

As the prospect was so favorable that this whole region of country would soon be in the hands of the Federal troops and occupied by them, I deemed it safe to return to my father-in-law's, in the south-eastern part of Tishomingo Co. I applied to Gen. Rosecrans for a pass through the lines for myself, wife, and child. Gen. Rosecrans went with me to see General Pope, and after introducing me and vouching for my loyalty, asked him for the pass I desired. Gen. Pope said that he had issued orders to the effect that no passes through the lines should be granted for a specified time. Gen. Rosecrans then proffered to send Captain Gilbert, one of his staff officers, with us beyond the lines. This he said was done in consideration of the kindness I had shown him and staff upon his arrival in Rienzi. He told me that the rebels were over there in the woods not more than a fourth of a mile distant, and that they were about to move upon them. He advised me to return to Rienzi till the rebels were driven farther south. We were then near Mr. McClaren's, seven miles from Rienzi, on the road to Booneville. I resolved to run the risk, as Mrs. Aughey was anxious to return to her father's. We started and had not gone far when the screaming shells and bursting bombs came howling through the valley. Then followed the rattle of musketry, and presently the impinging of steel. The din of battle sounded in our ears. Suddenly a shell, screeching like a howling demon, passed over us. The pomp and circumstance of glorious war were displayed to our startled gaze. A retrograde was as dangerous as a forward movement, and we persistently followed our leader, Captain Gilbert. Our child, not realizing the danger, laughed merrily at the grand panorama. Soon a charge was sounded and the rebels fled pell-mell, pursued vigorously by the victorious boys in blue. I had no fear for my own personal safety because of the excitement, but feared greatly that some of the missiles might injure wife or child. But they seemed to bear a charmed life, for though the air was full of messengers of death, and many whistled by in close proximity, none did us the least injury. Several times when a shell exploded near, our horse reared and plunged, to the imminent peril of the occupants of the vehicle. Before the noise of the battle had wholly ceased my wife pointed to a navy repeater lying on the ground. I descended from the buggy and secured it.

At this time all marketable commodities were commanding fabulous prices. Flour sold at $30 per barrel, bacon 40 cents per pound, coffee one dollar per pound; salt was nominally one hundred dollars per sack of one hundred pounds, but there was none to be obtained even at that high price. All manufactured goods were very costly. Upon the occupation of the country by Federal troops goods could be obtained at reasonable prices, but our money was all expended except Confederate bonds, which were worthless. Planters who lived beyond the lines of the retreating rebel army had cotton, but they feared to sell it as the rebels called it treason to trade with the invaders, and threatened to inflict the penalty in every case. As there was no penalty attached to the selling of cotton by one Mississippian to another, my Unionist friends offered to sell their cotton to me for whatever price I could afford to pay. I was also solicited to act as their agent in the purchase of commodities. I agreed to this risk because of the urgent need of my friends, many of whose families were destitute of the indispensable necessaries of life. I thought it was better that one should take a great risk than that many people should perish. By this arrangement my Unionist friends would escape the punishment meted out to those who were found guilty of trading with the Yankees; if discovered I alone would be amenable to their unjust and, under the appalling environment, extremely cruel and vindictive law, and my friends would thus save their cotton liable to be destroyed at any moment by a dash of rebel cavalry. I sold their cotton, procured supplies for the famishing, and thus relieved the wants of many. I did not charge one cent for commission fees, and expended one hundred dollars of my own money to furnish provisions for families utterly destitute, some of whom had not tasted food for days. One day I rode into Iuka to the head-quarters of Gen. Wm. Nelson. The Gen. told me that he learned that Norman's bridge over Bear creek was held by a force of rebels. He asked me if I could send one or two Union men to that place to ascertain the number and position of the troops holding that point. I replied that I could. I secured the services of Wm. and John Thompson, who were brothers and staunch Unionists, to accomplish this hazardous undertaking. Only one of them succeeded. He got through on the pretext that he was desirous of getting medicine for his sick wife. He gave the diagnosis, procured the medicine at a cost of three dollars, and returned. During his brief stay he learned the probable number and disposition of the troops stationed at the bridge, and discovered the vulnerable point and recommended a plan of attack. I conveyed his report to Gen. Nelson. The next night the attack was made and not a rebel soldier escaped death or capture. Thus was Norman's bridge captured and destroyed.

One day I rode over to Mr. Holland Lindsay's on business. I had learned that he was a rabid secessionist, but supposed that no rebel cavalry had come so far north as his house since the evacuation of Corinth. Mr. Lindsay had gone to a neighbor's. His wife was engaged in weaving. She was a coarse, masculine woman, and withal possessed of a strong prejudice against all whom she did not like, but an especial hatred of the Yankees rankled in her bosom. I sat down to await the return of her husband. Soon Mrs. Lindsay broached the exciting topic of the day, the war. She thus vented her spleen against the Yankees:

"There wur a Yankee critter company (cavalry) come along here last week. They hearn a noise an' thought our troops waz a comin' so they drawed up in two streaks of fight right in front ov our house. Arter a while they axed me ef I haddent seen no rebels scoutin' round here lately. I jes' tole' em it warnt none ov their bizness. Them nasty, no-account scamps callin' our men rebels. Them triflin', nigger-stealin' scoundrels. They runs off our niggers an' won't let us take 'em to Mexico an' the other territories."

I ventured to remark, "The Yankees are mean indeed, not to let us take our negroes to the territories and not help catch them for us when they run off."

The emphatic us and our nettled her, as none of the Lindsays had ever owned a negro, being classed by the white nabobs as poor white trash, nor did I ever own a slave.

She replied: "I've hearn that you is a tory." She became reticent, indeed quite morose. I concluded to ride over to Mr. Spigener's, to whose house Mrs. Lindsay had informed me her husband had gone. On the way I met Hill's cavalry. One of them halted me, inquired my name and business, which I gave. He informed me that Mr. Lindsay had gone across the fields home and that he was on his way to Mr. Lindsay's. When we reached Mr. Lindsay's house we saw him in the yard. I transacted my business with him as quickly as possible.

Some soldiers had gone into the house. Mrs. Lindsay told them that I was a double-dyed tory and advised my arrest. The cavalrymen were all around me. Davis, Lindsay's nephew, came out and ordered my arrest. He sent my horse to the stable. After supper my horse was brought and I was taken to camp. I was now a prisoner in the hands of my own and my country's enemies. Four men were detached to guard me during the night. They ordered me to lie down on the ground and sleep. The ground was wet and I had no blanket, so I insisted upon going to Mr. Spigener's, about one hundred yards distant, to secure a bed. They would not consent, but I started without permission. The guards followed me. Mr. Spigener gave me a bed, the guards remaining in the room watched me while I slept. The next morning I asked permission to see their captain, whose name was Hill. I asked to be allowed to return home, informing him that I had been arbitrarily arrested by some of his men. I said that I was a civilian and not amenable to military law. Capt. Hill replied:

"Are you a Unionist?"

"I voted the Union ticket, sir."

"That is not a fair answer. I voted the ticket myself. Now I am warring against the Union."

"I have seen no valid reason for changing my sentiments."

"You confess, then, that you are a Unionist?"

"I do. I regard the union of these states as of paramount importance to the people inhabiting them."

"You must go to head-quarters, where you will be dealt with as we are accustomed to deal with all the abettors of an abolition government."

A guard numbering fifteen were detached to take charge of me. The apparent leader was a soldier named Saccapee Vaudreuil, who claimed that he was a descendant of Pocahontas in the 10th generation. They then started to convey me to Fulton, the county seat of Itawamba Co., Miss. When we reached a cross-roads about 12 miles from the point of starting, we found a company in charge of a Unionist prisoner named Benjamin Clarke. We were then placed in charge of two men, Dr. Crossland, of Burnsville, and Ferdinand Woodruff. They were under the influence of liquor and were very insulting in their denunciations of all traitors to the Southern Confederacy. They detailed to each other a history of their licentious amours. Dr. Crossland was the father of a very pretty little girl whose mother was a poor white woman. We halted for dinner. They asked me to pay for it, which I did, they promising to refund the money when we reached Fulton. This they forgot to do.

On our arrival at Fulton we were taken to the head-quarters of Col. Bradfute, the commander of the post. My fellow-prisoner was examined first.

Woodruff stated that they had played off on Clarke. They had visited him as he was plowing in his field, telling him that they were Federal soldiers—they were disguised as such—Clarke assured them that he was a Unionist, and that he hoped soon to enlist in the Federal army. Bradfute became very angry upon hearing this, swearing that Clarke ought to be taken out and shot then, but he said a few days' respite would make but little difference, as Gen. Beauregard would not allow such a tory to live long. Said he, addressing the guards, "Had you hung Clarke you would have saved us some trouble and have done your country good service." The colonel, turning round, glared upon me with eyes inflamed with passion and liquor, and thus addressed me: "Are you a Unionist, too?"

"I am, sir. I have never denied it."

"Where do you reside?"

"My home is Rienzi, Tishomingo Co., Miss."

"What is your profession?"

"I am a minister of the Gospel."

"I suppose, then, that you go to the Bible for your politics, and that you are a sort of higher law man?"

"My Bible teaches, let every soul be subject to the higher powers, for there is no power but of God. The powers that be are ordained of God. Whosoever, therefore, resisteth the power, resisteth the ordinance of God, and they that resist shall receive to themselves damnation. I have seen no valid reason for resistance to the government under which as a nation we have so long prospered."

"I command you to hush; you shan't preach treason to me, and if you were to get your deserts you would be hanged immediately. Have you ever been within the Federal lines?"

"I have, sir."

"At what points?"

"Rienzi and Iuka."

"When were you at Iuka?"

"On last Saturday."

"Had the Federals a large force at that place, and who was in command?"

"They have a large force, and Generals Thomas and Steedman were in command."

"That is contrary to the report of our scouts, who say that there are but two regiments in the town. I fear you are purposely trying to mislead us."

"Gen. Steedman has but two regiments in the town, but Gen. Geo. H. Thomas is within striking distance with a large force."

"What was your business at Iuka?"

"I went there to pay a debt of fifty dollars which a widow—Mrs. Nixon Paden—owed. She wished to be paid in Confederate money before it became worthless."

"Have you a Federal pass?"

"I have none with me, but have one at home."

"How does it read?"

"It was given by Gen. Wm. Nelson, and reads thus: 'The bearer, Rev. John H. Aughey, has permission to pass backward and forward through the lines of this division at will.'"

"Where were you born?"

"In New Hartford, Oneida Co., New York."

"Yankee born," said the colonel, with a sneer, "you deserve death at the rope's end, and if I had the power I would hang all Yankees who are among us, for they are all tories, whatever their pretensions may be."

"My being born north of the nigger line, Col., if a crime worthy of death, was certainly my misfortune, not my fault, but the fault of my parents. They did not so much as consult me as to any preference I might have as to the place of my nativity."

Woodruff, one of the guards, now informed Col. Bradfute that I was a spy, and while the Confederates were at Corinth had, to his certain knowledge, visited Nashville, Tenn., carrying information.

I told Woodruff that his statement was false, and that he knew that it was utterly without foundation in fact.

At the close of the examination, Col. Bradfute and an officer, who the guards told us was Gen. Chalmers, spent fifteen or twenty minutes in bitterly cursing and denouncing all traitors, Yankees, and tories, as they termed us.

Gen. Chalmers wrote me from Washington City, while he was a member of congress, that he was not the officer who was present with Col. Bradfute. That on that day he was eight miles east of Fulton, busily engaged in making preparations for a battle with Gen. Philip Sheridan, which was fought on the next day; and he asserted that he would not have treated prisoners with so great insolence and severity. He also denied any complicity in the Fort Pillow massacre. This officer, at the instance of Col. Bradfute, wrote to Gen. Pfeiffer. He absented himself for a short time, and I, from my position behind his chair, could read the letter. The following sentences occurred in the document: "An avowed Unionist. Has done our cause much harm. Advocates reconstruction at this late day. A pestilent fellow. Has in our presence uttered treasonable sentiments, and seems to take pleasure in doing so, He has held treasonable correspondence with the enemy, and has more than once acted as a spy. We can furnish testimony to establish all the above charges." We were then placed under guard and sent to the head-quarters of Gen. Pfeiffer, in Saltillo. We were brought into the august presence of this redoubtable general. When he read the letter handed him by the guards, he soundly berated us, and then sent us out a mile and a half from town, where we were placed under guard for the night in a small plat of ground surrounded by a chain. Quite a number of prisoners were there under guard; it was a sort of guard house, except that there was no house. No supper was furnished us, and the bare, cold ground was our bed and the blue canopy of heaven our covering.

The next morning we were brought into the presence of Gen. Pfeiffer. I asked for breakfast. This was refused. I offered to pay a dollar for a meal, as I was very hungry. To this he deigned no reply. I then offered three dollars for a lunch for myself and Clarke. This offer was arrogantly refused. He said he had no supplies for traitors at any price.

Said he, "I learn that you were born in New Hartford, New York, brought up in Steubenville, Ohio. How long have you lived in the South?"

"I have lived in the South eleven years."

"Where have you lived?"

"In Winchester, Clark county, Ky., Baton Rouge, La., Memphis, Tennessee, Holly Springs, Miss. My home at present is Rienzi, Miss."

"Are you a slave-holder?"

"I am not."

"Will you take the oath of allegiance to the Confederate States of America?"

"I will not."

"Have you recently taken the oath of allegiance to the United States of America?"

"I have."

"Where and when?"

"Gen. Wm. Nelson administered to me the oath June 8th, 1862, at his head-quarters in Iuka, Miss."

"Do you regard that oath of any binding force?"

"I do, most assuredly."

"Did you take it voluntarily?"

"I certainly did."

"Do you know that in taking that oath you became guilty of treason against the Confederate States of America, and the Republic of Mississippi?"

"I could not be a traitor to a cause I never espoused, nor betray the interests of a government which I have always denounced as a usurpation.

I profess to be a loyal citizen of the state of Mississippi and of the United States of America, and I hope to see this state, whose true interests I have ever endeavored to promote, return to her allegiance to the Federal Union which she has for the present endeavored to repudiate. I hope the sober second thought will lead her to see and repent her folly. Had the secession ordinance been submitted to the people and a free ballot and a fair count allowed, then we would have voted it down by a majority of more than two to one."

"Are you a higher law man?"

"Yes, I believe in the command, 'Let every soul be subject unto the higher power,' the powers that be."

"Well, the Confederate authorities are the higher powers, and the powers that be. The Confederate government is the government de facto, and by the Bible rule you ought to submit to it as a good citizen."

"Any insurrectionary faction usurping temporarily the reins of government, may have a de facto power to compel obedience to its behests by those who are willing to acquiesce rather than endure the penalty for resistance of its illegal and tyrannical exactions. Mobs in cities are often the powers that be, and a horde of bandits have often been the de facto rulers, terrorizing the people of a wide district, and for a time defying the civil authorities. I regard the Federal government engaged in quelling rebellion as the de jure government to which I owe allegiance. Those who are engaged in rebellion against this government are traitors to their God, recreant to their own best interests, and are guilty of treason against the best government the world has ever known."

"Do you know, sir, that all you have uttered has been recorded, and that you have spoken these words against your own life?"

We were then delivered to the guards, fourteen in number, and conducted to a hamlet near Verona, where were the head-quarters of Gen. Sterling Price. We were brought into the presence of Gen. Thomas Jordan, Gen. Beauregard's chief of staff. When he read the letter from Gen. Pfeiffer, handed him by one of the guards, he said, looking at me sternly:

"You, sir, are charged with sedition."

"What does sedition mean?"

"It means enough to hang you, you villainous tory. Where were you born."

"In New Hartford, near Utica, Oneida county, New York."

"Born in an abolition state, you doubly deserve to die, and no mercy or pity should be shown you."

"As to the guilt attached to my first seeing the light in the Empire state, if sin, it is not mine, but the sin of my parents. But you talk as a veritable son of folly, and in so doing you reproach God. Parents, native place, and clime. All appointed were by Him. But I glory in my native state. New York has never done anything to stain her fair escutcheon. She has never repudiated her just debts. She has never nullified Federal laws. She has never attempted to secede from the Union. Permit me, General, to ask you where you were born and educated?"

"I was born in Georgia, and graduated from the military academy at West Point, in your native state."

"New York may have, in some degree, tarnished her fair fame by nourishing in her bosom and allowing to be educated within her borders, a few traitors to the Federal government, but it is some palliation that it was not wittingly done."

"Do you call me a traitor to my face?"

"I make no personal application, but allow each one for himself to draw the inference his own conduct justifies."

"If you were so enamored of New York, why did you not stay there or return when Mississippi seceded, or when an act was passed by the congress of the Confederate States of America, entitled 'An act respecting alien enemies,' warning and requiring every male citizen of the United States, fourteen years old and upward, to depart from the Confederate States of America within forty days from the date of the president's proclamation, which was issued August 14, 1861, this proclamation excepting from its operation Delaware, Maryland, Kentucky, Missouri, District of Columbia, and the territories of New Mexico, Arizona, and Indian Territory."

"I regard Mississippi as still a member of the Federal Union, and the act of secession illegal and unconstitutional, and therefore void. I am a citizen of the United States of America. If the proclamation issued August 14, 1861, was aimed at and included the Unionists, we were recognized as citizens of the United States at that date, many months after the passage of the secession ordinance, and as we have as often as it has been offered, firmly refused to take the oath of allegiance to the Confederate States of America, and thereby become citizens of the Southern Confederacy, we are still, as you must acknowledge, citizens of the United States of America. If we are citizens of the Confederate States of America, why so persistently offer us the oath of allegiance. Many citizens of Germany, Great Britain and Ireland, and other foreign countries, have long resided in our country and have never taken the oath of allegiance, or become naturalized. Why not allow us to remain as residents within, but not as citizens of, the Confederate States of America?"

"By your own statement you are an alien enemy of our Confederacy, and have no rights that we are bound to respect. You clearly come within the scope of the law and proclamation. My plan would have been to suffer all alien enemies to depart in peace who were willing to accept the offer, and hang those who desired to stay and do us all the harm they could."

"The Unionists are a mighty host. In forty days they could not dispose of their property."

"No, they would not be allowed to take with them any of their property. Our congress passed a law to the effect that the property of all in the South who have a domicile in the North shall escheat to the Confederate States, and that any of our citizens who are indebted to citizens of the United States shall, upon payment of three-fourths of their indebtedness to the treasury of the Confederate States of America, be liberated from any claim upon them by their alien creditors."

"Perfidy personified! Now, sir, suppose the cause of the Union should triumph, what will become of those like you who have taken a solemn oath to support the government at whose expense you have been educated, and then in violation of that oath, and forgetful of her fostering care, as base ingrates have rebelled and with malice and prepense are endeavoring to subvert the best government on earth, a government which has never in person or property inflicted upon you a single injury, but has bestowed many favors, and superabundant blessings?"

"I will never ask clemency from a government I detest. There is no danger of abolitionism and Puritanism triumphing. Should they do so I would make my home in Brazil or Cuba. I will hear no more of your detestable palaver. Jefferson Davis, in clemency and mercy to the misguided, issued his proclamation; those who have not availed themselves of it must bear the terrible and just consequences."

"My friends who expressed their willingness to accept Jeff Davis' permission to leave, are either dead or languishing in gloomy prisons. It was only a piece of treachery on the part of your honorable president and his most honorable congress. But just give me a pass to go north and I will go instanter."

"The first pass you will get will be a free ticket to hell, where you would have been long ago if the devil had his due, or the Confederate officers had done their duty."

"Thanks, for your kind offer to give me a free ticket to the infernal regions. I was not aware before that you were the devil's ticket agent. You have me in your power and may take my life, but you cannot destroy the government. It will live long after you and I are dead. But what right, may I ask, have you, who believe in state sovereignty, you, a citizen of what you term the republic of Georgia, to leave your own nation, and crossing the foreign republic of Alabama, enter the republic of Mississippi, and interfere with me, one of its humble citizens, who has never breathed the air of your august republic to do you or any of the citizens of your foreign government any harm. This is an unwarranted and unlawful act, and evinces a high degree of presumption upon the part of an alien—a foreigner who has not, I opine, been naturalized since his advent into our nation, the independent, sovereign republic of Mississippi."

"Did you oppose the secession of Mississippi?"

"I did, but I now favor it. I trust that she will soon become convinced of her folly and secede from this confederation and resume her allegiance to the Federal union."

"That tongue of yours will not long give utterance to such vile and treasonable sentiments, you ought upon your capture to have been sent to hell from the lowest lateral limb of the nearest tree. Corporal of the guard, take charge of the prisoners."

We were soon under way to Tupelo. When we reached this town we were conducted to the office of the provost marshal. We underwent an examination here in presence of officers of high rank, Gen. Braxton Bragg, Gen. Hardee, and Gen. Sterling Price being among the number. Their insignia of high rank, their dignified bearing, their resolute demeanor, their searching and subtle questions, wisely put to elicit the desired information to secure our condemnation, awed me into reticence.

I perceived that my life hung in a balance, and realized as never before the necessity of exercising great discretion in giving answers so as not to provoke these officers (who had the authority to order my immediate execution), and thus avoid the doom which a single incautious word would doubtless precipitate.

I told General Bragg, in reply to one of his leading questions, evidently designed to force from my lips a confession of my guilt, that it was an admitted principle in law, that no one is required to criminate himself.

General Sterling Price, who had just completed a dispatch which he handed to a courier, ordering him to convey it as speedily as possible to some subaltern in Verona, with a sharp look and an air of triumph said, "Your answer, by implication, admits your guilt. You would, it seems, shelter yourself behind a provision of the common law, which is suspended in its operation by martial law, which supersedes civil law during the continuance of the war. Will you take the oath of allegiance?"

"I will not make any admission nor confession, nor will I take the oath of allegiance."

"Well," said General Bragg, "we will await the testimony. From the tenor of this paper which I hold in my hands, there seems to be an abundance of it. We have too long been lenient with this dangerous class in our midst. I am inclined to punish them hereafter to the extent of my authority and the demerit of their treasonable conduct."

Clarke trembled like an aspen, and utterly refused to make any statement. I felt greatly depressed. I was hungry, thirsty, greatly fatigued, and mentally disquieted, knowing that my wife would be much distressed because of my ominous absence, the cause of which she could only conjecture.

We were then taken into the presence of the commander of the post. The provost marshal's name was Paden—the name of the commander was Clare. Gen. Thomas Jordan was now present, as well as the former named officers of distinguished rank. General Jordan made a statement. I feared from the interjected utterances of Gen. Bragg that we would be shot or hung at once. He was very angry, and several times declared that we deserved immediate execution. At length, in apparently great excitement and indignation he called the officer of the guard, and I feared the worst, but he only ordered him to take us to the dungeon. We were speedily committed to prison. When we entered, two men, Capt. Bruce and Lieut. Richard Malone, men who had been elected to these positions by their fellow prisoners, received us with a cordial greeting. We told them that we were perishing from hunger and thirst. Bruce and Malone set two of the prisoners at work to prepare something for us to eat. Bruce, addressing us, said, "Our bill of fare is not very extensive nor inviting. We have no coffee, nor molasses, nor sugar, nor salt, nor beef, nor vegetables. In these war times we must not be epicures nor expect the luxuries of life, but be content with what we can get,—just what is indispensable in prolonging existence. We are allowed to do our own cooking, but that, in the kindness of heart of the Confederate authorities, is accorded as a favor, an indispensable sanitary regulation. We have but little exercise, they say, and exercise being conducive to health, cooking promotes that object. We will soon have ready for you some corn-bread and a little meat. The meat makes up in strength and odor what it lacks in quantity, and the parasites will impart a freshness to it so that you will think of fresh meat while chewing it." The prison was filthy in the extreme, and full of vermin, even our food was infested. No brooms were furnished us, and we could not sweep the floor. No beds or bedding were provided, and we were compelled to sleep upon the floor without covering and nothing but the hard planks underneath us. When night came a space on the floor was assigned to Clarke and myself. We lay down on our hard bed and tried to sleep, but our slumbers were sadly disquieted by the cold and filth and hardness of the floor, and the graybacks, with which our clothing was already infested. The building had been an old grocery. Now it was metamorphosed into a prison. Where we lay the floor was saturated with molasses. When I tried to rise in the morning I could not. My coat was apparently hermetically fastened to the floor. Clarke was in the same condition. He, through the aid of a fellow prisoner, succeeded in freeing himself from the adhesive floor. He then assisted in extricating me, but a part of my coat remained attached to my wooden couch.

The crimes charged upon the prisoners were desertion, trading with the Yankees, adhesion to the Federal Government or Unionism, enacting the spy, refusing Confederate bonds and money, piloting the Yankees, the utterance of treasonable language, etc. The crime of the negroes, mulattoes, quadroons, and octoroons was endeavoring to escape from Dixie-land and the Iron Furnace of slavery, via the underground railroad. These remained till their masters, learning of their arrest, came for and released them. On the evening succeeding our incarceration two prisoners had been led out and shot. I soon learned that this was not an unusual occurrence. Nearly every day one or more suffered death as the punishment of their patriotism. Many of the prisoners wore heavy fetters. Some were handcuffed, had fetters on their ankles, and were chained to bolts in the floor. Often, without previous warning, the guards came, accompanied by an officer or two, usually two officers, and marched the poor prisoners to the fatal spot and shot them to death or ended their existence by suspension from the gallows. The two prisoners who were shot a few hours after we entered the prison were named Jerome B. Poole and Calvin Harbaugh. Being Unionists, they refused to take the arms offered them, when they were arrested and brought in as conscripts. Poole was from Brazella, and Harbaugh from Shuqualak, Noxubee Co., Miss. They were then suspended by the thumbs till they begged the officers to order them to be shot, as they preferred death to such excruciating torture. After the endurance of every refinement of cruel torture, they were at length brought to Tupelo, tried, and condemned to be shot to death. They inferred by a remark made by one of the officers who brought us into prison that I was a minister. Poole came to me and told me that they would be shot at sunset, and wished me to explain to Harbaugh more fully the way of salvation. He had tried to do so in a feeble way, but feared that he had not made it sufficiently plain to the mind of his friend. Harbaugh then asked me what he must do to be saved. I replied, "Believe on the Lord Jesus Christ and thou shalt be saved. You must exercise faith in Jesus Christ. Come to Jesus just as you are, not waiting to cleanse your soul from one dark blot. Do not tarry till you are better. Away from Christ you will only become more guilty. Come with all your guilt and fear oppressed, and say God be merciful to me a sinner. Ask him to receive you and forgive you, and adopt you into his family and make you one of his dear children by adopting love and grace for Christ's sake."

Harbaugh asked, "What is faith in Jesus Christ?"

"Faith in Jesus Christ is a saving grace whereby we receive and rest upon him alone for salvation as he is offered to us in the gospel."

"But Poole says I must be born again—that I must have a change of heart."

"The bible tells us that whosoever believeth that Jesus is the Christ, is born of God. Ye are all the children of God by faith in Jesus Christ. Therefore if a man be in Christ he is a new creature. He is born again. And as Moses lifted up the serpent in the wilderness, even so must the Son of Man be lifted up, that whosoever believeth in Him should not perish but have eternal life. Whosoever believeth then has eternal life, and whosoever has eternal life surely sees and enters the kingdom of God, so that whosoever believeth is born again. For God so loved the world that he gave his only begotten Son, that whosoever believeth in Him should not perish but have everlasting life. God loved and gave, we believe and have, and this is all of it to attain life and experience the new birth."

"I do believe on Jesus Christ and accept him as my Savior. I have never been baptized. Will you baptize me?"

"Yes, I will, gladly."

Capt. Bruce asked one of the guards to call an officer. When the officer came he sent a prisoner under guard for water. Harbaugh now told me that his father was a Baptist minister, and that be had taught him that the true scriptural mode of baptism was by immersion. An officer was called to whom the request was preferred that I should be allowed to immerse the prisoner in Old Town creek near by. Old Town creek is a tributary of the Tombigbee river. The officer returned stating that the military authorities absolutely refused to grant this request, believing it a ruse to secure an opportunity to effect an escape. Harbaugh said that he would submit to baptism by pouring or sprinkling, though he did not believe it to be the scriptural mode. He trusted that the good Lord would look upon the sincerity of his intentions to obey his command, which he was doing to the extent of his ability and opportunity. He did not think the Lord would require an impossibility.

In the presence of the prisoners and in the most solemn manner possible (the circumstances enhanced the solemnity), the ordinance was administered.

Just at its close food prepared by the prisoners was brought and offered these men. They took it in their hands, but ere it was tasted the sun began to dip his disk beneath the western horizon, the dreaded squad appeared before the door. These men, putting away the food untasted, said "We go to eat bread in the kingdom of God. Pray for us that we may have grace to deport ourselves with becoming dignity and propriety in our last moments. Farewell till we meet before the great white throne. You will probably come soon, for our foes are cruel as the grave."

The officers unlocked their gyves, led them out, and we saw them no more. A half dozen captured slaves seated in a corner of the prison, led by a young octoroon, sang some hymns. They called them spiritual songs. The following, to the tune, Old Folks at Home, was very melodiously and sweetly rendered:

OUR FATHER'S HOME.
Far over Jordan's rolling river,
Eternal day.
There's where my eyes are turning ever,
There's where the angels stay.
All through this vale of sin and sorrow,
Patient we roam,
Still trusting for the happy morrow,
Bright in our Father's home.
    Chorus.
All our heavy load sits lighter
Every storm we bide.
Oh! brothers, how the way grows brighter,
Near to the Savior's side.
Far from his tender arms benighted,
Dark was our way.
Still every precious promise lightened,
Where could the spirit stay.
Down at the foot of Calvary's mountain,
Pilgrims we come,
Oh, may we through that crimson fountain,
Come to our Father's home.
    Chorus
One lovely form among the sainted,
Heavens within,
Stands on my vision ever painted,
Stretched on the cross for sin.
When shall we hear his voice commanding,
Come, higher, come,
When in his golden courts be standing,
With our beloved ones at home.
    Chorus.

Chapter Three

Our privations were so great from a lack of good, wholesome food and pure water—for the scanty supply of water allowed us was tepid and foul—and from a want of beds, cots, couches, or something better than a filthy floor whereon to sleep, that I resolved upon an attempt to escape at the risk of my life. I felt sure that I could not long survive the horrors of this prison-pen. As soon as my arrest became known to the 32d Mississippi regiment, encamped in the suburbs of Tupelo, the officers called upon me. Col. Mark Lowrey, Capt. L. A. Lowrey, the Col.'s brother, Major Arnold, and Adjutant Irion. This regiment was raised in Tishomingo Co. One of its companies, the Zollicoffer Avengers, having been raised in Rienzi, where I had been for years the proprietor and president of the Rienzi Female College. The daughters of many of the officers of this regiment had been educated at this college during my connection with it. Owing me a debt of gratitude as they professed, could I expect less than the manifestation of deep sympathy with me in my sad condition—confined in a gloomy dungeon, deprived of the comforts, yea, even the necessaries, of life, and menaced and insulted by the officers in whose power I was? Some of these officers had publicly expressed themselves under great obligations to me for the thorough moral, mental, and physical training their daughters had received while under my care. In proof of this I have their own statements published in the public journals of the day. Whatever may have been my hopes, they were doomed to disappointment. These summer friends, so obsequious in my prosperity, conversed for a time upon indifferent topics, never alluding to my condition, and I did not obtrude it upon their attention, except that Capt. Lowrey, looking around upon the prisoners clanking their chains as they moved uneasily, trying to secure a less painful posture, said this is war—grim-visaged war with all its attendant horrors. When they left they said, "We will call soon again." I replied, "Do so, gentlemen, you will always find me at home," yet I was hoping they would not—my mind was bent upon and occupied with the high resolve of escaping or dying in the attempt, and even then I was maturing a plan to compass that end.

A young gentleman and his sister, by virtue of a pass, entered our prison. They conversed with the prisoners freely. An officer escorted the young lady to the part of the prison which I occupied. She enquired naively: "What is the charge against this prisoner?" The officer replied that I was an avowed Unionist. She said to me, "Are you a merchant?" I replied that I was a minister.

"Of what church?"

"Of the Presbyterian church."

"We are Presbyterians," said she.

She then made inquiries about Reverends Wm. A. Gray, of Ripley, Jno. H. Miller, of Pontotoc, Jas. Stafford, of Danville, Dr. E. T. Baird, of Crawfordsville, J. N. Carothers, of Okolona, R. Henderson, of Danville, and others. While she conversed with me the officer visited another part of the prison. She then said *taisez vous*, and slipped into my hand a note. She gave me her name as Miss Daisy Carson.

The note was written with a pencil, and read:

"We sympathize deeply with you. We will aid you in any way you may suggest. We live two miles from Tupelo due—[the cardinal point indicated was so defaced that it was illegible]. If you could reach our house you would find all possible assistance. We are true blue. Ambrose Kavanaugh will visit the prison soon, if he can secure a pass. Ernest Travis, of Verona, informed us of your imprisonment. I met you at Mr. Price's, in Ripley, but you may not remember me. My friend, Miss Jane Kendrick, often speaks of you. Chew and swallow this as soon as you have read it. I take a great risk in this matter, but I am of a romantic turn and love adventure. After the war and the triumph of the government it will be pleasant to recount our exploits in behalf of the suffering patriots. *Taisez vous, Votre amie.*

"CHARLOTTE CORDAY,

"My *nom de guerre.*

"P. S. —Prof. Yarbrough lodged with us one night. We sincerely hope that he has safely reached his destination ere this. Do not become dispirited, you have hosts of friends and are doubtless under the kind protecting care of Jesus.

" 'Tis' late before
The brave despair.
Stand Firm for your country,
It were a noble life,
To be found dead embracing her.
There is strength,
Deep bedded in our hearts, of which we reck
But little.
"Very respectfully,
"C. C."

A prisoner came to me and said, "Chaplain, I have been informed that I will be shot tomorrow, and I am not prepared to die."

"What was your offense?"

"I was a Unionist—was forced into the army. I deserted, they followed me with blood-hounds. When the hounds came near I got my back against a tree, and with a knotty club of pecan wood I killed six hounds. The cavalry came up and fired upon me. I fell, wounded in the head and left arm. The wounds were not very severe. They brought me to Tupelo, and I had my trial yesterday by court-martial. My captain, who just now left, informed me that on tomorrow I would be shot as a deserter."

"What is your name?"

"My name is John R. Witherspoon. I was born in Sumter, South Carolina, but have lived in Bolivar, Tennessee, for ten years. I have a wife and seven children, six are girls. The baby, John R. Witherspoon, Jr., is my only boy. My oldest daughter, Gertrude Maud, named for her mother, is fifteen years old. She is a good scholar, has a talent for music and painting. All my children are devotedly attached to their parents. What will become of them God only knows. I own one hundred acres of land in McNairy Co., Tennessee. My wife's mother gave her a colored girl. I am a poor man and will leave my family dependent. I am a member of the Presbyterian church, but have been living in the neglect of duty for some time, and now I must die unprepared."

"What caused your neglect?"

"I became a candidate for office, and as it was customary to treat a great deal when canvassing the district, I did so. I formed convivial habits that were disastrous to devotional duties. I became negligent and absented myself from the church. My wife and family are faithful, and many prayers are sent up to heaven in my behalf. O, if I were rescued from this impending doom I would, by the grace of God, no longer neglect duty."

I pointed him as well as I could to the Lamb of God that taketh away the sin of the world. We went up into a corner of the prison and knelt down. I prayed God to heal his back-sliding and restore to him the joy of His salvation, then asked him to offer up a prayer in his own behalf. He did so in language and with an unction that surprised me. At the close he earnestly implored God to spare his life for the sake of his dear family. He asked to be longer spared that he might atone in some degree for his past remissness in duty by devoting all the days of his allotted time to faithful service in his heavenly father's vineyard. I asked him if he entertained any hope. He replied that he did, and wished he could live to test its genuineness, but he had some fear.

And now came still evening on. Mr. Witherspoon volunteered to go for water. He took two buckets, one in each hand. Two guards accompanied him, one on each side. He drew the water and started back. It was now dark; when he reached a clump of bushes he dropped one bucket and raising the other he dashed it in the faces of the guards, and sprang for the bushes. The guards speedily brought their muskets to bear, fired in the direction of the fugitive, and instead of pursuing at once, ran to the tents of some officers and gave the alarm. The whole camp was soon intensely excited and hundreds joined in the pursuit. A cry would be heard, "Here he goes." A few minutes later in an opposite direction the same cry would be taken up. Unionists impressed into the service did this to contribute to the escape of the prisoner. He made good his escape, and succeeded after some time in getting his family conveyed to the North, through the kindness of Major General Hatch. An account of his escape has been published. He encountered much difficulty in avoiding the bloodhounds. At one time he heard their howling in his rear, and not more than a mile distant. He came to a field in which cattle were grazing. He sprang upon the back of an ox, and using a goad he compelled the ox to carry him across the field in a direction that broke the trail and baffled pursuit.

His final adventure, his last peril before his safety was insured, may be worth narrating. One day as he lay concealed in a ditch he heard in the remote distance in the direction whence he came the faint howling of hounds. The sound became more and more distinct, till he became convinced that they were pursuing him and had found his track. He arose from his moist bed, and hastened onward with all the speed his enfeebled condition would permit. He had not gone far till he descried another fugitive a short distance in advance. He called upon him to halt. The man obeyed. He gave his name as John Denver. The vigilantes of the vendetta, as they called themselves, had attacked his house last night. He had defended himself. They fired through a window, wounded him and killed his little daughter Nellie. He rushed out, slew the murderer of his child, and wounded two others. They beat a hasty retreat. He had lost an ear, and had a flesh wound in the left thigh which made travel difficult. He was on his way to Corinth to get assistance from the Federal commander, so that he and his family might go North. The howling of the hounds indicated to him that the vigilantes had been reinforced and were in pursuit of him. As rapidly as possible these panting fugitives made their way toward Corinth. The hounds gained upon them. Mr. Denver had two revolvers. He gave his companion one of them, and they both resolved to sell their lives as dearly as possible. The hounds were but a mile distant, when, to their joy, they suddenly met a regiment of Federal cavalry on a scouting expedition. They as quickly as possible explained the situation of affairs. The colonel ordered the regiment to fall back out of sight. He ordered a company to dismount and conceal themselves in the chaparral, he sending their horses back. He requested Witherspoon and Denver to climb two small trees and await their pursuers. He then joined the company in ambush. When the pursuers came up they ordered the fugitives to come down from the trees. There were twenty of the vigilantes. They asked Witherspoon who he was. He replied, "A prisoner from Tupelo, escaping to the Federal lines." After a few moments' consultation, they told these men that they had but five minutes to live; and if they wished to say their prayers they might spend the time in that way. They had but one rope, which they had brought to use in hanging Denver, but one of their number furnished a halter, taking it from his horse's neck. Two men approached, threw the nooses over the heads of their victims and adjusted them. They then selected two lateral limbs protecting from a tree near by, threw the ends of the ropes over them and were awaiting the order of Jack Clinkskales, their leader, to consummate their murderous purpose, when a volley from the ambushed Federal troopers made sixteen of them bite the dust. The four survivors rushed to their horses, but a second volley caused them to fall bereft of life. The bodies were scrutinized closely to be sure that life was extinct. They were then piled up in the chaparral, and the hounds killed. Upon the return of the regiment a few hours after a drove of wild hogs were found feeding upon them. Thus perished a hand of desperadoes not fit to live, less fit to die. Mr. Denver's family were brought into Corinth in an ambulance, and soon after came North to Evansville, Indiana. Mr. Denver enlisted in the Federal army, and did effective service in his country's cause. Mr. Witherspoon also enlisted in the Federal service. He died on the field of honor. He was instantly killed on the 1st day of the battle of Gettysburg. Mrs. Witherspoon thus wrote me:

"My dear husband often spoke of you, and had hoped to meet you again, but Providence otherwise ordered it. His death is a sad bereavement to me and the dear children. But God makes no mistakes, and I bow submissively to His will. He has promised to to be the husband of the widow and the father of the fatherless. I trust implicitly in the promises of a covenant-keeping God. The tone of my dear husband's piety was very different after his imprisonment in Tupelo. He seemed to think that he could not do too much to show his gratitude to the God who in his providence delivered him from the execution of the death sentence already pronounced by the court-martial, and which only lacked a few hours of fulfillment at the time of his escape. Pray for me and my dear children, that we may be enabled to bear with becoming resignation this afflictive dispensation of Divine Providence, and that it may be sanctified to the highest and holiest interests of our souls, work in us the peaceable fruits of righteousness, and while looking to things unseen and above a far more exceeding and eternal weight of glory. We will, Providence permitting, move soon to Cincinnati. My daughter Gertrude has secured a position as teacher in one of the public schools of that city. We would be happy to have you visit us at your earliest convenience.

Your friend,

MRS. G. M. WITHERSPOON."

OLD PILGARLIC. An elderly gentleman was ushered into prison on the morning of the 2d of July, 1862. He seemed anxious to convince the officer who accompanied the guard that he was mistaken in regard to some abstruse question. As soon as the officer left, I approached the prisoner, and after gaining his confidence, drew from him his sad history. His true name was Prof. Lorimer Vickroy Yarbrough, a native of Fincastle, Va. He had resided in Austin, Texas, and New Orleans, La. He loved the old flag, and resolved to reach the North, in company with his son Oscar. By some means suspicion was aroused, and they were taken from the steamboat at Vicksburg, Miss., and thrown into prison, where they languished for months. At length, through the aid of Unionist friends they escaped from prison, and in due time from the city of Vicksburg.

Prof. Yarbrough had a friend named Leroy Paden, living in Hazelhurst, Miss., upon whom he could depend for aid. He also held a note overdue for two thousand dollars, upon a gentleman who resided in Brookhaven, in Lincoln county, Miss. Could he collect the money due on this note it would assist him materially in making his way to the North. On the border of Copiah county, they were arrested by a committee of vigilantes, and thrown into an extemporized prison. Here they were immured six weeks and fed on corn bread and water. At length, Oscar enlisted in a company bound for the seat of war in Virginia, with the intention of deserting upon the first favorable opportunity. His father was still held a prisoner. Now malarial fever of a malignant type supervened. During its progress reason left her throne, but a naturally vigorous constitution triumphed, and the prisoner began to convalesce. Hearing the attendants say he had known nothing for three weeks, Prof. Yarbrough resolved upon a ruse which he hoped would give him an opportunity to escape. He would, by the use of incoherent expressions and singular conduct, feign madness. In the course of time, health returned, and the military authorities sent him to Gen. Beauregard at Tupelo. Gen. Beauregard believed him to be a malingerer, and sent for two alienists to decide upon his sanity. On the 12th of June, 1862, the commission to determine the sanity of the prisoner convened. A number of officers of high rank were present.

I will give the account of the examination in Yarbrough's language:

"I was brought in under guard, a seat furnished to me, and the bizarre farce commenced.

"Gen. Beauregard enquired, 'What is your name?'

" 'My name, Capting, air old Pilgarlic.'

"Gen. B. —'What does that mean?'

" 'It means old Baldhead. You see, Capting, I hain't got no har on top of my head. I was born so, and when some growed on, a nigger girl spilled some rusma on my crown, and I hain't hed no har sence.'

"Gen. B. —'Well, old Pilgarlic, you are in a bad fix.'

" 'Yes, Capting, and ef I hed as soft a skull as sum of these here young chaps, I could raze har to sell.'

"Gen. B. —'Where do you live?'

" 'I live in a cabin with a stick chimly, in Arkansaw.'

"Gen. B. —'Does your chimney draw well?'

" 'Yes, Capting, it draws the 'tention of every fool that passes on that trail.'

"Gen. B. —'Are you a married man?'

" 'Not now, I ain't, but I spect to be before long, fur you see, Capting, I hev the refusal of mor'n half a dozen widders.'

"Gen. B. —'Where did you say you were from?'

" 'From every place but this, an' ef you'll jis send them fellers away with the guns an' bayonets I'll be away from this in a giffy, that is, providin' you takes this jewelry off'n my legs an' wrists.'

"Gen. B. —'Pilgarlic, what's your opinion about this war?'

" 'I thinks, Capting, that no Southerner ort to fight agin liberty, nor no Yankee agin his country.'

"Gen. B. —'Where's your son?'

" 'Well Capting, I duzzent know. He give me the slip. I spec he went off ter the war.'

"Gen. B. —'Well, sir, your son attempted to desert to the enemy, and he now lies in prison with a ball and chain attached to his ankle.'

"I then commenced to sing as loudly as I could:

Spread all her canvas to the breeze,
Set every threadbare sail,
And give her to the god of storms,
The lightning and the gale.

"The General ordered me to cease. I heeded him not, and sang:

When a deed is done for freedom,
Through the broad earth's aching breast
Runs a thrill of joy prophetic, trembling on
From east to west;
And the slave, where'er he cowers,
Feels the soul within him climb
To the awful verge of manhood,
As the energy sublime,
Of a century bursts full blossomed
On the stormy stem of time.

"The alienists felt my pulse and inserted a thermometer into my mouth, which I crushed between my teeth. I then sang, or rather shouted vociferously:

Oh! For an hour of youthful joy,
Give me back my twentieth spring,
I'd rather laugh a bright-haired boy,
Than reign a gray-haired king.

"At this juncture Gen. Beauregard ordered the guards to make me hush. I then yelled, for it could not be called singing:

Prudent on the council train,
Dauntless on the battle plain,
Ready at the country's need
For her glorious cause to bleed.

"By the general's order the guards bound and gagged me. The alienists differed in opinion as to my sanity. One regarded me as a malingerer, the other declared that I was in a state of mental aberration which bid fair to culminate in incurable insanity. I was confined under guard in a room in a hotel in Tupelo till yesterday, when I was incarcerated in this dungeon."

Gen. Beauregard was now superseded by Gen. Braxton Bragg. Gen. Bragg had been but a short time in supreme command when he reviewed the testimony in the case of Prof. Yarbrough. On the 11th of July, 1862, the order came for his execution. He was taken from our prison to the fatal spot where so many brave Unionists had ended their lives. His request that they would not blindfold him was granted. He faced the muskets with an unblanched countenance. A volley rang out upon the evening air, and the professor fell pierced by the bullets of the squad. When his struggles ceased and he was pronounced dead by the sergeant, the corpse was given into the custody of Billingsly and Kaiser, conscripts, from near Tallaloosa, Miss., and relatives, they claimed, of the professor. They bore the body tenderly to a house in the suburbs of Tupelo. These men were Unionists, and had been forced into the Confederate service. This family, whose name was Montreal, were pronounced Unionists. When the putative corpse was laid upon the couch prepared for its reception, an examination revealed that one ball had shattered the left arm so that amputation would have been required had no other wound caused death. A ball had glanced from the ribs, another ball had passed through his clothing. The limbs had not assumed rigidity, and it was evident that the professor was not dead, but only in a state of syncope. From this condition he slowly rallied. Billingsly understood surgery, and with the aid of some Unionist neighbors Prof. Yarbrough's arm was amputated, and upon his recovery, which was rapid, he was conducted by night from one Union neighborhood to another, till at length he reached La Grange, Tenn., which was in the possession of the Federal troops. Among the first to visit him were his son Oscar, now a captain of a company in a Federal regiment, and a nephew, Charles Barry, formerly of D'Arbonne, La., now an officer in the Union army, Gen. Beauregard's statement in regard to the capture of Oscar Yarbrough being false.

The following letter will unfold some of the more thrilling incidents of his final escape:

Rev. John H. Aughey:

DEAR FRIEND — Having learned through John H. Stanton that you are chaplain of Gen. Benjamin Grierson's old regiment, the 6th Ill. cavalry, I send you by him this short letter. Please inform me how you escaped from Tupelo. I heard Gen. Bragg tell Major Grosvenor, when he tried to say something in your defense, that you would be hanged on Tuesday of the next week as sure as there was a God in heaven. He said you deserved to suffer a hundred deaths for your disloyal speeches and your many treasonable acts. That there was a ghost of a chance for you seemed incredible, chained as you were, and so vigilantly guarded, far away from the Federal lines and surrounded by the great rebel army. Do write me at once and tell me all about your escape. It must have been well-nigh miraculous. The first intimation I had of your escape was an extract from the New York Tribune of an address delivered by you in Cooper Institute in that city, from which I learned that you had succeeded in effecting an escape, but the particulars were not given.

After I was able to travel I was conducted from one neighborhood to another, till at length I reached the Federal lines. At one time we thought it best to travel in daylight. There were ten of us in company, eight of us Unionists endeavoring to reach the Federal lines. Two were guides, Paden Pickens and

Paul Paden. We called at the house of a widow named Mrs. Violetta Markle. Her husband had been tried by a vigilance committee and shot, April 19, 1861, as a Unionist. We gave her the countersign *taisez vous*. She replied *oui, oui*, all right, and then after preparing a meal for us, she informed us that we were near a rebel camp, and advised us to take the route traveled by the guide, Solomon Frierson, who had called at her house yesterday on his return from a trip to the Federal lines, to which he had conveyed twenty Unionists from Oktibbeha and Pontotoc counties. After leaving Mrs. Markle's, Pickens climbed a tree and made an observation of the surrounding country. Two rebel encampments were visible, one to the north-east, another to the north-west. He thought that we might pass between them without much danger. We started on our way. At one point it became necessary to travel on a road a short distance so as to obviate the necessity of ascending a lofty and precipitous hill. We had just entered upon the road when we saw a company of rebel cavalry about half a mile distant. They had just appeared on the summit of a hill behind which they had been concealed from view. They descried us, and putting spurs to their horses came rapidly toward us. We gave up all for lost, and were about to break for the woods, when Paden, taking ropes from his pockets, told Bryson and Birney to put their hands behind them, when he securely bound them with the ropes. As soon as the cavalry reached us we went to one side of the road to let them pass. The captain, whose name was Pender, wished to know what this cavalcade meant. Paden replied that they had in charge these two tories, and were taking them to camp to surrender them to the general in command, that they might get their just deserts. "Good," said the captain, "I'll go back with you. Sergeant Buford, take command, and go on; I'll go back to camp with these men."

On the way back Paden proposed to the captain that we try these men now, and if they are found guilty shoot them. Capt. Pender agreed to this at once. He said that was the object of his expedition at this time—to quell the disaffected traitors to the Confederacy. He declared that it was he that had ordered the shooting of ten tory devils in the Poplar Springs neighborhood, led by one Methuselah Knight, as arrant a tory as ever lived. We then left the road, and coming to a copse of dwarf tamaracks, we held a trial, and upon their own confession convicted Bryson and Birney of treason against the Confederate States of America. Paden and Pickens asked the privilege of shooting the prisoners. This Capt. Pender granted. Upon the pretense that they had no pistols, Pender drew his pistols from their holsters and presented them to Paden. Paden handed one to Pickens. The prisoners were then bound to two saplings. Paden asked Pender to give the command. The captain told the prisoners that, in compassion to their souls, he would grant them five minutes to make their peace with God.

Birney said, "Captain, we have long ago made our peace with our God. Have you done the same?" Pender replied, "I have killed Union traitors enough to save me."

He then gave the command, "Make ready, TAKE AIM, FIRE." Pickens and Paden fired simultaneously, but not at the prisoners. Pender fell pierced by two balls, and in five minutes his soul had taken its flight to the bar of God. As Pender fell he said, "D—n the traitors," and without uttering another word his spirit left its clay tenement. It became necessary to kill the horse, as his presence would endanger our safety. Bryson and Birney were unbound, and we pursued our journey rejoicing, leaving Pender where he fell. Without further incident of importance we reached the Union lines, and received a cordial welcome.

Let me hear from you at your very earliest convenience.

Yours truly,
L. V. YARBROUGH,
Alias, OLD PILGARLIC.

Having determined to attempt an escape at all hazards, I thought it would be well to secure a companion who would undertake with me the perilous adventure. Two are better than one. After due deliberation, I selected Richard Malone, his piercing eye and his intellectual physiognomy led me to believe that if he should consent to make the attempt with me, our prospect for success would be enhanced. Upon broaching the matter to him, he drew from his pocket a paper containing the proper route to pursue, mapped out clearly. A Unionist friend had covertly conveyed it to him. Gray Walton was his name. For some days Malone had resolved to escape or perish in the attempt. With all the ardor imparted by a new born hope, we entered upon the formation of a plan of escape. We went out now upon every possible pretext. We no longer tried to avoid the guard that came to obtain detachments of prisoners to do servile labor. We were the first to present ourselves, our object being to reconnoitre, in order to learn where guards were stationed, so as to determine the best method of escaping through the town after leaving the prison, and of passing through the great army that environed us. During the day we made these observations, that two guards stationed on the western enclosure attached to the prison were very communicative and very verdant, that after relief they would come on duty again at midnight, that there was a building on the south side of the prison, sixteen feet distant from it, which extended beyond our prison, and beyond the enclosure in the rear of the prison in which the guards were stationed. We learned that the moon would set about 11 P. M. and we ascertained that there were no guards upon the south side of the prison during the day. I learned this by volunteering to go for water. Two guards accompanied me; as I neared the prison, having drawn the soft hat I was wearing down pretty well, I peered from under it and scanned the surroundings as closely as possible, observing where every vidette was stationed, and gaining by close scrutiny all possible information. We learned that one of the planks in the floor was in a condition to be readily removed. The building was placed on blocks, and the planks were nailed on perpendicularly, and the ragged edges did not in some places reach the ground. Apertures were thus formed by which we hoped, if once under the prison, egress might be secured. We then hoped to reach the building which was about sixteen feet distant, on the south side, and by crawling along close to it pass the enclosure on the western end of our prison in which the guards were stationed. Troyer Anderson, and De Grummond, Federal prisoners, assisted by Hermon Bonar, Prince Shelby, and Gaither Breckenridge, Unionists, managed to raise the plank from the floor and replace it loosely, so that it could be removed at the opportune moment.

Benjamin Clarke came to me and said, "Take me along with you." I referred him to Malone, who refused. Clarke came back, and told me that Malone would not consent, and begged me to try to prevail upon Malone to agree to take him with us. Said he,

"I have been tried and condemned, and should I be shot my poor wife and eight children will perish."

I went to Malone and asked him to consent to take Clarke along. Said he,

"No, Clarke has not nerve sufficient to face the glittering bayonet, which we may have to do, nor has he the tact necessary to make his way through this great army without detection. He would do something that would betray us, not intentionally, of course."

As Malone was inexorable, I told Clarke that he and Robinson must come half an hour after us. This they failed to do. They dared not make the attempt, which was indeed perilous. This was July 4, 1862. We improvised a 4th of July celebration. I was the orator of the day, and delivered a eulogy of our patriot fathers who had fought and bled to secure our country's liberty.

We may say of these noble men as was said of the cathedral builder:

The hand that rounded Peter's dome,
And groined the aisles of Ancient Rome,
Wrought with a sad sincerity;
Himself from God he could not free,
He builded better than he knew—
The conscious stone to beauty grew.

Yes, they builded better than they knew. They erected a temple of freedom which we trust shall be lasting as time. No weapon formed against it shall prosper. In the providence of God no parricidal hand shall be permitted to succeed in overthrowing this grand edifice, this glorious temple of our country's liberties. Let us endeavor to be worthy sons of these noble sires, imitate their virtues, prize the heritage bequeathed to us by them, and preserve it unimpaired as a blessing to our posterity forever.

Breathes there a man with soul so dead,
Who never to himself hath said,
This is my own, my native land,
Whose heart hath ne'er within him burned;
As home his footsteps he has turned
From wandering on a foreign strand?
If such there be, go mark him well,
For him no minstrel raptures swell.
High though his titles, proud his name,
Boundless his wealth as wish can claim;
Despite these titles, power, and pelf,
The wretch concentered all in self,
Living, shall forfeit fair renown,
And doubly dying shall go down
To the vile dust from whence he sprung,
Unwept, unhonored, and unsung.

Perish the hand that with parricidal intent would apply the torch of the incendiary to the fair fabric erected at so great a cost by our revered ancestors.

Ah, never shall the land forget
How gushed the life-blood of the brave,
Gushed warm with hope and courage yet
Upon the soil they fought to save.
Oh, is there not some chosen curse,
Some hidden thunder in the store of heaven
Red with uncommon wrath to blast the man
Who would compass our loved country's ruin?

A dishonored grave and a hell of torment will be the final fate of every traitor, and while he lives remorse will haunt the impious wretch.

Not sharp revenge, nor hell itself, can find
A fiercer torment than a guilty mind,
Which day and night, doth dreadfully accuse,
Condemns the wretch, and still the charge renews.

Such be the doom of all traitors. May Jehovah, God of nations, blast all treasonable designs against the best of governments, a government founded upon justice and equity, and promotive of all the holiest interests dear to the heart of every true patriot, and philanthropist, and only subversive of despotic principles which would impair human rights and overthrow constitutional liberty.

Yes, my native land, I love thee,
All thy scenes I love full well.—
Land of every land the pride.

It is your high prerogative and mine to be able to say, I am an American citizen.

Our glorious government will live and flourish and dispense innumerable blessings broadcast over a smiling land long after treason has been consigned to an infamous and gory grave.

We may not live to see this prediction verified, but

"It is sweet to die for our country,"

and to know that although we perish as patriot martyrs, our children and the millions yet unborn who are to come into the possession of this glorious heritage, will enjoy during the coming cycles of the future the perennial sweets of liberty, equality, and fraternity. May God speed the day when the enemies of our Lord and of our country's liberty shall be overthrown.

I see officers approaching who may not be able to appreciate and approve sentiments such as I am enunciating. Permit me, therefore, to close somewhat abruptly with this sentiment:

Our Banner: Now wave in strength its pennons fair,
In peerless grandeur round the world,
Proclaiming far that freemen dare
Defend the right with flag unfurled.
We then sang with a will,
My country, 'tis of thee,
Sweet land of liberty, etc.

J. A. H. Spear, of Ellisville, Ill., or Troyer Anderson, sang a patriotic song. I remember but one couplet:

We've lofty hills and lovely vales,
And streams that roll to either sea.

It was well received. Some of the Federal prisoners started,

Rally round the flag, boys,
Rally once again,
Shouting the battle cry of freedom.

The officers who had entered, now in great anger forbade any further patriotic demonstration. They carried off our flag which we had improvised, and told the guards to inform them if we disobeyed their orders.

At four o'clock P.M., our plan was fully matured. At midnight (the moon having set and the verdant guards being on duty) we would raise the plank, get under the floor, and, myself in advance, make our exit through one of the apertures upon the south side of the jail, then crawl to the building some sixteen feet distant, and thence continue crawling close to the building till we had passed the sentinels in the western enclosure, then rise and make our way as cautiously as possible to a point in a corn-field in view from the prison, and where was a garment suspended from a fence post. The one who arrived first must await the other. A signal was agreed upon to prevent mistake. The signal was to place the arms akimbo. The countersign, *taisez vous*, the response, *oui, oui*. If the guards ordered us to halt we resolved to risk their fire, for our firm resolve was liberty or death.

As soon as the prisoners learned that I was a minister, they with entire unanimity and great cordiality chose me chaplain, and I preached to them every evening as long as I remained with them. Night drew on apace. Thick darkness settled upon prison, camp, and town. Murky clouds o'erspread the sky and obscured the stars as we partook of our scanty allowance of corn-bread and water—foul, tepid water. I took this meal with the Federal prisoners who were temporarily incarcerated till after some formalities they would be sent to prison at Camp Oglethorpe, Macon, Ga., and other places. Their names were Jesse L. McHatton, Co. H, 59th Ill. Vols., J. A. H. Spear, Ellisville, Fulton Co., Ill., Brocket and Benedict, 35th Reg. Ill. Vol. Inft., Sullivan, Howell Trogdon, of St. Louis, Mo., M. Troyer Anderson, Foster, Lowery, and a German, who went by the name of Charlie, who wore a saddler's knife sewed on his coat sleeve, Wm. Soper, Co. D, 22d Reg. Ind. Vol. Inft., and De Grummond, of Galesburg, Ill. The breeches I wore were light colored. McHatton exchanged a pair of brown colored for mine, so that I might better evade the guards.

About ten o'clock Malone raised the plank, and I went under to reconnoitre.

I remained under the floor about ten minutes, having learned that there were no guards patroling the south side of the prison, as we feared might be the case after night. I had learned by observation, when returning with water, that there were none during the day. Just at the noon of night we heard the relief called. Malone and I tried to find the prisoners who were to raise the plank, but not being able readily to do so we raised the plank ourselves, and both succeeded in getting under without much difficulty. Malone having gotten under first was compelled, contrary to our arrangements, to take the lead. As he was passing through the aperture he made considerable noise. I patted him upon the back to indicate silence and warn him of danger. He reached back, gave my hand a warm pressure to assure me that all was right, and passed out. I followed. I heard Malone in advance of me, but it was so dark that I could not see him. As I reached the point opposite the sentinels in the rear, one of them, apparently on the alert, and startled by the noise, came to the side of the enclosure nearest me, and leaning over peered into the darkness. He remained a considerable time in that inquisitive attitude. I remained very quiet. At length he walked to the door and looked into the prison. I moved on as noiselessly as possible, passing all the sentinels. It required great presence of mind and vigilant care to pass them without attracting attention or exciting their suspicion. I reached the pre-arranged place of meeting, but Malone was nowhere to be found. I gave the preconcerted signals, but they elicited no response. Some mistake had been made, and after waiting a long time I was compelled to set out alone. Not being able to rejoin my friend, I regarded as a great misfortune. He had the chart to guide us, and after reaching a point fifteen miles north-west of Tupelo he would be familiar with the topography and geography of the country. I had frequently passed through Tupelo in the cars, but knew but little of the country off the railroad through which I must pass.

Somewhat depressed in spirits by the loss of my compagnon de voyage, I resolved to reach my family by the safest and most practicable route. I feared the hounds and the cavalry which would scour the country in search of us as soon as our escape became known. I was still in the very midst of the great rebel army, and found great difficulty in avoiding the videttes that seemed to be well-nigh omnipresent. I soon found that day was brightening in the east. I felt glad to think that I was no longer in the gloomy prison. I could say with the Psalmist, "I am escaped as a bird out of the snare of the fowler. The snare is broken and I am escaped. God hath delivered me out of the hand of my enemy." I looked to the east, and lo! the orb of day was peering above the horizon. I must find a place to hide. I speedily discovered a small but dense thicket amid a grove of tupelo trees. This grove gave name to the town of Tupelo. I secreted myself as covertly as possible. A tree with low branches was near; I would ascend this if the hounds should discover my track. After the excitement and consequent mental strain, I tried to woo tired nature's sweet restorer, balmy sleep, and had partially succeeded, when the noise and horrid din of the great encampment sounding in my ears startled me, and drove far hence the winged Somnus. Soon many soldiers passed and repassed me. I was still in the very midst of the great army, and liable to discovery at any moment. I broke off twigs and covered myself with leaves and branches of the underbrush surrounding me. I was within thirty yards of Old Town creek, an affluent of the Tombigbee river, or rather one of the creeks forming the Tombigbee. The soldiers had found a suitable pool for bathing, and they passed and repassed all day; on one side their path or trail ran only six or eight feet distant, on the other path was but fifteen or twenty feet distant from my lair. About nine o'clock A.M. I heard the booming of cannon all around me, proceeding from the various encampments. The passing soldiers, whose lowest tones were distinctly audible, said that the artillerists were firing salutes in honor of a great victory obtained over General McClellan in the peninsula of Virginia. According to their statements, his whole army, after a succession of losses during eight days' continuous fighting, had been completely annihilated at a place named Malvern, and they were quite sure that Stonewall Jackson would be in Washington City within a week. This sad news depressed me more by far than the thought of my own condition. The hours dragged heavily. At one time two soldiers came within two feet of me in search of blackberries. I feared that one of them would tread upon my feet as they passed out of the copse, but he did not, although he must have missed stepping upon my feet by but a few inches. About noon, judging from he vertical rays of the sun, two soldiers sat down at the point closest to me on the nearer path. They were almost in juxtaposition. Their lowest tones were frightfully audible. One of them informed his companion that he had been in Tupelo in the morning and that two prisoners had broke jail. They were Parson Aughey and Dick Malone. He said a big reward was offered fur bringin' 'em in dead or alive. He said: "I seed the cavalry start after 'em with two all-fired big packs of dogs. One pack went this away and the other that away. (I supposed he indicated the directions by pointing.) I'd give my wages fur six month to ketch ary one of 'em. Think uv the honor uv it, Jim, to ketch 'em afore the dogs and cavalry did. Ole Bragg wouldn't stop at a cool thousand or two. Ole Jurdan he were bad flustered. He was a cavortin' aroun' hollerin' out his orders at the top uv his voice, jest a makin' the air blue with his cussin'. I wouldn't be in them prison guards' place for no money. I seed them officers put the irons on 'em, an' they took 'em in ter that same jail thet the tories hed got out on."

The other replied, "It aint no use, Jack Simeral, fur you to talk about them fellers. I'll bet they's sharp an' they's safe a hidin' with sum of thar tory friends hours ago. I'll bet they aint two miles from town. Jack, you know the Clines an' Kaverners, they'd die ter save a Union man. They hid Jake Broome a month, an' your own cousin Tillie Jack, she carried him grub till the Union fellers got the thing fixt up an' sent him off ter the Yankees—Bill Hawkins a giden' a squad of em'."

"Well," said the other, "them dogs'll kum up with 'em if they hev haf a chance, an' they'll never make it to the Yankee lines, sure as my name's Jim Billick."

Soon one of them arose and struck a bush almost above my head. I thought that he had discovered me and was about to rise and run, when I heard him say to his comrade, "Bill, that was the biggest snake I've seen lately, a regular water moccasin, but it got off inter the bushes. I reckin' it's makin' fur the creek, kase they don't git far from water."

I began to feel somewhat uncomfortably situated when I learned that I was in close proximity to large and poisonous snake, but I would have much preferred meeting an anaconda, boa constrictor, or even the deadly cobra di capello, rather than those vile secessionists, thirsting for innocent blood. They too, passed on and left me to gloomy rumination. Presently a large number coming from the creek were about to enter this thicket in quest of berries when one of their number swore that there were no berries in that thicket. He had been there last evening with a crowd and cleaned them out teetotally. He then took them to a place where he said there were plenty of berries, much to my relief. I thought this 5th of July was the longest day I had ever known. The sun was so long in reaching the zenith, and so long in passing down the steep ecliptic way to the occident. But as all days, however long seemingly, come to an end, so did this. The stars came glittering one by one. I soon recognized that old, staunch, and immovable friend of all travelers on the underground railway, the polar star. Rising from my lair, I was soon homeward bound, guided by the north star and an oriental constellation. Plunging into a dense wood, I found my rapid advance impeded by the undergrowth, and had great difficulty in following my heavenly guides, as the overarching boughs of the great oaks rendered them invisible or dimly seen. I came to the creek—Old Town creek. At that place it was deep and wide. I found a place where a fallen tree partly spanned it. I walked on the trunk till I nearly reached its terminus, then I ran and jumped as far as I could. I alighted near the further shore, in water only up to my arm-pits. I speedily reached the dry ground and hastened onward. The water quenched my raging thirst, but I was very hungry, tired, and sleepy. I at length lay down at the foot of a large water-oak, resolving to take only a nap, and then rise and pursue my journey. When I awoke the sun was rising. I arose full of regret for the loss of so much precious time. Though somewhat refreshed by my sound sleep, my hunger was almost unendurable, and I was famishing from thirst. At length I descried a small log house by a roadside. In the distance I could see tents. Feeling sick and faint, I resolved to go to the house to obtain water, and if I liked the appearance of the inmates, reveal my condition and ask for aid. I never had much difficulty in discerning between a Unionist and secessionist family. The bile and bitterness of the rabid secessionist was patent, and readily revealed his true character. He gloried in making his proclivities known. The Unionist was ordinarily reticent, unless he was playing the role of a secessionist, and even then his theatrical performance was transparent to one who had himself found it necessary upon occasion to assume that guise, or to one who had mingled with both classes and had studied their idiosyncrasies.

I went to the door of the log edifice and knocked. A gruff voice said, "Come." I entered, but a glance revealed to me the character of the proprietor. I did not like his physiognomy. He looked the villain. A sinister expression, a countenance revealing no intellectuality except a sort of low cunning, bore testimony that it would be the extreme of folly to repose confidence in the possessor of such villainous looks. I asked for water, intending to drink and leave his rude domicile. He pointed to the bucket without speaking. A gourd dipper was floating upon the surface of the water which filled it. I drank and bade him goodbye, and took my departure, glad to escape so easily. I had proceeded but a few steps when I heard the command, halt! uttered in a stentorian tone. Upon looking backward I saw two soldiers within a few steps. One was presenting a double-barreled gun, the other was heavily armed. I asked the soldier who had given the command by what authority he halted me, to which he replied, "I know you, sir, I have heard you preach frequently, you are Parson Aughey, and you were arrested and lodged in prison at Tupelo. I was in Col. Mark Lowrey's regiment yesterday, and learned that you had broken jail, and now, sir, you must return. My name is Dan Barnes. You may have heard of me." I had indeed heard of him. His father had held the office of postmaster. His son had systematically robbed the mail, and for a long time eluded detection. A detective, at length, through a decoy letter, discovered his guilt. When he was arrested the letter with its contents was found upon his person. While being conveyed to prison he escaped from the officer, fled to Napoleon or Helena, Arkansas—was followed, brought back, and incarcerated in jail at Pontotoc. As the evidence against him was positive and admitted no doubt of his guilt, he would have been convicted and sent to the penitentiary, but fortunately for this criminal, at this juncture Mississippi seceded. The jurisdiction of the Federal authorities was regarded at an end—a nolle prosequi was entered in the case of Barnes, and he was liberated and soon after joined the Confederate army.

Soon Barnes came to me and said, "Parson, I feel sorry for you, I can sympathize with you for I was once in a tight place myself, and would have been much pleased to have found a friend to lend a helping band. Now, if you will pay me a reasonable sum I will afford you an opportunity of escaping." I distrusted Barnes' sincerity, but could not make the matter worse by accepting his proffered aid. He named two hundred and fifty dollars as the reasonable sum to secure his connivance at my escape. I proffered two hundred and forty dollars. It was accepted, and I paid it over to him. When he had secured the money, he said, with a sardonic laugh, "I was just playing off on you. You must go back to prison. I have no sympathy for d—d tories, and wish they were all in h—l." They then brought me into the presence of General Jordan, whose headquarters were still at the place where I had the misfortune to meet him at first. The proprietor of the log cabin was named David Hough. He accompanied Barnes and Eph. Hennon, as they returned me to the rebel authorities. Barnes proclaimed, as be passed through the camps, his good fortune, and received the congratulation of the soldiers. He received everywhere an ovation. It was a sort of triumphal march, which he enjoyed greatly.

I became the cynosure of all eyes. As Barnes would stop and recount his heroic and marvelous exploit in arresting me, the soldiers would crowd around me, gazing and hurling at me a torrent of questions. They wanted me to tell them where Malone was, and assured me that old Bragg would be d—d glad to see me. After running this gauntlet for hours, I was ushered into the august presence of Gen. Jordan. He said, "Where is Malone?" I told him that I did not know—that I had not seen him after I had left the prison. He refused to credit any of my statements. He told me that Malone would soon be brought in, dead or alive. He could not evade the bounds and the cavalry. He hoped to heaven that they might catch him speedily, that we might die together. He then ordered a guard to conduct me to a blacksmith's shop. He ordered the blacksmith to forge fetters—bands and chain—so large and strong that I might be so securely manacled as to prevent the least possibility of my giving them the slip till I had expiated my crimes upon the gallows. The blacksmith was ordered to put the bands on while red hot, and my boots were burnt in the process of ironing. It was quite painful, though the blacksmith was as gentle as possible. Gen. Jordan stood by with drawn sword, superintending the execution of his order.

The blacksmith said, "*Taisez vous.*" I replied, "*Oui, oui.*" He gave me his name, and embraced every opportunity of offering a word of comfort. He was a Unionist. He asked Gen. Jordan to allow me to go to his house and get something to eat, but his request was arrogantly refused. I think his name was Monday or Friday. I remember that it was the name of one of the days of the week. I thus associated it in my mind at the time. He told Gen. Jordan that he had never manacled a man, and was averse to obeying such an order. The General told him to go to work at once, or go to prison. The blacksmith only obeyed upon compulsion.

"Iron him securely, *securely*, sir," was the General's oft repeated order. The ironing caused me much pain, my ankles being long discolored from the effects. By wearing shackles so long, ulcers were formed which have left life-long scars. After I was secured by these manacles, they assisted me to remount the horse. I was compelled to ride sidewise. The irons prevented me from riding astride. I told Gen. Jordan that I had been told that iron had become scarce in the Southern Confederacy, but that he had given me an abundant supply. I was conducted under guard to Tupelo. Upon my arrival the provost marshal and commander of the post were much rejoiced to see me. They became hilarious. Barnes, in grandiloquent style, stated that I had attempted to bribe him, that he had listened to my proposition with indignation, and when he had gotten the money did what he regarded was his duty. The commander replied that all of the property of traitors was theirs, and commended Barnes for deceiving me after he had secured the bribe. He also recommended Barnes for promotion for his heroic and patriotic act in arresting me, and for his incorruptible integrity.

The Provost marshal said to me: "Why did you attempt to leave us?"

"Because, sir, your prison was so filthy, your fare so meagre and unwholesome, and your treatment so harsh, cruel, and vindictive, that I could not endure it and survive."

"Parson, you know the bible says, 'the wicked flee when no man pursueth, but the righteous are as bold as a lion.' You must have been guilty of crime or you would not have attempted to escape."

"I confess to the truth of some of the charges made against me, and yet hold that I am innocent of any crime against God or man for which I am amenable to the state or Confederate states. As to pursuit, I think two companies of cavalry with blood-hounds would indicate quite vigorous pursuit."

"You shall never be remanded to the prison you left; rest assured of that. Did any of the prisoners know of or aid you in your escape?"

"No, sir, none of them knew anything about it."

"Are you telling the truth?"

"I am."

"Where is Malone?"

"I know not. I never saw him after I left the prison."

"He cannot escape. He will be brought in, dead or alive. Why did you attempt to bribe Dan Barnes?"

"It was his own offer. I knew that his cupidity was great, and thought it no harm to accept his proffered venal aid. If Barnes had his deserts, he would now be immured in the penitentiary at hard labor."

"Did the jury that tried him acquit him?"

"No, the secession of Mississippi alone saved him. I refer you to Col. Tison. He, being marshal of North Mississippi, arrested Barnes. He found on his person the evidence of his guilt—the money and drafts stolen when he robbed the mail."

I might say here, that after this Barnes was in company with several soldiers, boon companions of his. One of them, named Maness, said to Barnes, in reply to some fanciful story that he had been telling, "Now, Dan, you know that that is a lie." Dan, in anger, said, "If you repeat that I will shoot you." Maness replied, "We all know it isn't true." Barnes immediately shot Maness, and then fled to Chepultepec, Alabama. Was pursued, overtaken, and arrested. On their return, near the place where Barnes had shot Maness, near Paden's mills, the guard, three of whom were brothers of the murdered man, held a consultation, which resulted in a decision to inflict summary punishment upon the murderer. He had escaped the penalty due his crime in robbing the mail, and they feared that if they returned him to the army he might escape merited punishment. They compelled him to dig his own grave, and then they hanged him and buried him in the grave he had dug. His doom was just, and no tears were shed over his tragic fate.

Some of the general officers entered the provost marshal's office. After a short consultation, one of them, approaching me, said, "You will be shot within an hour. If you have any messages for your friends you may write it, and I will see to its delivery."

I wrote thus:

TUPELO, MISS., July 7, 1863.

MY DEAR WIFE—I must die within an hour, so General Bragg has this moment informed me. This is the last letter you will ever receive from me. I die because I have pursued unswervingly what I regarded as my duty to my God and my country. I would not, even for the consideration of long life and the endearments of a happy home, prove recreant to duty and swerve from fidelity to a government that has never infringed my rights of person or property.

To the kind protecting care of a covenant-keeping God I commit you and our dear Kate and the unborn babe, whose face in this world I will never see. God has promised to be the husband of the widow and the father of the fatherless, and he is faithful who has promised. I die at the hands of cruel, implacable, and vindictive men, my own and my country's enemies. This is the hour and power of darkness, but it is my time to die. My hour has come. It is appointed unto man once to die. Of man the scriptures say, his days are determined, the number of his months is with thee. There is an appointed bound that he cannot pass. The wicked go when their cup of iniquity is full, the righteous when they have fulfilled the mission appointed them by Jehovah. Our Savior was slain by wicked men carrying out according to the freedom of their own will their own murderous purpose, as Peter declared at Pentecost, Him being delivered by the determinate counsel and foreknowledge of God, ye have taken and by wicked hands have crucified and slain. Kiss our darling Kate for me. I have no fear of death. I go trusting in Jesus. We will meet beyond the river. Farewell, a long farewell.

Your affectionate husband,
JOHN H. AUGHEY.

I wrote within the lines an occasional word in phonography, which read thus: Inform Generals Nelson and Rosecrans of my re-arrest and my sad fate.

I was then placed under guard and conducted to a small room in a hotel till preparations might be made for my death by shooting. Two guards remained in the room with their guns with bayonets fixed, with strict orders to shoot or bayonet me if I made the least show of an attempt at escape. There were two guards also stationed just outside the door, with the same orders, to be enforced if necessary.

I remained in this room an hour or more, supposing that as soon as the necessary arrangements for my execution were completed I would be led to death.

After a time orders came and I was marched into the presence of the officers. General Bragg said, "We have concluded to hang you."

I replied, "I deprecate that mode of execution. Do please shoot me."

He then said, "You will also have a trial, and if it results in conviction, of which there is no doubt, you will be hanged in the presence of the army."

The guards were then ordered to take charge of me. My chain was so short that I could only step about ten inches. I could just set my heel in stepping even with the toe of the opposite foot. They brought me to the same old prison. When I entered it, my old friends, the true, tried, and trusted prisoners who still survived, crowded around me. Captain Bruce addressed me in his facetious manner. In prison his wit had beguiled many a tedious hour. His humor was the pure Attic salt.

"Parson Aughey, you are welcome back to my hotel, though you have played us rather a scurvy trick in leaving without giving me or any of us the least inkling of your intention, or settling your bill."

I replied, "Captain, it was hardly right, but I did not like your fare, and your hotel was sadly infested with chinches, chiggers, ticks, and graybacks."

"Well, you do not seem to have fared better since you left, for you have returned."

"Captain, my return is the result of coercion. Some who oppose this principle when applied to themselves have no scruples in enforcing it upon others.
'No rogue e'er felt the halter draw
'With good opinion of the law,'
is an old saw, and the truth of proverbs is seldom affected by the lapse of time. I am your guest by compulsion, but remember I will leave you upon the first opportunity."

Upon hearing this statement, an officer present, named Cecil Hindman, with a bitter imprecation, said that when I next crossed the threshold of that building it would be to go to cross the railroad to the place of execution.

The prisoners gathered around me upon the exit of the officers, and I related to them my adventures. They then informed me of what had occurred during my absence. At roll call the next morning we were missed. Clarke was taken out to guide a company in search of you. The guards on duty during the night were put under arrest.

Our method of escape was speedily discovered and the guards were released, as they were not at fault. The floor was spiked down, the guards increased in number, and greater vigilance enjoined. The prisoners were questioned as to whether they knew of our escape or had in any way contributed to the effect it. We all positively denied any knowledge of or complicity in the escape. They asked me if I had given the officers any information about their knowledge of our designs and co-operation in effecting them. I told them that I had positively denied that any except Malone and myself were privy to our plans. Was this right? Is falsehood ever justifiable?

If I had revealed the aid received from my fellow prisoners they would have been severely punished; perhaps some of them capitally, at once. And my fellow-prisoners would have regarded me as a base ingrate, and would not a second time, as they did, have risked their lives to set me free and save my life. We ought to speak every man truth to his neighbor, but those secession-ists, thirsting for innocent blood, were in no true sense our neighbors, though too near neighbors, in regard to physical proximity, for our welfare. In order to save life we may take life, and may we not deceive by words, and be guilt-less, those who would use their knowledge to destroy the innocent? I asked Benjamin Clarke, when he was remanded to prison, to give us the particulars of the pursuit of Malone and myself by the cavalry and blood-hounds, to which request he assented.

Chapter Four

BENJAMIN CLARKE'S STORY.

"You were not missed till roll-call in the morning. Your name was the first on the roll. This man (laying his hand on the shoulder of a prisoner) is a great mimic. When he tries he can beat a mocking bird. He can mimic any man's voice. He can call up any animal or bird when he wants to shoot it. This man, Will Croghan's his name, sung out, 'Here.' Some of us that knowed you was gone looked round, thinkin' it was your voice. When they got to Malone's name, Jim Benton sung out present, but he wasn't no mimic, and the officer called out agin, Dick Malone, an' nobody answered. He then stopped calling the roll and sent out an orderly. It wasn't long till old Bragg, Hardee, and some other officers come into the prison in a hurry. The officer commenced calling the roll agin. Croghan was afeard to chirp, an' they found that you and Malone was gone. Bragg stormed round a spell, and afore long I was sent for. They told me to mount a horse a nigger was holdin'. I done so, and we all started off. They told me to guide them straight to Paden's mill. We had twenty-five cavalry men and forty dogs. They started with that many, seein' they might have to separate to follow different trails. How the hounds did howl and yelp. To give you a chance, I took 'em round by Bull Mountain, up one hill an' down the same, an' up another. They wanted to find some of your cloze in the prison to let the dogs git a scent. I thought Alex. Spear, that Federal prisoner from Ellisville, Illinois, an' you had traded pants, so you could git a dark pair so as to git by the guards, but they wazent none the wizer for me knowin' that. Well, nigh on to 4 o'clock in the evenin' we struck a trail. The hounds follered it lively. I waz awful feared it waz yourn, still I thought you wouldent be sich a fool as to go off on a straight shoot for Fulton, where they took us on our way here, an' where all the roads waz picketed. The trail was fresh, and the hounds got about a mile ahead. All at once we knowed they had treed their game, an' agin I jist trembled in my boots for fear it waz you. We loped along as fast as we could, but the ground got swampy an' the bushes waz thick, an' drekly we knowed the dogs hed come up with some big varmint, an' it was givin' 'em battle, and they waz gittin' the wust of the skrimmage. We hed an awful time to git through the chaparral, an' we had to go out of our way a long trip to git round a sloo. But when we did come up with the dogs they hed killed an awful big bar. But afore he knocked under he'd got his work in on the dogs, an' you may never b'leve me agin ef there wazzent fourteen dogs lyin' dead as herrin's an' some more completely uzed up. The best sentin' hound waz lyin' close to the ded bar, and the bar's jaws was clozed on one of his hind legs like a vise. We got his jaws loose, but the dog's leg waz mashed into a jelly, an' we hed to shoot him to put him out of hiz mizery. Well, these cavalry fellows swore they wazzent goin' to leave till they hed tried some of the bar steaks. They drug the carcass of the bar half a mile to a hummock, an' rolled up logs till they hed made a big log-heap, then sot it on fire, skinned the bar, sliced off the nice steaks, an' jist enjoyed themselves. 'Fore this waz done it waz very dark, an' the cap'n in charge of the squad sed he reckoned they'd best go inter camp fer the night. 'Twazent fur from Fulton. 'Bout midnight ten of these fellers stole off to go to Madam Dunderberg's, in Fulton. She kep a bagnio on the edge of town. They got into a row with some roughs that waz there an' hed monopolized all the girls, and Bill Snediker and Jo Rucker was killed, an' Nath Downs waz hurt bad. They had a tough time gitten back. The cap'n hed to leave Downs at a settler's cabin, an' sent the settler fer a doctor, but before the doctor kum Downs hed gone wher they don't don't need no doctors, fur as we know. Well, 'twas nigh about noon, an' the cap'n said we'd bury Downs decent afore we left, so we hed dinner fust of'n the bar, then we dug a grave 'en buried Downs with the honors of war. I thought about escapin', but there wazent the ghost of a chance. The dogs was allowed to tackle the bar, an there wazent much of bruin, as the cap'n called him, left after they had done satisfied their appetites. The cap'n, Hindman I think waz his name, was purty bad flustered. He'd give me his compass, an' I, hopin' to escape, pertended I'd dropped it accidental in the swamp. The cap'n waz mad as blazes, an' swore wus than old Van Dorn when he foun' out the parson and Malone hed broke jail. He told me I must git them to Paden's mill agin night, or he'd tie me up by the thumbs. I told him that was onpossible. He said onpossible or not it must be did. Well, we started off, bearin' northeast. We passed right by my house. I said, "Cap'm les make some inquiries here." We pulled up before the door, it opened an' my wife an' children come to the door. I got down of'n the horse an' they all gathered about me like so many bees. Lilly May, the baby, nestled her head in my bosom. Jim said, 'Pa, we've been workin' like beavers since you waz taken away from us. You'll find the crops all right. Ma helped us, too.' Just then the cap'n ordered me to mount my horse. 'Oh, pa,' the children shouted, 'Ain't you come home to stay?' but the cap'n hurried on, and the last sight I had of my wife and babes they waz all weepin' as ef their hearts would break, an' its the last sight of 'em I ever expect to have in this world.

He stopped to weep and we all wept in sympathy with him. "When we got to Mackey's creek," he continued, "near Paden's mill, we camped fur the night. Next mornin', bright an' early, we rode up to Mr. Paden's. The cap'n told Mr. Paden he had a disagreeable duty to perform. He had been ordered to search his premises for a prisoner—a son-in-law of hizzen that hed broke jail at Tupelo. Mr. Paden said he might search, but they would find no one. They searched the house upstairs and down, then sent a squad to the negro quarters, another to the mills, but their errand waz a bootless one.

Again he stopped to weep, we all wept with him. Saying, "Excuse me I could not help it," he continued: "Your wife sat on the sofa in the parlor, pale as death. Before we left she came to the door and looked at the hounds and listened to their howling. Her hands were clasped together. Once I saw her lips move. I thought she was praying. I stood near her, but I did not hear her speak. I think she couldent speak for sorrow. Oh, how my heart bled for her, an' how much I wanted to tell her that I believed you waz safe in the Federal lines, but I could not git a chance to do so without notice. I got a chance to say to her father, I believed you waz safe in Rienzi by this time, an' I told him to tell his daughter so, which I haint no doubt but what he did. We left an' come back in a hurry. The other company that went due north got back about the time we did. A squad of them reported that they caught Malone, but that he got away from them at a house where they went to git water. They fired on him, and have no doubt that they wounded him bad, an' think he never could make the Federal lines. Our cap'n told everybody he met that a big reward was offered fur you, an' described you the best he could, an' stuck up notices describing you an' offering a reward fur catchin' you. When they got back they put me back in prison, an' I waz very sorry to see you here. Well, we'll have a chance now to go to heaven together. I reckon there aint much show fur either of us."

M.T. Anderson said, "If I am ever exchanged I'll publish this from one end of the North to the other. I'll tell of the heroic endurance of the southern loyalists who prefer death to dishonor, who prefer an ignominious death to the guilt of treason against the best government the sun shines upon."

I approached a prisoner who was heavily fettered. Both hands and feet were bound with iron bands, and he was chained to the floor, the chain being fastened to a bolt. I learned that he was a Minorcan. I said, "You are a

Minorcan, I learn." He replied, "I have that honor, sir." After confidence had been established between us, he gave me his history, thus:

"My name is Louis LasCassas Lornette. My father is a native of the island of Minorca. He removed with his family and a large number of Minorcans to a town on the St. John's river, Florida, in the year 1826. There I was born May 8, 1828. My mother gave birth to triplets—all boys—Louis, Pierre, and Philippe. We always dressed alike, and bore a striking resemblance to each other. We were devotedly attached to each other and were inseparable companions. We became mighty hunters before the Lord. We pursued this vocation con amore, and the founder of Nineveh himself, the renowned Nimrod, could not have been more successful than we. At length the tocsin of war sounded—civil war. We had all attended the academy of a professor named Nathan Hale, of the state of Vermont. He was a great admirer of the great statesman, Daniel Webster. He had a copy of his speeches which we were permitted to read. We admired them much, especially his debate with Hayne, Calhoun, and others in the U.S. senate in regard to the right of a state to nuillify the laws of the national government, or to secede from the Union. We thought those statesmen were like pigmies in the hands of a giant. When the war came, and we were told that the government must be disrupted in the interest of human slavery, my brothers and I resolved, come weal or come woe, we would never, never be guilty of treason to subserve an institution we detested. Our parents had taught us to hate slavery with a perfect hatred. Many a poor hunted fugitive have we protected, and taught him how to defend himself from the terrible Siberian blood-hound. We had never entertained for a moment the idea that we ourselves would ever be the object of pursuit by these same horrible dogs. One night a company of cavalry surrounded our father's house, during a re-union of his family. We three brothers were seized, bound, and after various vicissitudes were placed in prison in New Orleans, La., on the charge of treason against the Confederate States of America. We were tried and condemned to be shot. They then offered us a pardon on condition that we would enlist in the Confederate army. They gave us one week's respite for consideration. We were permitted to occupy the same cell in prison. We debated the matter, pro and con. At first we thought it best to send in our decision in the negative at once. Pierre reasoned in this way: 'Would it not be well to accept their terms, take the oath, enter the army, and at the first favorable opportunity desert and make our way to the Federal lines.' 'But what about the oath?' said Philippe. 'An oath exacted under such circumstances is much more honored in the breach than in the observance,' replied his brother. In a moment of weakness we sent in an affirmative answer. We begged to be permitted to enter the same regiment and the same company. This request was denied. We were mustered in in different regiments, and thus separated widely. I was put in a Mississippi regiment. I deserted, hoping to reach the Federal lines. A company of cavalry, with a pack of fierce Siberian blood-hounds were sent out in search of me. I came to a planter's quarters. The colored people and I searched all one day, thus losing much precious time, to find some herbs with which I could have compounded a subtle poison, and by means of pieces of meat saturated with it, I could have destroyed a large pack of hounds. But we could not procure the herbs. They are indigenous to a low, swampy country. They abound in the everglades of Florida. The colored people furnished me with cayenne pepper, onions, and matches, and I felt comparatively safe. But one day I heard a pack of hounds behind me. I used every ruse and stratagem I could devise, but just as I felt assured that the trail was broken a company who had gone north in search of you, while returning, came upon me and ordered me to come down from the tree in which I had taken refuge, and here I am."

"What will be your fate?" I asked.

He replied, "They have discovered the regiment to which I belonged, and I am condemned to death by shooting."

About 11 o'clock A. M., Col. Gustave Feuillevert came into the prison. He was a planter, a slaveholder, and a friend of General Sterling Price. He was of French ancestry. Had formerly lived in Florida, and was an uncle of Louis Lornette, the prisoner. He recognized him at once, as Louis a few years before had visited his uncle and spent the summer with him. Col. Feuillevert, who was an ultrasecessionist, tried to induce some of the prisoners to promise to enlist in his regiment in case he secured their release upon that condition. He was not successful in a single instance. He then approached his nephew, Louis, who was sitting alone in the corner of the prison, and informed him that his brothers, Philippe and Pierre, were at his house in hiding. He said they had deserted from Florida regiments, and after many remarkable adventures had reached his house in as ragged and forlorn a condition as it was possible for men to be found. He detested their treason, but their aunt would save them at the peril of her life, and although he would not betray them he felt sorry and angry at their obstinacy. The colonel urged his nephew to abjure his allegiance to a government that made war upon the institutions of the South and refused to keep faith with the Southern states, and had measurably nullified the provisions of the fugitive slave law; but all in vain, Louis refused to swerve from his loyalty. The colonel bade his nephew adieu, and departed. The day of Louis' execution dawned. I conversed with him, prayed with him, took his last messages to wife and children, promising that if I survived the horrors of this prison I would faithfully deliver them, but of this I had little hope. Louis told me it was clear to his mind that God in His providence had sent me to this prison for such a time as this. Those appointed to die needed the presence of one who could point them to the Savior, and, as a humble instrument in the hand of God, prepare them for a dying hour. It was a source of poignant regret that he had, even for the hope of escape, taken the oath of allegiance to the Confederate States of America. His oath of allegiance to the state of Florida he thought was right and proper, as he understood it.

At noon the guards brought in a prisoner who had voluntarily surrendered himself, declaring that he was Louis Las Cassas Lornette and desired to rejoin his regiment. When confronted with the condemned Louis, they bore such a striking resemblance to each other that the officers were puzzled. Gen. Bragg would be absent from Tupelo for a few days, and Gen. Sterling Price, to whom the case was referred, granted a respite till Gen. Bragg's return. Each prisoner insisted that he was Louis Las Cassas Lornette, and refused to recognize the other. The officers took the matter under advisement, and thought it best to send the two prisoners to Gen. Bragg for his decision. Should they fail to carry out Gen. Bragg's orders promptly they feared the consequences. A regiment was detailed for this purpose. They went via Paden's Mills. Here they met a regiment of Federal cavalry; a skirmish ensued, several were killed, and their bodies lie buried in Mr. Paden's orchard. The Confederates fled and were pursued four miles. They left their prisoners in the hands of the Federals.

So Louis and Pierre still live to tell their children the trials and persecutions of the Southern loyalists. Philippe soon rejoined them in the North, and enlisting in the same regiment, they served faithfully till the close of the war. Philippe died May 8, 1866, of a wound received in the engagement which resulted in the capture of Fort Fisher. Not till the war was ended did their families rejoin them. Louis' and Pierre's and Philippe's families are citizens of California. Pierre had resolved to save his brother or perish with him. The affection of Damon and Pythias could not have been stronger. A kind Providence crowned the scheme to save his brother Louis with abundant success, and these elderly veterans, still as much alike as in their youth, save the scar of a sabre thrust which laid open the cheek of Louis, are still fighting their battles over at the urgent solicitation of their children and their grand-children and neighbors.

These brothers are still soldiers, faithful soldiers of the Cross. Louis dates his conversion from the time of his incarceration in Tupelo, and when he writes to me addresses me as his spiritual father, and speaks of himself as my son in the gospel, begotten in my bonds. Pierre and Philippe united with the regimental church at Beaufort, North Carolina, brought to Jesus by their brother Louis, and their Christian graces rapidly developed under the faithful ministrations of that godly pastor, Chaplain LaSalle Coligny, of Huguenot ancestry.

After being remanded to prison, I felt that my condition was utterly hopeless. For a time, as often as I approached the door, the guards would order me back. I preached to my fellow-prisoners every evening. The best possible order was maintained, as they stood or sat upon the floor and listened to the words of eternal life. A deep seriousness prevailed, and many believed, to the salvation of their souls. The songs of Zion resounded through the prison house, and a great concourse of soldiers assembled outside the guards in front of both doors. Several officers saw fit to come in during divine service. Some of them behaved decorously, but on one or two occasions, officers who neither feared God nor regarded man, nor the proprieties becoming gentlemen, interrupted the services by talking in a loud and insulting tone, and asking me how I liked my jewelry, pointing to my fetters. The prisoners protested against their rude and ungentlemanly conduct but without effect; they sent a remonstrance to the commander of the post, but he treated it with silent contempt.

We were a motley assemblage. All the southern states and every prominent religious denomination had representatives among us. The youth in his non-age, and the gray-haired and very aged man were there. The learned and the illiterate, the superior and the subordinate were with us. The descendants of Shem, Ham, and Japheth, were here on the same common level, for in our prison were Africa's dark-browed sons, the descendants of Pocahontas, and the pure Caucasian. Death is said to be the great leveler; the dungeon at Tupelo was a great leveler. A fellow feeling made us wondrous kind; none ate his morsel alone, and a deep and abiding sympathy for each other's woes pervaded every bosom. When our fellow-prisoners were called to die, and were led through our midst with pallid brows and agony depicted upon their countenances, our heartfelt expressions of sorrow and commiseration were not loud (through fear) but deep.

An officer entered. My name was called. I arose from the floor on which I had been reclining. I recognized him as my old friend, Col. H. W. Walter, of Holly Springs, Miss. After the ordinary salutations, he informed me that he was judge advocate of this army, and that he came to inform me of the day appointed for my trial, and to learn whether I wished to summon any witnesses, and whom. I gave him the names and addresses of several witnesses, but he refused to send for them, upon the plea that they lived too near the

Federal lines I replied that the cavalry that had gone in pursuit of me had visited those localities.

He then asked me what I wished to prove by those witnesses. I replied that I wished to prove that the specifications under the charge of enacting the spy are false; that Ferdinand Woodruff is a man of no moral worth; that Barnes is a mail-robber, and therefore not a competent nor veracious witness.

"Your own admissions," said the colonel "are sufficient to cause you to lose your life. Both charges against you will be fully established. The testimony as to your guilt is very clear and positive." He then read the charges and specifications:

"First charge.—Treason.

"First specification.—That Rev. John H. Aughey, a citizen of the state of Mississippi, and of the Confederate States Of America, stated to a member of Hill's cavalry, that if McClellan were defeated the North could raise a much larger army in the a short time; that the North would eventually conquer the South, and that he was a Unionist—this for the purpose of giving aid and comfort to the enemy.

"Second specification.—That when said Aughey was requested to take the oath of allegiance to the Confederate States of America, he refused, giving as a reason that England and France and himself had not as yet recognized the Southern Confederacy; stating also that he had voluntarily taken the oath of allegiance to the United States government, which he regarded as binding—this in North Mississippi.

"Third specification.—That said Rev. John H. Aughey was acting as a Federal agent in the purchase of cotton, and that he had received a large sum of gold from the United States government to pay for the cotton purchased.

"Second charge.—Enacting the spy.

"That said Aughey, while a citizen of the Confederate States, repeatedly came into our lines for the purpose of obtaining information for the benefit of the enemy, and that he passed through the lines of the enemy at will, holding an unlimited pass from Gen. Wm. Nelson, of the Federal army, granting that privilege—this in the vicinity of Corinth, Mississippi, in '61–2.

"Witnesses—Wallace, Ferdinand Woodruff, J. B. Coyner, Daniel Barnes, David Hough,—Williams, and J. R. Simonson."

I demanded a copy of these charges, which Col. Walter promised to furnish. He kindly bade me goodbye, and left the prison.

About 3 o'clock in the afternoon, I approached two prisoners who were heavily ironed. They were handcuffed, had bands and chains upon their ankles, similar to mine, and were also chained together and to a bolt in the floor.

I inquired for what offence they were incarcerated. The prisoner whom I addressed was a tall gentleman with a very intellectual expression of countenance and of prepossessing manners. He was pale and sad.

"We are charged with desertion."

"Did you desert?"

"I enlisted in the Confederate service for twelve months. At the expiration of my term of service I asked permission to return home, stating that I had learned from a trustworthy source that my family were suffering from a lack of the necessaries of life; that they lived in Tennessee, which is occupied by Federal troops. Confederate money there has no purchasing power, not being worth the paper on which it is printed; that I desired to relieve my family from their distress, and as my term of service had expired, I demanded my discharge. This they refused, stating that the Confederate congress had passed a law requiring all soldiers who had enlisted for any term, however short, to be held to service during the war, and that all who left before its close would be considered guilty of desertion, and if arrested would be shot. Regarding the law as a tyrannical enactment, and of no binding force, I attempted to return to my family, but was arrested and committed to this prison."

"What will be your fate?"

"I don't know, but fear the worst. At our trial Gen. Bragg said some salutary examples must be made to deter soldiers from deserting, or the army would waste away as snow before the bright beams of the vernal sun. His bile and bitterness overflowed in acrimonious invectives."

The other prisoner's statement was a perfect counterpart of his comrade's.

The first was named Melville Baillie, of Raleigh, Tennessee, and the other Polk Childress, of Hickory Wythe, Tenn. Their friend, Parley Van Horn, of Colliersville, Tenn., they left sick at the home of his cousin, Felix Grundy Ayres, in Byhalia, Miss., who thus escaped. I left them and walked to the opposite side of the prison, when I observed a file of soldiers drawn up in front of the prison. Two officers entered, and walking up to the prisoners with whom I had just been conversing, unfastened their chains, and ordered them to follow. As the officers passed Capt. Bruce, he asked, "What are you going to do with these men?" "Going to shoot them," was the reply. They then showed him the warrant for their execution, having written across it in red letters, "condemned to death." When the prisoners reached the door, the file of soldiers separated, received the prisoners into the space in their midst, marched them across the railroad, and shot them.

Thus was perpetrated an act of cruel tyranny that cries loudly to heaven for vengeance. Two families, helpless and destitute, were thus each deprived of its head, upon whom they were dependent for support, and abandoned to the cold charity of a selfish world. The wages earned by a year's service in behalf of the wicked, cruel, and vindictive Confederate states, was an ignominious death and a dishonored grave. The widow and the fatherless cry to heaven for vengeance, and their cries have entered into the ears of the Lord Of Sabaoth.

The judge advocate of the army, Col. H. W. Walter, returned to the prison and called my name. I speedily confronted him. He brought a copy of the charges preferred against me.

He said: "My wife feels a deep interest in you. She is very anxious in some way to secure your acquittal. I received a letter from her today, a portion of which I will read you: 'Mr. Aughey's many friends in Holly Springs, and I am of the number, earnestly request you to do all you can for his release, that will comport with the interests of our government. Remember that he is a minister of the gospel, and deserves all the courtesy, consideration, and kind treatment due to one who has faithfully and zealously fulfilled his high calling in our immediate vicinity—at Waterford and Spring Creek. Our dear friend, Mrs. Louis Thompson, has a mother's affection for him, and will visit him if permitted, that she may minister to his comfort and intercede for his release. He has often been our guest and has ever deported himself as a Christian gentleman, sans peur et sans reproche,' etc."

He informed me that my trial had been deferred until Monday. He said, "You will be tried on Monday and hanged on Tuesday at 2 o'clock P.M."

"Colonel, if my death is a foregone conclusion, you may as well reverse the order, and hang me on Monday and try me on Tuesday."

"I have examined the testimony against you. I know the intention of the officers. Your own admissions are sufficient to condemn you. It is my duty as judge advocate to do all I can for the prisoner, and as a friend I would take pleasure in securing your acquittal, if that result would comport with the interests and safety of the Confederate states. But you have done us all the harm you could. Winfrey and Armstrong, young soldiers from Choctaw county, have informed me all about your seditious language and conduct while a pastor of churches down there. They will appear against you. The full extent of the injury you have done our cause in North Mississippi can only be conjectured, but it was to the extent of your ability and opportunity. Woodruff, Barnes, Crossland, Capt. George, David Hough, Wallace, and J.B. Coyner, have given sufficient testimony to Gens. Bragg, Beauregard, Jordan, and Price, of your treasonable exploits to fill a volume. At one time Gen. Bragg became so angry at the recital of your Norman Bridge feat, that he came near ordering a detail to hang you at once without the forms or farce of a trial. And he would have done so, only Gen. Sterling Price interposed and insisted that as you were a minister of the gospel the right thing to do was to give you a fair and impartial trial. As you were chained and closely guarded in the very midst of this great army, escape was not possible, and a few days' respite could not by any possibility injure the Southern Confederacy. Gen. Jordan, who is Beauregard's chief of staff, declared that he ordered and inspected the ironing, and that he would vouch for the security of the prisoner, for a few days at least. At another time, when Dr. Crossland recounted your insolence to Gen. Pfeiffer, at Brooksville, Gen. Bragg could scarcely restrain his wrath, and was upon the point of ordering your immediate execution. He thought Gen. Pfeiffer did wrong to allow you to express treasonable sentiments and to denounce the Confederate cause. Your execution will be as conspicuous as possible. It will take place in the presence of two brigades, composed of soldiers, many of whom are personally acquainted with you. There are many Unionists up there in North-eastern Mississippi, and a salutary example will not be lost on them. Some of them are in our army here perforce, and will witness an execution suggestive of their own fate if they should be guilty of treasonable language or conduct. Your crimes will be read to them and commented on by Major General Hardee, if present, or Gen. Mark Lowrey, in case of his absence."

"Colonel, I am a civilian. What right have they to try me by military law. The civil court has jurisdiction, and not a court-martial."

"All citizens of the Confederate States between 18 and 35 have been declared in the army, by congressional enactment, and have been required to report themselves at the head-quarters of the commander of the nearest military district within a given time, or be considered deserters. Have you complied with this law?"

"No, I have not. You have furnished me a copy of the charges against me, with the specifications. Desertion is not one of the charges."

"No, there are charges enough without that. I only mention it to show you that that enactment gives military jurisdiction over all citizens of military age. All your interests are with the South. It is your adopted home, though like myself you are of northern birth. Why did you not cast in your lot with the dominant class, for whose society you are fitted by literary culture, and not with that class which is giving us so great trouble, and whose treasonable utterances and acts we must suppress with an iron hand. Our own safety requires that we tolerate no longer the traitors in our midst. We must confiscate their property and exterminate them as we would venomous serpents."

"Jefferson Davis, in his inaugural address, quoting from the Declaration of

Independence, declares that when governments become destructive to the ends for which they were established it is the right of the people to alter or abolish them. Was it the end for which our government was established to foster the interests of human slavery? If so, and you deem it right to protect those interests, go and fight in their defence, but do not endeavor to compel me and the great majority of the southern people who own no slaves to fight for your interests, and to become the foes of a government that has never trespassed upon our rights, a government which has no superior upon the face of the earth. You may murder me, but you cannot murder the government. If I had a thousand lives I would gladly lay them all upon the altar of my bleeding country."

"Parson, recanting your opinions would not save you now. You have forfeited your life, and I will not insult you by characterizing your crimes by their true names."

"Who said anything about recanting? I have no desire to recant truthful principles. You may express your opinion of my crimes, if you wish, and give their true names."

"Well, your crimes are, treason, enacting the spy, base ingratitude to your benefactors, and those who have heretofore reposed confidence in you, by siding with their enemies."

"Colonel, I have given a fair equivalent for all that I have received, and I have injured no one wittingly, in person, property, or reputation. My present condition indicates that the ingratitude is all upon the other side. I have labored faithfully for eleven years to promote the intellectual and moral and religious interests of the southern people, and they thus repay me with bonds and imprisonment, and they intend to pay the last installment by putting me to an ignominious death on the scaffold."

"Parson, I will call tomorrow, and should you have any requests to make, such as conveying messages to friends, disposition of property, or benefit of clergy at your execution, I will fulfill them for you."

"I would be glad to have Rev. James A. Lyon, D. D., of Columbus, to be present at my execution, also Rev. James Pelan, of Macon."

"I will telegraph them at once."

"I will prepare messages for my wife and other friends by tomorrow evening."

"I will secure their delivery at the earliest possible moment."

"Thanks, Colonel."

Soon after Col. Walter left, Col. Clare came in and asked me whether I had been president of a female college in Rienzi. I replied in the affirmative. "Tis strange," said he, "that one who has been so favored, and one who has accumulated property in the South, should prove a traitor to his adopted country and become its enemy."

I replied that I had given a fair equivalent for every dollar I had obtained from the citizens of the South; that for eleven years I had labored faithfully as an educator and minister of the gospel to promote the educational, moral, and spiritual interests of the southern people in the states of Kentucky, Tennessee, Louisiana, and Mississippi, and that now I was receiving my reward by being chained, starved, and insulted, and that they intended soon to pay the last installment by putting me to death ignominiously on the scaffold. I denied being an enemy to my country or to the South, I regarded those who would promote divisions and overthrow the government as the real enemies of the South who were imperiling all her best interests. If my advice had been followed the South and the whole country would now be enjoying its wonted peace and unparalleled prosperity, and would not have suffered W. L. Yancey and other demagogues to precipitate a desolating and ruinous revolution.

He replied, "Ingrate, traitor, wretch, I have no sympathy for you." He then called upon all the supernal and infernal powers to blast my soul in everlasting death and confine it forever in fiery torments.

The prison walls echoed and re-echoed his blatant blasphemy. The prisoners stood aghast, and with faces blanched with fear for my safety, plucked me away and crowded the space between me and this vile blasphemer, who, with hand upon the hilt of his sword and pistol belt alternately, seemed ready to wreak his vengeance upon me.

At this moment Major Irion entered, and was informed by this minion of Jeff Davis that he had relieved his mind by giving me a "good cussen." He left the prison with this officer, cursing as he went.

Perhaps I should have been more circumspect—more reticent, and thus prevented this outpouring of the vials of Confederate wrath by this cursing Shimei. At this moment Gen. Braxton Bragg and several officers of high rank entered. A distinguished French officer was visiting this country on a tour of inspection. He desired to visit this prison, and this was the occasion of their visit. When they came to the place where I was standing, Gen. Bragg said,

"This man dies on Tuesday next."

"What is his offence?" inquired the officer.

"He is a prisoner of state, and is guilty of treason."

"Are they all state prisoners in this prison?"

"All except a few prisoners of war, who will be removed to another prison in Macon, Ga., in a few days."

"This is a bastile, I suppose, but what has this prisoner done?"

"What has he not done, would be a more pertinent question. He has thrown all the influence of his official position as a minister of the gospel into the scale of opposition against our government."

"He is a minister, then?"

"Yes, a Presbyterian minister, of Northern birth and education."

"Ministers are usually regarded as non-combatants."

"Yes, but by word and deed and sermon and pen and every species of treasonable act and utterance, he has done our cause infinite harm. He is far from being a non-combatant."

"What is his name?" [Producing a note-book].

"He spells his name A-u-g-h-e-y. I am not sure of its pronunciation."

"Oh, yes, General, I recognize that name as of French origin. We have the name in France—a family of Huguenots. Many of that family were banished because of their opposition to the religious traditions of our empire, and some of them, after the revocation of the edict of Nantes, fled to the British Islands, and to Germany and Holland, to avoid the penalty affixed to disobeying the ecclesiastical regulations of our country. He comes by his refractory opinions and conduct legitimately."

Gen. Bragg is a cadaverous, plain-looking man. He has bushy black eye-brows and piercing eyes. He stoops slightly in walking, and his stubby iron-gray beard and his receding forehead give him a plebeian look. He is cruel as the grave. Nearly every day he shoots some of his own soldiers, often for trivial offences. Cruelty is plainly written in indelible characters upon every lineament of his features, which are stern and almost savage in their expression.

After a thorough inspection of the prison our distinguished visitors retired.

I approached two elderly, gray-haired men, who sat in the north-west corner of the prison. These old gentlemen had become fast friends, and wept at the thought of their bleeding country's woes, brought on by designing, scheming politicians (not statesmen) in the interests of an institution subversive of all the inalienable rights of man. They gave me their history. The older gentleman, John Champe, was the youngest son of a revolutionary sire. His father had been chosen by Washington to effect the capture of Benedict Arnold after his treason, so as to save the life of Major André. This, because of untoward circumstances, he could not accomplish. But the effort was a gallant and heroic one, and merited and received high commendation from Gen. Washington. This is his story:

"I resided in Tuscumbia, Ala. I had four sons. Three of them had joined the

Federal army. One night an attack was made on my house. My youngest son and I defended ourselves, but after killing four of our assailants, they burst in the door. We fled by the back door, and endeavored to reach the Federal lines. A company pursued us with blood-hounds. They overtook us. We fought with desperation. We killed five hounds and four of the soldiers. We expended all our ammunition. We were both severely wounded. They hung my son to the limb of a tree, and left the body to be devoured by the birds of prey. They put me in irons and brought me here. Why they spared my life I know not. The surgeon informs me that my wound in the breast will prove fatal in a short time. It gives me great pain. I would like much to see my aged wife, who, alone and surrounded by bitter foes, is mourning our absence."

The other said. "My name is Carter Braxton. I was named for my grandfather, a signer of the Declaration of Independence. My home is in Obion county, Tenn. My four sons are all in the Federal army. This is the cause of my imprisonment. They asked me if I were a Unionist, and I replied that it was a principle of law that no one was bound to criminate himself. I have had my trial. They proved that I had refused to take Confederate money, that I have traded with the Yankees, that my four sons were in the Federal army, that I was not a slaveholder, that I refused to take the oath of allegiance to the Confederate states, that after the reduction of Fort Donaldson I had told one George Sarbaugh that it would take more than one Southerner to whip five Yankees."

While he was yet speaking, the officer entered, and this old gentleman and a prisoner named Jason Chenault were unchained and marched to the fatal plat and shot. Chenault was a Kentucky Unionist, who had come to Mississippi to collect money due him for mules sold the year before. He was arrested, charged with enacting the spy, found guilty, and shot. I might record the sad fate of Nicholas Vedder, Bynum, Sorrell, and Oswald, all shot at the same time, for avowed Unionism, but space is wanting. I may place upon a permanent record in the near future the biographies of these and other martyrs to the holy cause of our country's integrity imperiled by traitors.

I preached every evening. One evening my text was I. Kings xviii. 21: "How long halt ye between two opinions." As none of us had a hymn book, I composed these hymns for the occasion. I parceled them out by couplets, and all joined in the singing:

How long! O, sinner, wilt thou halt,
How long! Remain in guilty doubt,
While heaven and earth and air and sea
The Lord is God, responsive shout.

Whilst thou art halting, sin grows strong,
And lust and passion rule thy soul,
And all the powers of hell combined
Still hold thee 'neath their stern control.

O, sinner, choose in this thy day
To serve the Lord who loves thee well,
Oh! choose to walk in wisdom's way
And break thy league with death and hell.

Then will the host of heaven rejoice,
Then will the powers of darkness rage,
But thou, a soldier of the cross,
Wilt a successful warfare wage.

And when the glorious victory's won,
Thou wilt a king, a conqueror be,
Wear on thy brow a diadem,
And have a right to life's fair tree.

HYMN AFTER SERMON.
Spirit of the living God,
Water now the precious seed,
Slay the sinner with Thy sword,
Comfort to Thy saints afford.

Satan, like the birds of prey,
Strives to catch the seed away,
Cares in countless numbers come,
Shines with scorching heat the sun.

Thus we see our Savior's foes
Strive to blast the seed he sows.
In the hearts of young and old,
Prosper it, a hundred fold.

Holy Spirit, Father, Son,
Aid us till our work is done;
Then, instead of worthless leaves,
We shall bring our precious sheaves.

Two young men, John N. Maple, of Verona, Miss., and Samuel Melvin, of
Tallaloosa, Miss., the former a Primitive Baptist, the latter a Methodist, held
a discussion on the doctrine of foreordination. Some point in my sermon
occasioned it. They both appeared to believe in the doctrine, since the term
was used in the Bible. Melvin said the decrees of God were founded upon His
foreknowledge. In the case of Paul, God foresaw all the contingencies and
knew because of His prescience how they would eventuate, and based His

decree that Paul should stand before Cæsar upon that foreknowledge. Maple affirmed that God knew that Paul would stand before Cæsar because He had decreed it. That He did not stand aside an indifferent spectator to observe how affairs would result, and then decree that they should take place, as He foresaw they would happen anyhow. That all that God does in time He always intended to do, and all that wicked men do He always intended to suffer or permit them to do. He would allow them to do wickedly in the exercise of the freedom of their will, only so far as He chose to overrule their wickedness for the promotion of His declarative glory, and the remainder of wrath He would restrain. Beyond the boundary of His will He would hem them in by His providence, and say, so far shalt thou go and no farther. Foreordination is founded upon the will of God, and not upon His foreknowledge of what man will do or what He foresees will happen. At the close of their debate it was found that neither had convinced the other of his error, nor anyone else.

A man of Herculean frame, whose height was six feet eight inches, occupied the space on the floor next to mine as sleeping quarters. This space he called his dormitory. He gave me his history thus:

"I am a native of East Tennessee. I was born in Tellico Plains, Monroe Co., measurably brought up in Conasauga, Polk Co. I married Miss Tennie Paden, bought a farm near Dandridge, of one Geo. Cogsil, and moved on it in the year 1860. My own name is Hermon Bledsoe. I was chosen a delegate to the mass convention of Unionists, held June 17, 1861, in Greenville, Tennessee, to protest against the tyranny inaugurated over us by the rebel authorities. I was a member of the committee which prepared the following address, which was adopted by the convention with entire unanimity. We first detailed the facts of the election, how in Middle and West Tennessee the people were overawed, bullied, persecuted into an adoption of the ordinance; how the secessionists had prepared for the furtherance of their schemes, though the state had voted No Separation; how no provision was made for examining the returns otherwise than by a disunion governor, whose hold on power depended upon the success of the secession program; how volunteers in the secession army were allowed to vote within and without the state, contrary to any law; how discussion was forbidden in those sections where the secession vote was triumphant, while every Union paper there was crushed out; how a military despotism was ruling in spite of the wishes and rights of the people. The address then went on to say, in behalf of the loyal Unionist majority:

" 'We prefer to remain attached to the Government of our fathers. The Constitution of the United States has done us no wrong. The congress of the United States has passed no law to oppress us. The president of the United

States has made no threat against the law abiding people of Tennessee. Under the Government of the United States we have enjoyed, as a nation, more of civil and religious freedom than any other people under the whole heaven. We believe that there is no cause for secession nor rebellion on the part of the people of Tennessee. None was assigned by the legislature in their miscalled declaration of independence. No adequate cause can be assigned. The select committee of that body asserted a gross and inexcusable falsehood in their address to the people of Tennessee, when they declared that the Government of the United States had made war upon them.

"'The secession cause has thus far been sustained by deception and falsehood, by falsehood as to the action of congress; by false dispatches as to battles that were never fought and victories that were never won; by false accounts as to the purpose of the president; by false representations as to the views of Union men; and by false pretenses as to the facility with which the secession troops would take possession of the capital and capture the highest officers of the Government. The cause of secession or rebellion has no charms for us, and its progress has been marked by the most alarming and dangerous attacks upon the public liberty. In other states, as well as our own, its whole course threatens to annihilate the last vestiges of freedom. While peace and prosperity have blest us in the Government of the United States, the following may be enumerated as some of the fruits of secession.

"'It was urged forward by members of congress who had sworn to support the Constitution of the United States, and were themselves supported by the Government; it was effected without consultation with all the states interested in the slavery question, and without exhausting peaceable remedies. It has plunged the country into civil war, paralyzed our commerce, interfered with the whole trade and business of our country, lessened the value of our property, destroyed many of the pursuits of life, and bids fair to involve the whole nation in irretrievable bankruptcy and ruin. It has changed the entire relations of states, and adopted constitutions without submitting them to a vote of the people, and where such a vote has been authorized, it has been upon the condition prescribed by Senator Mason, of Virginia, that those who voted the Union ticket must leave the state. It has advocated a constitutional monarchy, a king, and a dictator, and is, through the Richmond press, at this moment recommending to the convention in Virginia a restriction of the right of suffrage, and in severing connection with the Yankees, to abolish every vestige of resemblance to the institutions of that detested race. It has formed military leagues, passed military bills, and opened the door for oppressive taxation, without consulting the people, and then, in mockery of a free election, has required them by their votes to sanction its usurpations, under the penalty of moral proscription or at the point of the bayonet. It has offered a premium for crime in directing the discharge of volunteers from criminal prosecutions, and recommending the judges not to hold their courts. It has stained our statute book with the repudiation of Northern debts, and has greatly violated the Constitution, by attempting through its unlawful extension to destroy the right of suffrage. It has called upon the people in the state of Georgia, and may soon require the people of Tennessee, to contribute all their surplus cotton, corn, wheat, bacon, beef, etc., to the support of pretended governments alike destitute of money and credit. It has attempted to destroy the accountability of public servants to the people by secret legislation, and set the obligation of an oath at defiance. It has passed laws declaring it treason to say or do anything in favor of the Government of the United States, or against the Confederate states, and such a law is now before, and we apprehend will soon be passed by, the legislature of Tennessee. It has attempted to destroy, and we fear will soon utterly prostrate, the freedom of speech and of the press. It has involved the Southern states in a war whose success is hopeless, and which must ultimately lead to the ruin of the people. Its bigoted, overbearing, and intolerant spirit has already subjected the people of East Tennessee to many petty grievances; our people have been insulted; our flags have been fired upon and torn down; our houses have been rudely entered; our families subjected to insult; our peaceable meetings interrupted; our women and children shot by a merciless soldiery; our towns pillaged; our citizens robbed and some of them assassinated and murdered. No effort has been spared to deter the Union men of East Tennessee from the expression of their free thoughts. The penalties of treason have been threatened against them, and murder and assassination have been openly encouraged by leading secession journals. As secession has been thus overbearing and intolerant while in the minority in East Tennessee, nothing better can be expected of the pretended majority than wild, unconstitutional, and oppressive legislation; an utter contempt and disregard of law; a determination to force every Unionist in the state to swear to the support of a constitution he abhors, and to yield his money and property to aid a cause he detests, and to become the object of scorn and derision as well as the victim of intolerable and relentless oppression.

" 'In view of these considerations, and of the fact that the people of East Tennessee have declared their fidelity to the Union by a majority of about twenty thousand votes, therefore we do resolve and declare.'

"Here followed a series of patriotic resolutions, and the appointment of a committee to prepare a memorial, asking the consent of the legislature of Tennessee to consent to the separation of East Tennessee, and those counties of Middle Tennessee which desired it, from the rest of the state, that they may be formed into a separate state.

"Brownlow, Maynard, Etheridge, Nelson, Hawkins, Johnson, etc., led the Unionists. It was not long before those Unionists and protestants against wrong were flying for their lives, and were hunted down like wild beasts. The leaders disappeared from observation, and the people could only become quiescent in a state of affairs which, in the presence of the armed minions of the Southern Confederacy, they were powerless to prevent.

"I was placed on the proscribed list, and was compelled to hide in a cavern with other Unionists. One night I visited my family, which consisted of my wife and twin babes, Mark and Paul. A band of guerrillas, lying in ambush in the chaparral near my residence, surrounded the house, and rushing through the door, which for the moment I had forgotten to fasten, took me prisoner. They searched my person and found several copies of the address above given, and some letters in a drawer, which were construed unfavorably by these cruel men. They handcuffed me and took me to the chaparral copse. They held a brief trial, which resulted in my conviction and condemnation to death. Immediate preparations were made for my execution. Douglas Flinn declared that hanging was too good for such a wretch as I. Jim Bainbridge coincided with him in opinion. 'What do you want done with him?' said Bob. Torrence, who commanded the gang. 'Let us burn him at the stake, like Col. Brown's Sam last week, for assaulting a white girl.' 'All right,' said Torrence. 'All in favor of burning this d—d renegade, this Lincolnite, this tory and traitor, say aye.' A vociferous aye resounded. 'All opposed, no.' Only two voices responded in the negative. Sam Lovell took off the handcuffs and bound me to a sapling with the rope with which they had intended to hang me. The trial had begun in the gloaming, and now darkness had enshrouded all the land. Flinn ran and gathered an armful of dry sticks and deposited them in a pile at my feet. Soon many were engaged in gathering fagots. Flinn declared that this was the happiest night of his existence. He would soon have the pleasure of seeing this miserable traitor going up like Elijah in a chariot of fire. 'So mote it be,' growled Jacob Embry, in a sepulchral tone. George Goshen, Peter Peters, and J. B. Coyner were dispatched to Aunt Sylvia Caldwell's for a firebrand with which to ignite the pile of fagots. I commended my soul to God and calmly awaited death. Flinn approached me with a pile of (as he said) very dry wood. He approached quite near, and dropping the fagots he placed a knife handle between my teeth. The large blade of the knife was open. He then ran to and mounted a stump about fifty yards distant, and commenced to deliver a harangue laudatory of the Southern Confederacy, and denouncing all traitors, wishing them in the bottom of the lowest hell.

"With some effort I managed to sever the cord binding my wrists. I then cut the cord bound around my waist, and quietly and quickly made my escape. The crowd around Flinn, who was doubtless a Unionist in disguise, were cheering vociferously, which aided my escape, as the noise drowned the crackling of the fagots as I removed or trampled upon them on the farther side from the stump orator and his auditors. Soon the men with the fire arrived and applied it to the heap around the sapling. Looking back from a hill about two miles distant I saw the flames rising higher and higher, till a large space was illuminated. Suddenly I heard fierce yells of disappointment and rage, emanating from the throats of this infuriated and disappointed crowd of demons incarnate, maddened to frenzy by my escape. I traveled by night, but lay concealed during the day.

"When in hiding near Siluria, Shelby county, Alabama, I heard the sound of a wood-chopper's ax, quite near, and peering from the copse in which I was concealed, I saw a slave at work felling a tree. Soon he began to declaim a piece:

> " 'The hillsides in places are white I know,
> But the whiteness is not occasioned by snow.
> It is only the petals of apples and cherries
> And peaches and plums and all sorts of berries,
> Just falling in sport from their bowers,
> As if to represent April showers'

" 'Now,' said he, apparently well satisfied with his effort, 'Dat's 'bout as good as young Massa Josiah hisself could spoke it.'

"I called, 'Halloo, uncle!' as he rested for a moment from his labor, with arms akimbo. 'Who am dat calling?' he cried out, with some degree of trepidation. As he looked in my direction, I beckoned him to approach me. When he came near I said, 'To whom do you belong? Where do you live?' He replied, 'I belongs to Major Cayce, of Talladega. He bought me and my wife of Col. Shorter, of Choccolocco, Calhoun county, last year. I was borned the slave of Parson Lagow, of Emuckfaw. When I wuz six months old, master died, an' ole lady Rudisil bought me at the sale fur $500. I lived wid her at Chepultepec till I waz ten years old, den she died, and I wuz sold agin to Gov. Peyton Claiborne, of Sylacauga. I'se bin around sum, but I'se never bin out en the state of Alabam. I buys my time from my now master, Major Cayce, for twenty-five dollars a month. I lives in that cabin up yonder on the hill.' He pointed with the index finger of his right hand to a cabin almost lost to sight in the distance, nestling among the trees in a grove surmounting a hill of great height. He named it cosy cot, and the name was not a misnomer.

"I revealed my condition to this quadroon slave, and he and his kind wife fed and lodged me for a week, till I was sufficiently recovered from my fatigue to continue my journey.

"Should opportunity ever be afforded for reciprocating the kindness of this slave husband and wife, Isam and Tabitha, I will gladly avail myself of it, and do them all the kindness in my power.

"I continued my journey, and with but little of incident or adventure worth narrating, I at length arrived at the home of my cousin Jerry Humboldt, in Selma, Ala. My cousin was a staunch Unionist, a stalwart, uncompromising friend of the United States government and the old flag, the star-spangled banner, the emblem of freedom and the inalienable rights of man.

"Every day dangers thickened around us. We were compelled to devise a plan of escape to the Federal lines. Twenty-five of us set out together, under the guidance of Leander Browning. At Talahatta Springs, Clark county, a band of guerrillas, or partisan rangers, as they called themselves, overtook us as we were camping for the night. We fought them long and well, till we had slain nearly twice our number of our pursuers, then, as the darkness grew denser, the remnant of us, wounded and bleeding, fled.

"I was captured at Sanwilpa, was taken to Tuscahoma, put into a guard house. Soon after I was conveyed to Pushmataha; thence I was removed to this dungeon in Tupelo, Miss. I adroitly concealed my identity, and though under violent suspicion nothing definite was proved against me. To save my life, I have agreed to take the oath of allegiance, and join the rebel army. I may soon be able to desert and reach the Union lines. My nom de guerre is Ralph Benton."

"Have you any conscientious scruples about the propriety of taking an oath with the deliberate intention of violating it?"

"Not any. It may save my life. At least deliver me from this prison. Deception is certainly justifiable in a case like this. The rebels have violated every oath that they have ever taken. Shall we keep faith with them? Naught but Punic faith for them. As soon trust a rattlesnake as a rebel. I hope to reach the Union lines and offer my services to General Pope as a volunteer in his army."

On the next day my friend was permitted to take the oath and enter the rebel army. He had several copies of the address concealed about his person, as he thought beyond the reach of rebel search, one of which he gave me. I retain it as a sacred memento. A rumor reached me through Philip Henson, a Federal spy, that my friend was under violent suspicion by the rebels, and was caught in his attempt at escape, and shot by order of Gen. N.B. Forrest. Concerning this rumor, Gen. Jefferson C. Davis told me that a soldier in his command bore the name and answered the description of Hermon Bledsoe; that he was a deserter from the enemy; that he was severely wounded in a skirmish, and that his recollection was that his wound proved fatal.

One of my fellow-prisoners became suddenly insane. He frothed at the mouth, rolled his eyes wildly, and butted his head against the walls of the prison. His paroxysms were very violent in the presence of the officers. I sat near him, and after observing him for awhile I came to the conclusion that he was a malingerer. Presently an officer entered, at that instant the crazy man was seized with another paroxysm. He became very violent. The officer watched him for some time and then said, "We must remove him to the hospital that he may die there, for there seems little hope of his ultimate recovery, he is so sick and crazy and fierce."

This man's name was Bovard Willis, a Unionist, of Biloxi, Miss. After the officer's departure he quieted down in a very short time. I approached him and said:

"Willis, I do not profess to be an alienist, but I know that you are no more crazy than I am. I will not betray you. What is your motive in feigning madness?"

He replied, "If I am taken to the hospital I will have a far better opportunity of escaping. I voted against secession, I led the Unionists in our county, I became very obnoxious to the secessionists, and there is no hope for me but escape."

In the evening he was removed to the hospital. The next morning he was missing. He had unfortunately left some clothing in the hospital. The company that went in search of him let the hounds smell the garment. Soon they struck his trail and followed it to the creek. Willis, upon reaching the creek, waded in it three miles, and thus baffled his pursuers for several hours. In the afternoon they recovered the trail and followed it rapidly for several miles. By this time Willis had reached a house ten miles south-west of Tupelo. He went to it at a venture. He asked for water. The proprietor seemed to know by intuition the character of this wanderer. He told his wife to prepare some food for this stranger. While he was eating, the howling of the hounds was heard. Willis rose in great trepidation. His host at once interpreted the reason. No plan seemed feasible for the concealment of the fugitive. Mrs. Quay suggested the closet as a hiding place, but her husband thought it unsafe, as it was in a part of the house so exposed that it would be among the first places searched. The blood-hounds finding the track fresh were pursuing with great speed.

Mr. Quay said, pointing to a tree about two hundred yards distant, "If you could reach that tree, you would find a secure asylum till your pursuers had gone on, or returned supposing they were on the wrong trail. The horses are in the field, if I can only get one up in time and carry you over to the tree and get back before they reach us you will be safe."

Just then the hounds broke out afresh into loud howls and sharp yelps.

"They are too near for that that" said Willis, "I am lost."

"Pa," said little Violetta Quay (who was only six years old), "you just tote that man over to the tree."

"I'll do it," said her pa. He stooped down, and Willis perched himself upon his shoulders and was borne to the tree, and in an incredibly short space of time was concealed amid the foliage of the loftiest branches of this mighty king of the forest.

Quay had just time to return and enter his house when the hounds bounded into his yard, their fierce yelps betokening that they knew that the object of their pursuit was near. Soon the pursuing cavalry entered the yard, and dismounting, began unceremoniously a thorough but bootless search of the house and premises. They questioned strictly each member of the family, but they were all woefully ignorant. The officer in charge asked little Violetta if she had seen any stranger about lately. She replied, "If I had I wouldn't tell you. I just wish the poor man would come here, I'd hide him if I could from those awful dogs." The hounds were completely baffled. They would not leave the track indicated by the scent of Willis' garment for any other. After two hours of fruitless endeavor to recover the track, they left Mr. Quay's house and returned.

Willis was now among friends. After some night spent in hiding, Willis was conveyed by nocturnal journeys from one friendly post to another, till he reached the Federal lines at Memphis, Tenn. Willis did not change quarters till the guides were ready to enter upon their perilous task of guiding a band of Unionists, of which Willis was one, to the Federal lines. He said, "There is no place so safe as where the hounds have been." And so the experiment proved the adage true. Willis was not molested in this sylvan retreat, though the whole country north to the Federal lines was repeatedly traversed by cavalry and hounds.

M. T. Anderson, of Millersburg, Holmes Co., O., came to me and said:

"Mr. Aughey, I am very sorry for you. There is hope for me. I am a prisoner of war. If I survive the horrors of imprisonment I will be exchanged, but for you, a prisoner of state, there is no hope except by eluding the vigilance of the guards and making your way through this great army, and traversing a long stretch of hostile country to the Federal lines. Now, sir, I am not superstitious, but I had a dream last night that has deeply impressed me. I thought that I was caught up into heaven, into the midst of the Paradise of God, and as I stood dazed amid the splendors of the city of the Great King, and bewildered by the light and resplendent glory that emanated from the great white throne, and Him that is seated thereon, I heard a voice saying, 'Who will go for us to earth, and deliver my servant from bonds and imprisonment and impending death, that he may longer proclaim my gospel?' Suddenly there appeared before the throne a form of wondrous beauty, apparently a young man—of radiant countenance; from every feature beamed love and peace and good-will, who said, 'Here am I. Send me. I will go and deliver him and bring him safely to the desired haven.' 'Who art thou?' said the recording angel, who sat hard by the throne of God. 'I am Ariel, the lion of Jehovah, who am made strong to deliver his chosen ones from all their enemies that rise up against them to destroy them. I delivered Peter from Herod's dungeon, and many saints who were shut up in prison have I released,' and he was bidden to perform the mission. And then I heard the voice of a multitude saying, 'Go, and Jehovah, merciful and gracious, mighty and strong to deliver, give thee abundant success.' And all the host of heaven responded, 'Amen.' Then a voice said to me, 'Return and make known the vision to my servant, who in bonds is breaking to thee and those with thee the bread of eternal life.' I awoke trembling and astonished.

"Now, I entertain more than a mere presentiment of your escape. I am so fully impressed with the truth that my dream was a revelation of God's will concerning you, that I firmly believe that these wicked men will not be suffered in the providence of God to take your life. I predict that many, many years of successful labor in your Master's vineyard are before you; many souls, by your instrumentality, are to be brought into the fold of Christ and the kingdom of heaven."

"I wish you may not be a false prophet, and that your dream may not be verified. The eye of faith alone can discern a ray of hope. Sight shows a prison, strong and closely guarded, a mighty army of watchful and malignant foes, chains, fetters, guards on the alert, pickets, patrols, videttes, blood-hounds innumerable, my sun of life apparently on the horizon's verge. The hour of my departure fixed. Many, many miles intervening between my prison and a place of safety—a city of refuge. A physical frame enfeebled by starvation and surrounding horrors which have been endured for many weary months, which are lengthening into years. It does indeed require strong faith to discern a ray of hope or glimmer of light to irradiate the future. Next Tuesday ends all, my foes have decreed. If God in his providence has longer life in store for me I will be spared. But I feel that I have received dying grace, and dying grace is reserved for a dying hour. However, should any plan of escape present itself, I will not be slow to avail myself of it. But my only hope is in escape. The vindictive Confederate authorities are determined to put me to death at the hour mentioned by Col. Walter. They are implacable and unmerciful, and it irketh them to await the appointed hour. I would like much to live for my dear wife's sake, and our dear infant's sake. By this cruel deed of rebel hate, my wife will be widowed and my child made fatherless. But God has promised to be the husband of the widow and the father of the fatherless. To his covenant-keeping care I commit them both, and the babe unborn."

Feeling assured that my departure from this terrestrial sphere was near, I sat down upon the floor of my dungeon and slowly penned the following letter to my wife:

My Dear Mary:

The Confederate authorities announce to me that I have only a few more days to live. When you receive this letter the hand that penned it will be cold in death. My soul, divested of the body, will have passed the solemn test before the bar of God; I have a good hope through grace that I will then be rejoicing amid the sacramental host of God's elect, singing the new song of redeeming love in the presence of Him who is the chief among ten thousand and the one altogether lovely. Mary, meet me in heaven, where sorrow and tears and temptation and sin are unknown, and where the wicked cease from troubling and the weary are at rest. If General Bragg will permit my body to be taken in charge by my friends, I will ask your brother, D.R. Paden, and cousin, Capt. Jas. H. Tankersley, to convey it to you. Bury me in the cemetery at Bethany church. That was my first ministerial charge. Plant a cedar at my head and one at my feet, and there let me repose in peace till the archangel's trump shall sound, summoning the dead to the judgment of the great day, and vouchsafing to saints the long hoped for redemption of the body. As to my Property has all, by Confederate laws, been confiscated, and after years of incessant toil I leave you penniless and dependent, but I implore you to trust in God. To his kind, protecting care I commit you and our dear little Kate. Jehovah has promised to be the widow's husband and the father of the fatherless. Rest assured the Lord will provide. Only trust Him and love Him with your whole heart and soul and mind and strength. I know that it shall be well with them that love God. Be not faithless, but believing, and though clouds and darkness surround you at present, well-nigh obscuring the spiritual sky whence hope emanates, yet be assured a more auspicious day will dawn, and God will bring you safely to your journey's end, and our reunion in heaven will be sweet.

Our dear little daughter, Kate, bring up in the nurture and admonition of the Lord. Teach her to walk in wisdom's ways, for all her ways are pleasantness and all her paths are peace. Her infant mind may be compared to wax in its susceptibility for receiving impressions, and to marble for its power in retaining those impressions. That she may be satisfied early with thy mercy, O, God, that she may rejoice and be glad all her days. Teach her to remember her Creator in the days of her youth, before the evil days come in which she shall say, I have no pleasure in them. Make the Bible, the precious Bible, her constant study, and let its words be as household words to her. Inspire her mind with a love of the Book which is able to make wise unto salvation. See to it that the words of Christ dwell richly in her soul, that she may be filled with knowledge and wisdom and spiritual understanding. Pray for the Holy Spirit to bless your labors and counsels. Without his blessing all your labor would be in vain. Pray that the third Person of the adorable Trinity, the Spirit of the living God, may take up his abode in her heart, to abide with her forever. As my duties in regard to instructing our child will devolve solely upon you, take for your guidance in this respect Deut. vi. 5–9. Let your example be such as you would wish her to follow. Children are much more inclined to follow example than precept. Exercise care in this respect, for as is the mother so is her daughter.

I regret that my family, from the force of circumstances, will be compelled to remain in a section where, by many, my course of conduct which led to my death will be considered disgraceful. But this cannot be avoided. The time, I feel sure, will come when, even in Mississippi, I will be regarded as a patriot martyr. My conscience is void of offence as regards guilt in the charge preferred against me. When the wicked bear rule the people mourn. What cruelties are being perpetrated by rebels against God and their country. How long, O, Lord, how long shall the wicked triumph? How long will God forbear to execute that vengeance which is his, and which he will repay in his own good time? I have an abiding confidence that the right cause will prevail, and though I shall not live to see it, for my days are numbered, yet I firmly believe since God is a God of justice and an avenger of the righteous who serve him faithfully, that the rebel power will be destroyed utterly.

"Truth crushed to earth shall rise again—
The eternal years of God are hers—
But error wounded writhes in pain
And dies amid his worshipers."

I write this letter amid the din and confusion incident to a large number of men crowded into a narrow compass and free from all restraint.

This letter will be conveyed to you by friends. The names of those friends you will know hereafter. My real estate will be restored to you when the Union cause triumphs. That it will do so ultimately is beyond the possibility of a doubt. Give my love to all my friends. Remember that I have prayed for you and our dear Kate unceasingly during my imprisonment, and my last utterances on earth will be prayers for your welfare. Farewell, God bless you and keep you and our dear child from all harm.

Your affectionate husband,
JOHN H. AUGHEY.

I then wrote my obituary, which I placed in the hands of Mr. De Grummond, a Federal prisoner, by whom it was to be sent to the Philadelphia Presbyterian for publication. I copy a portion of it:

OBITUARY.

Died in Tupelo, Itawamba county, Miss., July 15, 1862, Rev. John H. Aughey.

The subject of the above notice suffered death on the gallows at the hands of the Confederate military authorities, on the charges of treason and enacting the spy. John H. Aughey was born in New Hartford, Oneida county, N.Y., May 8, 1828. Removed with his parents to Steubenville, O., July 4, 1837. Is an alumnus of Franklin College, New Athens, Ohio. His theological instructors were, Revs. L. A. Lowrey, Winchester, Ky.; Jahleel Woodbridge, Baton Rouge, La.; John H. Gray, D. D., Geo. W. Coons, D. D., and Rev. J. O. Steadman, D. D., Memphis, Tenn.; Rev. Chas. S. Dod, Rev. H. H. Paine, and Rev. S. Irwin Reid, Holly Springs, Miss. Was licensed to preach the gospel by the Presbytery of Chickasaw, October 4, 1856. Ordained to the full work of the ministry by the Presbytery of Tombeckbee, April 19, 1861. Was married January 22, 1857, by Rev. R. Henderson, to Miss Mary J. Paden, of Iuka, Miss., who, with one child, a daughter, born September 3, 1858, survives him. God blessed his labors by giving him many souls as seals to his ministry. After eleven years labor in the South as an educator and minister of the gospel, having never injured a citizen of the South in person or property, he fell a victim to secession hatred, and died a felon's death, because he would not become a traitor to the government which had never in a single instance trespassed upon his rights of person or property. He rests in peace and in the hope of a blessed immortality beyond the grave. "Take ye heed, watch and pray, for ye know not when the time is." Mark xiii. 33.

"Leaves have their time to fall,
 And flowers to wither at the north wind's breath,
 And stars to set—but all!
 Thou hast all seasons for thine own, O! Death."

ADDRESS TO MY SOUL.

O! my soul, thou art about to appear in the presence of thy Creator, who is infinite eternal, unchangeable in his being, wisdom, power, holiness, justice, goodness, and truth. He cannot look upon sin. He is a sin-avenging God, and thou art defiled by sin. Thy transgressions are numerous as the stars of heaven. Thou art totally debased by sin and thy iniquities abound. Thou art guilty of sins both of omission and commission. Justice would consign thee to banishment from heaven and to everlasting destruction from the presence of the Lord and the Glory of his power. Guilty, helpless, wretched as thou art, what is thy plea that sentence of eternal death should not be pronounced against thee?

THE SOUL'S REPLY.

I plead the merit of the Lord Jesus Christ whose blood cleanses from all sin, even from sins of the deepest dye. I plead the atonement made by Him who made an atonement for sin, who bore my sins in his own body on the cross of Calvary and wrought out a perfect righteousness which I may obtain by simple faith. No money, no price is demanded. This I could not pay, for all my righteousness is but filthy rags, and I must perish were any part of the purchase price demanded. Nothing in my hand I bring. My salvation must be all of grace, or to me it would be hopeless. I trust that Christ will clothe me in the perfect, spotless robes of his own righteousness and thus present me faultless before the throne. With this trust I go to the judgment seat, assured that the soul that implicitly trusts in Jesus shall never be put to shame. He is faithful who has promised.

MILITARY DUNGEON,
TUPELO, MISS., July 11, 1862.
My Dear Parents:
Life is sweet, and it is a pleasant thing to behold the sun. All that a man hath will he give for his life. Having promise of the life that now is. The life is more than meat. They hunt for the precious life. These quotations from the Word of Life show the high estimate that is placed upon life. My life is not precious in the eyes of these virulent secessionists, for their military rulers declare that on the 15th inst. my life must terminate. Yet a few days and me the all-beholding sun shall see no more in all his course. Mourn not for me, my dear parents, as those who have no hope. For me to live is Christ, and I can say also with the apostle, and to die is gain. I fear not those who, when they have killed the body, have no more that they can do. But I fear Him whose fear casteth out every fear. When these lines are read by you he who penned them will be an inhabitant of the Celestial City, the New Jerusalem. He will have a palace home by the crystal sea, and be the possessor of a kingdom and a crown as eternal in duration as the throne of Jehovah. He will be reposing in his Savior's bosom in the midst of the Paradise of God.

Next to God my thanks are due to you, my dear parents, for guiding my infant feet in the path of wisdom and virtue. In riper years I have been warned and instructed. By precept and example I have been led, until my habits became fixed, and then, accompanied by your parental blessing, I sought a distant home to engage in the arduous duties of life. Whatever success I have achieved, whatever influence for good

I may have exerted, are all due to your pious training. I owe you a debt of gratitude which I can never repay. Though I cannot, God will grant you a reward lasting as eternity. It will add to that exceeding and eternal weight of glory which will be conferred upon you in that day when the heavens shall be dissolved and the elements shall melt with fervent heat. I die for my loyalty to the Federal Government. I know that you would not have me turn traitor to save my life. Life is precious, but death, even death on the scaffold, is preferable to dishonor. Remember me kindly to all my friends. Tell Sallie, Violetta, David, Lizzie, Mary, and Emma, my dear sisters and brother, to meet me in heaven. I know that my Redeemer lives. Dying is but going home. I have taught many how to live and how to die happily. Now by example I am called to teach them how to die as becometh the Christian. May God in mercy grant that as my day my strength may be, and that in my last moments I may not by slavish fear bring dishonor upon my Master's cause, but may glorify Him in the fires. Remember me to my old, tried, true, and trusted friend, Henry Spence. I have no doubt you are constantly praying for me. I will soon be in that glorious home where prayer is lost in praise, faith is changed to sight, and death is swallowed up in victory. Farewell till we meet beyond the river.

Your affectionate son,

JOHN H. AUGHEY.

To David and Elizabeth Aughey, Amsterdam, Jefferson county, Ohio.

CENTRAL MILITARY PRISON,

TUPELO, ITAWAMBA CO., MISS., July 11, 1862.

Hon. Wm. H. Seward:

DEAR SIR—A large number of citizens of Mississippi, holding Union sentiments, and who recognized no such military usurpation as the so-called Confederate States of America, are confined in a filthy prison, sadly infested with vermin, and are famishing from hunger—a sufficient quantity of food not being furnished us. We are separated from our families, and not suffered to hold any communication with them. We are compelled under a strong guard to perform the most menial services, and are often grossly and flagrantly insulted by the officers and guards of the prison. The nights are very cool, after the torrid heat of the day. We are not furnished with bedding, and are compelled to lie down upon the hard floor of our dungeon, where refreshing sleep is not possible. When exhausted nature can hold out no longer our slumbers are broken, restless, and of short duration. Our property is confiscated and our families left destitute of the necessaries of life, all that they possessed, yea, all their living having been seized by the Confederates and converted to their own use. Heavy iron fetters are placed upon our limbs, and daily some of us are led to the scaffold or to death by shooting. Many are forced into the army, instant death being the penalty in case of refusal, thus constraining us to bear arms against our country, to become the executioners of our friends and brethren, or to fall ourselves by their hands.

These evils are intolerable, and we ask protection through you from the United States Government. Please present our humble and earnest petition to his excellency, Abraham Lincoln, president of the United States, that he may take it under advisement and if possible afford us speedy relief. The Federal Government may not now be able to release us, but we ask the protection which the Federal prisoner receives. Were his life taken, swift retribution would be visited upon the rebels by just retaliation; one or more rebel prisoners would suffer death for every Federal prisoner whom they destroyed.

Let this rule hold good in case of Unionists who are citizens of the states in rebellion. The loyal Mississippian deserves the same protection accorded the loyal Rhode Islander or Pennsylvanian. We ask also that our confiscated property be restored to us, or, in the event of our death, to our families. If it be destroyed, we ask that reparation be demanded from the rebel authorities, or that the property of known and avowed secessionists be sequestered to that use. Before this letter reaches its destination the majority of us will have ceased to be. The judge advocate, Col. H. W. Walter, of the rebel army, has informed the writer that he must die on the 15th inst. We have therefore little hope that we individually can receive any personal benefit from this petition, even though you should regard it favorably and consent to its suggestions, but our families who have been robbed, so cruelly robbed, of all their substance, may, in the future, receive remuneration for their great losses, and should citizens of avowed secession proclivities who are within the Federal lines be arrested and held as hostages for the safety of Unionists who are and may be hereafter incarcerated in Tupelo and elsewhere, the rebels will not dare put another Unionist to death.

Trusting that you will deem it proper to take the prayers presented in our petition under advisement, and afford us the protection desired, we remain, with high considerations of respect and esteem your oppressed and imprisoned fellow-citizens,

JOHN H. AUGHEY,
BENJAMIN CLARKE.
B. D. NABORS,
JOHN ROBINSON,
And thirty-eight others.

Two young men, Donald Street and Samuel Maynard, informed me today that they had been impressed into the rebel service. They had been taken prisoner at Corinth by General Pope, and had taken the oath of allegiance to the Federal Government, to which their hearts had always been loyal. Recently they had been arrested by Parson Ellis and six other guerrillas, near Rienzi, and being brought by them into the rebel camp, they refused to rejoin their regiments, and in consequence were immured in this dungeon. From the threats of the officers they expected to be shot at any moment. They had used every means to banish the thoughts of death—had forced themselves to engage in pleasantry and mirth to drive away the sadness and gloom which oppressed them when alone, and when they recalled the delights of their happy homes which they would never see again. I counseled them to prepare to meet their God in peace, wisely to improve the short time granted them to make their peace, calling, and election sure. They replied that they hoped all would be well. They had long since confessed Christ before men, and hoped for salvation through his merit alone. Still, they could not help feeling sad, young as they were, in the near prospect of death. They were both in their 20th year.

While I was gone for water, these men were taken to their doom and I never saw them more.

One morning, as I lay restless and sore, endeavoring to find some position which would be sufficiently easy to permit me to secure, even for a few moments, the benefit of tired nature's sweet restorer—balmy sleep, the thought occurred that it would be well to attempt an escape, though it should result in death from the fire of the guards; this would be by far preferable to death by strangulation at the rope's end, and in the presence of a large concourse of hooting, jeering, yelling, infuriated rebels. I had just finished the preparation of the following address, to be delivered from the scaffold if not forbidden. I gave a copy to M.T. Anderson, who desired it for publication upon his exchange:

ADDRESS TO BE READ FROM THE GALLOWS.
My Unionist Friends:
Hear the words of a man about to die. Last words are of solemn import. Keep them in remembrance. Follow the counsels given, if they commend themselves to your judgement. The Confederate officers have brought you here to witness my fate, that you may thus learn the penalty they deem proper to be inflicted for inflexible adherence to patriotic principles. They declare that I am guilty of treason. Who are the traitors? I affirm that those who would subvert the integrity of the government founded by our patriotic ancestors, are the real traitors. Our politicians, I will not call them statesmen, would first overthrow the best of governments, and then construct from its ruins a government whose corner-stone shall be human slavery. Will it stand? Forbid it, Almighty God! forbid it, heaven. The millennium dawn is too near for God to permit to prosper a government organized to maintain a barbaric relic of the dark ages, and to preserve intact an institution subversive of all the rights of man. Human slavery is made a fundamental feature of the Confederate States of America—the corner-stone, as Alexander Stephens terms it. Should we who have no slaves risk life and limb in the interests of slave-holders, and at their bidding war against a government that has never trespassed upon our rights? I, for one, prefer death, and gladly welcome its embrace rather than to violate the monitions of conscience, the voice of reason, the decision of judgment, and the teachings of pious and patriotic ancestors. You believe in state rights, so do I. State sovereignty and national supremacy.

They are not incompatible. State and nation each sovereign in its own sphere. One needs not and has not trenched upon the prerogatives of the other. E pluribus unum, one composed of many. Distinct as the billows, yet one as the sea. Forced into the army as conscripts, you are not warring against the government by choice. Accept deliverance when it comes. See to it that the republic receives no detriment at your hands. The time is not far distant when the last assassin's dagger shall be stricken from his rebellious hand. How earnestly I have prayed to be permitted to see the downfall of treason, but God in his wisdom declines to grant my petition. The government will live and flourish long after all its foes are dead, buried, and forgotten, for the memory of the wicked shall rot. It will dispense blessings to your posterity and mine, till the angel of Jehovah, standing with one foot on the sea and the other on the solid land, shall, with trumpet voice, proclaim that time shall be no more. It is the last, the best, and most benign government ever bestowed upon man by Him who establishes the nations and fixes their boundaries and ordains their duration. Our government would be unworthy of respect were it impotent to enforce obedience to its wise, humane, and beneficent laws, and to perpetuate its existence, if necessary, by the complete overthrow of all opposing forces. The government under which we have as a nation so greatly prospered is the ordinance of God. The wheels of the chariot which bears it onward will ever revolve. He who stands in the way of its progress will be crushed as sure as fate.

Although in durance vile, and in rebellious ranks perforce, your conscience, your judgment, the teachings of true wisdom, the word of God that enjoins obedience to lawful authority, the patriotic utterances of Washington and his compatriots, should be the chart to direct you in the path of duty in every emergency. Firmly resolve that the republic, through you, shall receive no detriment. The government has done you no harm. Reciprocate with grateful hearts the benefits received from its benignant laws and beneficent institutions. When treason dies an ignominious death, be present to bury its gory corpse beyond the possibility of a resurrection. I see before me many who were with us on the high hills and in the deep glens devising plans to resist the detested conscription. Many of your comrades are in the ranks of the patriotic army aiding in crushing the hydra serpent head of treason and rebellion. See to it that they suffer no harm at your hands. May their lives be precious in your sight.

"Oh, Liberty, how many crimes are committed in thy name," exclaimed one well known to fame, but we are murdered by the craven hordes of treason to promote the fancied interests of chattel slavery, of human bondage.

I die, but the sacred cause I humbly represent will not perish with me on this scaffold. The roots of the tree of liberty, moistened by the blood of the noble phalanx of hero-martyrs who have perished here in Tupelo and on other fields, made classic and sacred by the outpouring of the precious blood of true Southern patriots, will strike deep and spread wide, and will send up through every pore the vital fluid which shall keep forever fresh and green the leaves of that sacred tree planted by our fathers in the primeval forest, under whose wide-spreading branches they and their children, and, we trust, their remotest posterity, will find safety and freedom and perennial happiness.

These, our murderers, would dig up the tree of liberty and plant in its stead the deadly upas tree of human bondage. Its roots would reach down and take hold upon perdition. The inalienable rights of man would perish beneath its blighting shade.

Shall we tamely and basely surrender our God-given heritage of freedom to save our lives imperiled by treason's minions? Shall we basely betray a cause dearer to us than life, for the sake of eking out a miserable, cowardly existence, purchased at the cost of our manhood and of every virtuous and holy principle? Shall we sell our birthright for a mess of pottage, and thus ignobly receive, as a boon graciously accorded by these fiends incarnate who are thirsting for our blood, a few years' longer lease of life, till nature calls us to pay the inevitable debt, and we slink into dishonorable graves?

No. A thousand times, no. My free soul, not trammeled by the fetters that blind and torture my body, gladly, joyfully embraces death, exultingly leaping into its outstretched arms in preference to the acceptance of life on terms so vile, so ignominious, that were I to do so, high heaven with ire would spurn my wretched soul, when seeking admission into Paradise, from all association with the spirits of the pure and good, and consign it to the doom of those who rebelled in heaven and on earth against the God who ordained the powers that be, to whom, when ruling by divine appointment, all are commanded to be subject.

The glorious cause, in the interests of which I lay down my life, will ultimately triumph. Truth crushed to earth will rise again. Entertain no doubts on this subject. Rebellion will be utterly subverted as sure as the God of justice reigns, who will ever prosper the cause approved in heaven.

> For right is right, since God is God,
> And right the day must win;
> To doubt would be disloyalty,
> To falter would be sin.

May God subvert rebellion by the speedy overthrow of all its enemies and the restoration of civil and constitutional liberty to the people of these distracted, discordant, belligerent, and rebellious Southern states. Liberty calls upon each one of you to do your duty, that her blessings may be dispensed to and enjoyed by all.

They love her best who to themselves are true, And what they dare to dream of dare to do.

Remember my advice heretofore given on many a high hill and secluded, lonely glen, at the solemn midnight hour. I am now ready to be offered up, and the time of my departure has come. I only exchange earth for heaven—a life of warfare for a victor's crown. Dying is but going home. Farewell, my friends, till we meet beyond the river where pain and sorrow, sin and death are felt and feared no more. My own and my country's enemies cannot reach me there to harm me. Those holy gates forever bar pollution, sin, and shame. None can obtain admittance there but followers of the Lamb. My prayer is that of the good Dr. Valpy:

> In peace let me resign my breath
> And Thy salvation see;
> My sins deserve eternal death,
> But Jesus died for me.

I have complied with the conditions upon which salvation is promised. I have exercised faith in the Lord Jesus Christ. I have exercised loving trust and trusting love, and have the assurance that Jesus is my loving, precious Savior, in whose delightful presence I am about to appear. So I have nothing to fear.

> Once to every man and nation
> Comes a moment to decide,
> In the strife of truth and falsehood
> For the good or evil side;
> Truth is now upon the scaffold,
> Wrong is now upon the throne,
> Yet this scaffold sweeps the future,
> And behind the dim unknown
> Standeth God within the shadow,
> Keeping watch above his own.

Weep not for me but for yourselves and your children. God in his righteous retribution will visit in vengeance for the great sins of this rebellious people. Our blood will be required at their hands. Those of you who can do so, escape for your lives, for this wicked people shall be crushed in the wine-press of

Jehovah's wrath, and will be compelled to drink to the dregs the cup of divine vengeance.

Though the mills of the gods grind slowly they grind exceeding small;

Though with patience He stands waiting, with exactness He grinds all.

I must close. Your friend and fellow-citizen of the state of Mississippi, and the United States of America,

JOHN H. AUGHEY.

The prisoners who were shot suffered death in the following gruesome manner: A hole was dug, I can scarcely dignify it by the name of grave. The victim was ordered to sit with his legs dangling in it. The file of soldiers took position in front of their victims, when three balls were fired into the brain and three into the heart, and the body falling into this rude excavation was immediately covered with earth. At first coffins were used, but of late these had been dispensed with, owing to the expense, and the increasing number of executions. In some cases the soldiers purposely missed their aim. It was an odious duty which they endeavored to shun, and only performed it upon compulsion. If the corpse was to be delivered to friends they invariably tried to aim so as to wound without taking life, and many of the condemned have, by feigning death, escaped in this way.

Gen. Bragg's name was a synonym for cruelty. He shot many of his own soldiers for trivial offenses, and upon the poor Unionists he had no mercy. One of his officers said to me, "So many men are put to death by Bragg, and executions have become so common that now when they occur they scarcely excite remark." He was a martinet who never failed to punish the most trivial offenses with great severity.

I had not long meditated upon this subject when I arose, resolved upon immediate death or liberty. Of two evils I chose the less. My intentions were communicated to several prisoners, who promised me all the aid in their power. My fetters were examined, and it was the opinion of Amos Deane and Amzi Meek that with proper instruments my bonds could be divested of the iron rods which secured the chain rings. A long-handled iron spoon, my knife, which had a file blade, and a file which one of the prisoners had procured from a Unionist visitor, were secured, and two were detached at a time to work upon my manacles. We went to a corner of the prison, and a sufficient number of prisoners stood in front of us to prevent the guards from observing the proceedings. We changed our location frequently to avoid suspicion, and when officers entered, labor was suspended till their exit. Several prisoners were shot today, and six Unionists were incarcerated. A reign of terror had been inaugurated only equaled in its appalling enormity by the memorable French revolution.

Spies and informers in the pay of the rebel government prowl through the country, using every artifice to lead Unionists to criminate themselves. After this they are dragged to prison and to death. The cavalry dash through the country making raids, burning cotton, carrying off or wantonly destroying the property of citizens, and committing depredations of every kind.

Several prisoners resolved to attempt to escape with me. Our plan was to bring in from the enclosure in the rear of the prison the ax with which we cut and split wood for cooking, and if possible to raise a plank in the floor by cutting away the wood and drawing the spikes, a sufficient number to stand around those who did the work to prevent observation, and to make a hilarious noise so as to drown the sound that would be made. Then in the night we would get under the prison and make our way out on the north side through the guards who were off duty. At this time there were three guards in front of each door, and two on the south side of the building. On the north side of the prison there were no guards on duty, it not being thought necessary if the other sides were vigilantly guarded. There were, however, several hundred guards who, when off duty, slept on this side of the prison.

When relieved they came there to sleep, and those whose turn it was went on duty. They were constantly coming and going, and during the whole night they kept up an incessant noise. My friends labored unremittingly during the day to remove the irons that secured the chain ring. Those who stood around us to prevent the observation of the guards standing in front of the doors told stale jokes and laughed at them immoderately, so as to drown the noise of the filing. The sun was now setting, but the ax had not yet been brought into the prison. Jimmie Tevis had hidden it under his blouse and tried to pass the guards with it, but they detected him by the protruding helve, and made him return it. Now the extra guards had gone on duty. There were three in front of each door. The doors had been removed. The apertures we called doors. A guard was seated on each threshold, and one inside the building promenaded the floor backward and forward throughout its entire length all night. During the day no guards were on the thresholds, nor in the building.

While deliberating upon the best plan to pursue, since we had failed in securing the ax, Gen. Jordan and Col. Clare entered. I was standing in the middle of the floor, midway between the doors, eating some rice which had been surreptitiously conveyed to me. A note accompanied the mess, deftly enclosed. It read: "From your sincere and sympathetic friend, Mrs. Lydia Runyan." Gen. Jordan came directly to the place where I stood, and holding a lantern in front of my face, said, "You are here yet, are you?" I gave an affirmative nod. "Well," said he, to Col. Clare, "I must examine this fellow's irons to see what is their condition." Suiting the action to the word, he put his hands down, and ascertaining that they had been tampered with, he endeavored ineffectually to pull off the bands. He did not notice that I could slip the chain rings off. "These irons," said he, "are very insecure. Who helped you to put them in this condition?" I made no reply. After waiting till he was assured that I intended none, he turned to Col. Clare and said: "Colonel, have these irons welded, put handcuffs upon him, and chain him to that bolt in the floor. The gallows shall not be cheated of their due."

Col. Clare said, "Must I do it tonight?"

"Yes, tonight. Do it at once."

"But," replied the colonel, "it is nearly nine o'clock, and I can't find a black-smith to weld the irons on his ankles. The forges are out of blast at this hour."

"Well, wait till morning, but do it bright and early."

"All right," replied Col. Clare, "I'll have it done by sunrise or before."

After these officers had taken their departure, the prisoners crowded around me and affirmed that they believed that there was a spy in the house in the guise of a prisoner. With entire unanimity they held the opinion that Aleck Stephens was the man. He was a red-haired, low-browed, grim-visaged, freckle-faced, hard-featured, villainous specimen of the genus homo, who sat reticent in a corner, peering from under his bushy eyebrows, and rejecting all familiarity or kind offices tendered by his fellow-prisoners. All realized that I must escape that night or it would be too late. When chained to a bolt in the floor, with securely welded anklets and wearing hand-cuffs, I would be in an utterly helpless condition. There were eleven guards on duty: three in front of each door, one seated upon each threshold, and one promenading the house, which was lighted during the whole night. There was also a special police force on duty, as some Federal prisoners who were in prison till some formalities took place would be sent in the morning to Columbus, Miss., and it was feared that they might attempt to escape ere they were sent farther south. I was seated with some Federal prisoners, sending messages to my friends. I told them that I would slip off my chain, run by the guards, and that it would draw their fire and be shot; that perhaps my mangled corpse would be brought into the prison in a few minutes. I asked them to be sure to inform my friends of the manner of my death. With this request they promised faith-fully to comply. I said, "Farewell, perhaps forever," and arose to make the hazardous attempt.

At this moment a young man whom we nicknamed "Mississippi" ran up to me and said, "Parson, I think I have found a way by which you may escape." His true name, I think, was Leonard Humphrey.

Said I, "What is it?"

He replied, "I was out in the front enclosure, and I saw a hole by the step under the jail, and I think you could get under."

"Why," I replied, "that would be impossible. The three guards standing in front would see me; the guard seated in the doorway would see me; in their presence it would be impossible to get under the building without discovery."

"I thought of that, and while you was preaching I was fixing up a plan, and by golly, I think we can get you off." We were permitted to go into the front enclosure, three at a time, at pleasure, during the day, and on moonlight nights till ten o'clock. He continued, "I must have help." He soon secured the requisite number, who, at the risk of immediate death, upon discovery, agreed to run the risk for my sake. May the Lord reward them.

He then detailed his plan. When the guard promenading the house approached we talked about the price of cotton or some indifferent topic. When he went from us we resumed the business in hand. We all promised implicit obedience.

Just at 9:45 four of us went out. I went out clanking my chains, to lull suspicion, and they did not order me back, as they had done so often before. The rule required that but three be permitted to be in the enclosure at one time, but they providentially did not enforce the rule this time. My three fellow-prisoners stood between me and the guards, and entered into a fierce discussion with them in regard to the comparative merit of Mississippi and Tennessee troops. The enclosures, in front and rear, were formed by stakes surmounted by poles. Their form was actually a parallelogram, whose dimensions were about ten by sixteen feet. The guards became much excited, and the discussion was becoming loud and acrimonious. Howell Trogden, a prisoner, sat inside and held the guard in conversation, who was seated on the threshold. I sat by the aperture under the building, removed my chain, put my legs under the building, and leaned my head upon my elbow, my elbow upon the step, upon which rested the guard's feet, who was seated upon the threshold of the prison door. My fellow-prisoners, in a wordy war with the guards, were diverting their attention, with every appearance of success. I reflected that a few moments would decide my fate. If detected in this forlorn hope, this last attempt with any prospect of success, I must end my life ignominiously upon the scaffold. In the early morning my anklets would be securely welded; I would be handcuffed and chained to a bolt in the floor of our gloomy dungeon. Then all hope must end, and soon my corpse would be borne into the presence of her whose tears were flowing, and who refused to be comforted, because of my ominous absence.

'Tis ten o'clock; I hear the order for the relief guard. They come; I see their bayonets glittering in the bright moonlight. The set time, the appointed moment, pregnant with my fate, had arrived. I offered an ejaculatory prayer to Him who sits upon the throne of heaven for protection at this critical moment. The guards stood within ten feet of me. Now they look steadily at me. I return their gaze. The relief guard has confronted them. They turn to receive it. At that moment I moved backward under the building and disappeared from view. The new guard enter upon their duty. The old guard, without a backward glance, march away. The prisoners are ordered into the dungeon. The guards see but three, and know that that is the highest number permitted by regulation order within the enclosure. They did not suspect that four had been suffered to be out, in violation of orders. I was under the prison, but there were vigilant guards on every side. We were in the midst of the great rebel army. The din of a multitude sounded in my ears. It seemed almost impossible even now to escape detection. Burdette Danner had thrown me his canteen, but it struck against the prison wall. It glittered in the bright moonlight; I was famishing from thirst, but I feared to seize it, though I knew that it was full of that precious liquid whose price was now estimated far above rubies. I did not wish to take any unnecessary risk. The hand protruding from under the prison would probably be observed by the guards and excite their suspicion. I could hear their lowest tones. After awhile one of them said, "Gilmore, I always do forget the countersign." The other replied, "It is 'Braxton' for tonight." Though uttered in an undertone, I caught it. "Well," replied his comrade, I thought it was 'Braxton,' or 'Bragg,' or something like that. I won't forgit it agin."

I crawled to the north side of the prison, and found that there were three apertures which would admit my egress. Upon reaching the first, I found that the guards were so numerous and so close, that it would be extremely hazardous to run the risk at this point. Crawling to the second, I remained till there was comparative quiet. But at the instant I was about to creep out, a soldier, who was lying with his face toward me, sat up and commenced coughing, and continued to cough at intervals for more than an hour. Finding it unadvisable to run the risk of detection at this point, I made my way with considerable difficulty to the third and last aperture, near the rear of the prison, and not far distant from the guards in the rear enclosure. Here exhausted nature could hold out no longer, and I slept. How long I know not. The vermin and the cold awoke me. Presently I heard one soldier say to another. "It is 3 o'clock in the morning and we will have to go on duty." I felt confident that then was my time or never. Morning would soon appear, and my escape would be discovered and my re-arrest follow. Commending myself into the hands of God, and pleading that he would mercifully keep me from detection, and grant me safe conduct through this mighty host of watchful foes, I arose from under the building, and in passing two sleeping soldiers lying within four feet of the prison wall, I struck my foot against the head of one of them. I had not walked for so long a time without a chain, which necessarily compelled me to make such short steps, that I reeled as if under the influence of intoxicants, when freed from it. This made me swerve from my intended course and strike with my foot the head of the somnolent guard. He awoke, and looking at me in the bright moonlight, said, "D——n you, don't do that again." He turned over and resumed his slumbers. He doubtless mistook me for one of his comrades, who, in his awkwardness, had made the unintentional assault.

In prison I had purchased a shirt, paying eleven dollars in gold for it, which resembled that worn by many rebel soldiers. This doubtless contributed to my escape, by warding off suspicion, which would have been aroused at once, if I had appeared in their midst in citizen's dress. I was also wearing McHatton's dark-colored pants. After proceeding a few steps I sat down by a stump, around which a number of guards were collected, some standing, some sitting, and some reclining. To appear at ease I took my knife from my pocket and commenced to whittle the stump and to whistle. This apparent unconcern may have deceived them, and contributed to ward off or allay suspicion. It was an almost unparalleled wonder that some of them did not observe me emerge from underneath the prison, as the moon was shining brightly and they were very near the prison wall in great numbers. Doubtless God had held their eyes or obscured their vision. I soon arose, returned my knife to my pocket, and wound my way cautiously among the various groups, endeavoring to reach the corn field to which I had made my first escape. I endeavored to see every vidette before he perceived me. I had some narrow risks in passing them. As I came near the corn field, a vidette, who had been concealed behind a tree, appeared, evidently with the intention of halting me if I approached nearer. I halted without the order. If he had given the command to halt, I should have given the countersign, Braxton, which I had learned while under the prison, and then have made some excuse for wandering away from my comrades. To avoid suspicion I resorted to a ruse which I cannot narrate. It proved successful. I, after a time, started toward the prison, till seeing videttes in front, I fell upon the ground and deflected from my course toward the prison. After passing through many perils and hair-breadth escapes, as the least blunder would have proved fatal, I reached dense woods and bore south-west. Kneeling down under a larch tree, I returned God thanks for thus far crowning my efforts with success, and most earnestly besought Him to continue His kind protecting care, to choose my path before me, and make it safe, that I might rejoin my family and friends in safety. I had asked Him in prison to lengthen my life by fifteen years, as he did Hezekiah's.

I now pursued my journey rapidly in a south westerly direction, choosing that which led directly from my home for two reasons. The cavalry, with the blood-hounds, would not probably be sent in that direction. After listening attentively while in prison to the reveille and tattoo, and the din from the surrounding camps, I thought the coast was clearest in that direction, and that I could, by taking that route, with the greater ease evade the rebel pickets. I hastened onward with all possible speed, avoiding roads, till the sun arose. As I was rapidly traveling along a narrow path, I suddenly met a negro. He was scared. So was I. I, in a peremptory tone, addressed him in quick succession, the following questions:

"Where are you going? Where have you been? To whom do you belong? Have you a pass?"

"I belong," said the boy, trembling, "to Col. Kohlheim, I have been to wife's house, and am gwine back to Massa's."

He handed me his pass which read: "The bearer, Tabor, has permission to go to Major Smith's to visit his wife and return. Good till tomorrow evening, ——— ."

"Well, sir," said he, as I handed back to him his pass, "you see it am all right wid me."

Concluding that it was not all right "wid" myself I hurried on. Tabor called to me ere I had gone twenty yards. I halted. He came up and asked me if "dis bill (presenting one on a Tennessee bank) was good." "Good as the bank," said I, and hurried speedily leaving the path and turning into a dense woods. Traveling on till about 12 M., judging from the vertical rays of the sun, I came to an open champaign country, through which I could not travel with safety, in daylight. I sought a place in which to hide, and discovering a ditch which bisected a corn-field, I concealed myself in that. Many passed near me during the day. I was very hungry. Sullivan and Soper, Federal prisoners had each given me, before leaving prison, a small piece of bread, which they had in their haversacks when captured. I found both pieces were saturated with tobacco. The prisoner with whom I had exchanged pants used tobacco, and had carried some in both pockets. As tobacco is very offensive to me, its presence upon my bread caused me to lose it. I reflected on the best course to pursue in order to secure the greatest degree of safety in my flight. I though at one time it would be best to go west until I reached the Mississippi river, then hail a gun-boat and thus be saved, but I reflected that I was a long, long distance from that river—that there was the great Mississippi bottom to pass through, which was full of lagoons, lakes, bayous, and swamps, and that it was infested with bears, rattlesnakes, vipers, bull-snakes, centipedes, tarantulas, and venomous reptiles and wild beasts of many kinds. I would also have to swim across the Yazoo and Tallahatchie rivers, which I feared I could not do, enfeebled as I would be when I reached those rivers, and encumbered as I was with the heavy iron bands. The day ended and the night came. The stars, those beautiful nocturnal luminaries, came out in silent glory, one by one. Fixing my eye upon the polar star, the underground railroad traveler's guide, I set out bearing a little to the west of north. I soon reached the thick woods and found it very difficult to make rapid progress, in consequence of the dense undergrowth and obscure light. The bushes would strike me in the eyes, and often the top of a fallen tree would compel me to make quite a circuit. Soon, however, the moon appeared in her brightness—the old silver moon. But her light I found to be by far less brilliant than that of the sun, and her rays were much obscured by the dense foliage overhead, hence my progress was necessarily slow, labored, and toilsome. During the day I had slept but little, in consequence of the proximity of those who might be bitter foes, and also because of the unpleasant position I occupied, as the ditch in which I had concealed myself was muddy and proved a very uncomfortable bed. I therefore became weary, my limbs stiff from travel and from the pressure of the heavy iron bands. Sleep overpowered me, and I lay down in the leaves and slept till the cold awoke me. I slept an hour and a half, as I judged from the moon's descent. The nights are invariably cool in Mississippi, however sultry may have been the weather during the day. Arising from my uneasy slumber I pressed on. My thirst, which had for some time been increasing, now became absolutely unendurable. I knew not where to get water, not daring to go near a well for fear of arrest. I must obtain water or perish. At length I heard some sucking pigs and their dam at a short distance from me in the woods. There seemed to be no alternative. I must either perish or obtain some fluid to slake my raging thirst, so I resolved to catch one of the little pigs, cut its throat, and drink the blood. I searched for my knife, but ascertained that I had lost it. I was therefore reluctantly compelled to abandon my designs upon the suckling's life. As I went forward, the sow and her brood started up alarmed, and in their fright plunged into water. I followed fast and found a mud-hole—a perfect lob-lolly. The water was tepid, foul, and mingled with the spawn of frogs. Removing the green scum, I drank deep of the stagnant pool. My thirst was only partially allayed by this foul draught, and so returned. As day dawned, I found some sassafras leaves, which I chewed to allay the pangs of hunger, but they formed a paste which I could not swallow. I remembered that this day was the holy Sabbath, but it brought neither rest to my weary frame, nor composure to my agitated and excited mind.

The course decided upon as safest and best was to go far to the south and west, and there wait till the cavalry had returned from their search for me, then by a very circuitous route to endeavor to reach the Memphis and Charlestown railroad, find some Federal outpost on that road, and thus be saved. About ten o'clock I came to an open country, and sought a place to conceal myself. I found a dense copse on a hillside, and hid within its friendly depths. I had about departed to the realm of dreams when I heard the voice of song. A human voice quickly aroused me. I peered out from my lair, and on an opposite hill I saw a gigantic Ethiopian making his way laboriously. He had a plank in his hands, there was one underneath him upon which he was walking. When he reached the end of it, he laid down the plank he bore in his hands, stepped upon it, and reaching back he lifted the other plank, and thus he wended his way. He accompanied his task by singing a song heard often upon every southern plantation:

My ole missus promise me,
Dat when she die, she'd set me free,
But she dun dead this many year ago,
An' yer I'm a hoin de same ole row.
Run, nigger, run, de patter-roller ketch you,
Run, nigger, run, hit's almos' day.

I'm a hoin across, I'm a hoin aroun',
I'm a cleanin up some mo' new groun',
Whar I lif so hard, I lif so free,
Dat my sins rises up in fronter me.
Oh, run, nigger, run, de patter-roller ketch you,
Run, nigger, run, hit's almos' day.

But some ob dese days my time will come,
I'll year dat bugle, I'll year dat drum,
I'll see dem armies a marchin' along,
I'll lif my head an' jine der song.
I'll hide no more behind dat tree,
When t he angels flock ter wait on me.
Oh, run, nigger, run, de patter-roller ketch you.
Run, nigger, run, hit's almos' day.

As he laid down his plank and stepped upon it, it slid from under his feet and he fell prone upon the ground. He jumped up and sang:

"If Charley slip upon his track
Der's danger de hounds will bring him back,
Oh, run nigger, run, de patter-roller ketch you,
Run, nigger, run, hit's almos' day."

Thus he improvised his song as he wended his weary way. He was trying to evade the hounds by thus leaving no scent for them to follow. As he passed me he sang:

"De pore white trash dey lives an' grows,
Dey noze far less dan the nigger noze."

Then he sang the chorus with a will:

"My name's Sam, I don't care a d—n,
I'd radder be a nigger, dan a pore white man."

He look around in alarm, and muttered, "Old Charley alwa's dun furgit hizsef when he sings dat song." He then passed onward in silence, carrying his planks with him.

A singular noise attracting attention, as I gazed up the hill I saw a man descend from a tree and look around warily. As he passed near me, I called out, in a low tone, *Taisez vous.*

Quickly glancing in my direction, he replied, "*Oui, oui.*"

I bade him come to me. He did so. He had been in hiding for a month, and becoming hungry he left his lofty perch to procure the food that would be left at the designated spot by his wife or eldest daughter. He told me to await his return and he would share his food with me, and he assured me of all possible aid. As he emerged from the jungle, a man with fierce aspect confronted him. He told him to throw up his hands. I had accompanied him and was about to retreat with all possible speed, but the thought of abandoning my friend restrained me. I determined to stand by him and abide the result. My friend refused to throw up his hands. He said he preferred to die there and then in preference to submitting to be bound. This man, who I learned was known as Col. Ned Barry, ordered us to march in front of him, or if we hesitated he would let its have the contents of his revolvers. We obeyed, hoping to escape by darting into the woods at some suitable point, or by some providential deliverance.

As we neared a large tree, Col. Barry said: "Israel Nelson, I've been prowlin' around arter you for more'n three weeks. Now, sir, you got ter go two miles from here, an' Gen. Yerger will be d--d glad ter see yer." He turned around to make this little speech. As he closed, and was about to advance, a dusky form suddenly sprang from behind the tree, a bludgeon descended swiftly upon the Colonel's skull, and our would-be captor lay unconscious at our feet. We found cords in his pockets and securely bound our fallen foe. Soon he returned to consciousness, and begged piteously for his life. We took possession of his weapons.

A little boy of ten years of age appeared on the scene. He came to find his father. He told him that ma wanted him to come to the house at once, there was strangers there to see him. What should we do to secure our own safety. Nelson proposed shooting both father and son. We took them both to the copse, and with the aid of this Ethiopian, who had appeared at an opportune moment, gagged both father and son, and bound them to the same tree. I urged Nelson to escape with me, and to leave these persons bound. He replied that he must see his wife, and that he would go to the trysting place, and she would probably be there, or in case she was not there, he would find a note secreted near by. The note was there, but contained no special information. Nothing but words of comfort and affectionate sympathy.

We heard hounds, and feared to return to our prisoners for a long time. The African, Charley, had left us, and as night had dropped down upon the scene we cautiously returned to the copse.

I hope never again to witness such a ghastly sight. The mangled remains of father and son were still adhering to the tree. Fierce hounds had torn them to pieces. I could no longer stay to gaze upon this sad tragedy. Nelson told me that he had resolved to shoot them both, as his safety and mine would be compromised by sparing their lives. I am glad that the terrible necessity was obviated. Nelson refused to abandon his family, and I could no longer delay, so hastened onward.

The dismal night passed away. I found a place to hide—a ditch as usual. I slept, and saw in my dreams tables groaning under the weight of the most delicious viands, and brooks of crystal waters babbling and sparkling as they rushed onward in their meandering course, but when I attempted to grasp them they served me as Tantalus of olden time was served, by vanishing into thin air or receding from my grasp. While lying here, I was occasionally aroused by the trampling of horses grazing in the fields, which I feared might be bringing on my pursuers. Once the voices of men mingled with the sound of prancing steeds upon a little bridge some twenty feet distant, induced me to look out from my hiding place, and lo! two cavalry men, perhaps hunting for my life, passed along.

When the sun had reached the zenith, I was again startled by voices, which approached nearer and still nearer my place of concealment, till at length the cause was discovered. Several children, both black and white, had come from a farm house about a quarter of a mile distant to gather blackberries along the margin of the ditch. They soon discovered me and seemed somewhat startled and alarmed at my appearance. I soon saw them gazing down upon me in my moist bed, with evident amazement and alarm. Pallid, haggard, unshaven, and covered with mud, I must have presented a frightful picture. As soon as the children passed me, fearing the report they would carry home, I arose from my lair and hastened onward. After traveling three or four miles I came to a dense woods bordering a stream, which had ceased running in consequence of the unprecedented drought that had for a long time prevailed throughout this section of Mississippi. The creek had been a large one, and in the deep cavities some water still remained. Though warm and covered with a thick green scum, and mingled with the spawn of frogs, I drank it from sheer necessity, tepid and unwholesome as it was. It did not allay my thirst, but created a nausea which was very unpleasant. After traveling several hours, I came to a place where was a depression in the ground. I thought I might possibly find water. Soon the sight of water gladdened me, but it was stagnant and covered with a thick, greenish, yellowish scum. As I approached it I was startled by seeing the tracks of someone who I thought might have been a fugitive like myself. By closely observing the footsteps and the surroundings, I discerned this to be the place I had left hours ago. I was traveling in a circle. My bewildered brain had lost its power to locate the cardinal points.

Chapter Five

About 4 o'clock P.M. I was startled by the baying of blood-hounds behind me, and apparently upon my track. Before escaping from jail I had been advised by my fellow-prisoners to procure some onions, as these rubbed upon the soles of my boots would measurably destroy the scent. These could only be procured by visiting a garden, and I feared to approach so near a house. I had not left any clothing in prison from which the hounds could obtain the scent so as to recognize my track, and my starting in a south-western direction was an additional precaution against blood-hounds. Having heard them almost every night for years, as they hunted down the fugitive slave, I could not mistake the fearful import of their howling. I could devise no plan for breaking the trail. Daniel Boone, when pursued by Indians, succeeded in baffling the dogs with which they pursued him by laying hold of overhanging branches and swinging himself forward. One slave on Dick's river in Kentucky, near Danville, Boyle Co., ran along the brink of a precipice, and dug a recess back from the narrow path. Crawling into it, he remained concealed till the hounds reached that point, when he thrust them from the path. They fell and were dashed to pieces upon the jagged rocks below. Some slaves, before escaping, provide themselves with a large supply of cayenne pepper. When the hounds are heard in pursuit they set down their heels with considerable force so as to make as deep an impression as possible, they then sprinkle their tracks with the cayenne pepper. The hounds, in rapid pursuit, inhale the pepper. It produces such pain and irritation that they will not pursue any fugitive for months, and even then with caution so great that they are nearly worthless as negro dogs.

None of these plans were practicable, and I believed death imminent, either from being torn to pieces by the hounds or by being shot by the cavalry who were following hard after them. Climbing a tree, I resolved to die rather than be taken back to Tupelo to suffer death on the gallows in the presence of a hooting, howling, mixed multitude of infuriate demons. I knew that upon my refusal to come down from the tree a volley from their carbines would end my life. The tree into which I had climbed was a large black oak; a juniper tree stood on a knoll between the oak and the route by which my pursuers would approach. The oak would afford perfect concealment from observation till my pursuers stood underneath the tree, then, by peering into its umbrageous recesses on all sides, my presence would be discovered. Oh! how I wished for my navy repeater, that I might sell my life as dearly as possible—that ere I was slain I might make some secessionist bite the dust. I thought of the couplet in the old song:

The hounds are baying on my track,

Christian, will you send me back?

A feeling of deep sympathy arose in my heart for the poor slave who, in his endeavor to escape from the iron furnace of southern slavery, encountered the blood-hounds, and was torn to pieces by them. A fellow feeling makes us wondrous kind. A touch of sympathy makes all the world akin. Now I hear the deep-mouthed baying of the hounds. The pack is large, and they realize that the object of their search is near. I see them now on the crest of the hill but a mile distant. Down the hill they plunge. The cavalry follow hard after them. Men and dogs seem intent upon their fell purpose. Soon they will seize their prey, their hapless victim is almost within their grasp. These fierce dragoons are mentally gloating over the reward which they will receive for their bloody work. Success will be achieved ere ten minutes elapse. All hasten forward to be in at the death. Must I die as the fool dieth? Like Jezebel, my blood lapped by dogs, and my body devoured by these fierce blood-hounds and those wild swine feeding near? My friends will never learn how I perished, and 'tis better they should not know the horrible circumstances attending my death. Oh! that I could see my dear wife and darling Kate, to kiss them a final farewell ere the tragic scene closes forever all my hopes of, and aspirations for, a long and happy life in their society. Now the hounds appear on the further brink of a ravine, a few hundred yards distant, a ravine I had crossed a short time before. Their loud baying, their quick, sharp yelps rang with frightful clearness on the summer air. All hope of escape died within my bosom. There seemed to be a pack of forty fierce hounds as they leaped down the steep declivity. I waited in terrible suspense their advent on the hither bank. The cavalry, with rattling sabers and glittering carbines, appeared on the farther bank, and halting on the brink found the declivity too steep to attempt the descent on horseback. A number dismounted and speedily disappeared within the ravine. Two gray foxes, driven from their covert by the noise of pursuit, ran by the tree in which I was concealed, and plunged into a cacti copse. A half-dozen men appeared upon the crest nearest me. The hounds were yet howling down in the glen. They were bearing eastward, up the ravine, and soon the dismounted dragoons recrossed, and remounting began to follow in that direction. On, on they went, with precipitate speed. The howling of the hounds and the yelling and horrid noise indicated that they were receding in the distance. Fainter and fainter the breezes bore to my ears the echoes of pursuit, till at length they were lost in the distance, and I was mercifully saved from a violent and horrid death. How had Divine Providence interposed in my behalf! It long remained a mystery. A negro fugitive, escaping from slavery, had crossed my path—had gone up the ravine. The hounds will always leave the track of a white man for that of a negro. On the next afternoon they caught the poor slave, who had concealed himself in a tree, and returned him to bondage. His master lived in Natchez, Adams Co., and this boy, Jingo Dick, had absconded three months before his capture.

I climbed down from the oak, and sat under the juniper tree. I sat under it, a long time, returning thanks to God for my deliverance from a horrible death, yet depressed with the apparently hopeless prospect of ever evading my pursuers and reaching a place of ultimate safety.

Soon a mocking bird from a neighboring tree began to sing. He seemed to mock me in my agony. When he ceased, a bird perched in the highest branches of the same tree poured from its little throat a song of hope—the sweetest song I ever heard, and then another and another joined in glad refrain, till the whole grove grew vocal with their notes of joy. My soul, responsive to these glad strains, grew hopeful, and I, leaving more than half my weary burden of care, trudged on, homeward bound. After awhile I became bewildered, but soon peeping from a flowery dell I saw the yellow compass flower. Its polary property I knew. And true as the magnetic needle it pointed the way to the desired haven. Coming to a hazel dell I saw the patriotic pimpernel. Its flowers of red, white, and blue were closed, and I knew that a storm was impending. Soon the sky became overcast. Dark, threatening, murky clouds o'erspread the sky and shut out the sun. Oh! that the rain might fall in torrents. I could then assuage my burning, raging thirst. On a distant hill I saw it falling, but only a few drops reached me, and my consuming thirst remained unquenched. I had the same sensations as Burton, one of the explorers of the Dark Continent. He says, "For twenty hours we did not taste water, the sun parched our brains and the mirage mocked us at every turn." As I jogged along, with eyes shut against the fiery air, every image that came to my mind was of water; water in the cool well, water bubbling from the rock, water rippling in shady streams, water in clear lakes, inviting me to plunge in and bathe. Now a cloud seemed to shower upon me drops more precious than pearls, then an unseen hand seemed to offer me a cup, which I would have given all I was worth to receive. But what a dreary, dreadful contrast. I opened my eyes to a heat-reeking plain and a sky of that deep blue so lovely to painter and poet, so full of death to us whose only desire was rain and tempest. I tried to pray but I could not. I tried to think, but I had only one idea—water, water, water. A cup of cold water. Oh! how precious. No comparison is adequate to express its worth. But I will trust Him who is able to supply all my needs.

Becoming confused again in regard to the cardinal points, I fortunately came to a cemetery. In all Christian lands the headstones at the graves are to the west. I took my bearings and traveled on in a north-easterly direction. The Savior said, in Matt. xxiv. 27, "As the lightning cometh out of the east, and shineth even unto the west, so shall also the coming of the Son of Man be." The early Christians supposed that this verse taught that Christ, at the second advent would appear in the east. Hence the burial of the dead so that in rising on the resurrection morn they would face the east. While steadily pursuing my weary way the faint howling of a distant pack of hounds coming from the direction in which I was traveling caused me to halt in consternation. I was ascending a lofty hill, and was nearing the summit, when these ominous sounds were heard. It was evident they were not in search of me, for they were coming south, but they might accomplish my destruction as certainly as if they had been commissioned to effect this object. I hastened to the summit of the hill. A lofty umbrageous oak, a venerable forest king, with lateral branches near the ground, stood on the highest eminence. As the increasingly distinct baying of the hounds indicated their rapid approach, I resolved to climb this tree. With less difficulty than I had anticipated I succeeded in doing so. Higher and higher I ascended, till I reached the lofty coronal of leaves that decked this mighty monarch of the woods. A grand panorama was spread out before me. Two miles distant, in the east, the tents of a great encampment were spread out in full view. The sentries were at their posts; the roads on all sides were picketed; a general review was in progress, and the bustle and excitement of camp life was evident in all its appointments. A company of cavalry with blood-hounds were just coming in from the north. They had twenty-five or thirty men in charge, in citizens' dress, evidently Unionists. They were driving these men before them on the double quick. Presently I saw one fall prone upon the earth. Three or four cavalry men dismounted, and pricking him with their bayonets, compelled him to rise. He staggered on a short distance and fell again. A second time they used their bayonets, when one of the prisoners left his companions, and running to the fallen man, thrust aside the bayonets. The guards on foot presented their carbines. A puff of smoke indicated that they had discharged them. This man, who seemed desirous of aiding his fellow-prisoner, fell upon the prostrate form of the fallen man, whom they now transfixed with their bayonets. After a few moments spent in inspecting their victims, they remounted their horses and rejoined their company. But what startled me most was the sight of a large company of hunters, composed of ladies and gentlemen, who, spread over a considerable space, in high glee and with loud and boisterous halloos were pursuing a bear. They were coming rapidly toward me from a point due north. That they would pass near me was evident. The bear was but a half mile in advance of the hounds, and they were gaining rapidly upon him. I perceived that the bear's strength was waning. He seemed to be running in a direct line toward the tree amid whose friendly foliage I was concealed. A planter, whose residence was upon a hill to the west, had heard the hounds, and I saw him hastily make preparations to join in the chase. Colored men brought out several saddled horses; a number of hounds were unleashed and unkenneled, and several men mounted the horses, and with guns in hand hastened away to join in the chase. I observed that from the direction they took they would not be likely to intercept the bear. On, on, they rode, and ere long joined the hunters in pursuit. The bear, with failing strength, reached a point about three hundred yards from my tree, and turning his back against a tree, stood at bay. The dogs, as fast as they approached, were driven back, howling in agony. As the bear was on the opposite side of the tree, I could not see the battle. It became fierce, and the mingled growling of the bear and the howls and yells of pain upon the part of the discomfited dogs made for a time a perfect pandemonium. The bear seemed on the point of gaining a victory, but the hunters rode up, called off the not reluctant hounds, and a volley from their carbines laid bruin dead at their feet. I could hear their conversation distinctly. The planter invited the hunters to come over and spend the night with him. He promised to send some of his slaves to flay the bear and care for the meat. The visitors' dogs were taken care of by the planter. They were leashed in his yard; but his own hounds were allowed to roam at will all night. The negroes came down from the house, skinned and dressed the bear, and it seemed to be attractive labor to them. The hounds came under the tree and barked furiously. One of the colored men said be believed there "was coons up dat tree, or dem dogs wouldn't bark so fierce." One of them said he believed he'd "go and tell master dat dere was coons in dat tree." Off he started, and soon came back to tell de boys to "kum up an' take keer of sum dogs dat de bear had almost killed." About ten o'clock I came down from the tree and pursued my journey in the direction of the polar star. I experienced greater difficulty in descending the tree than in the ascent. My limbs were weary; the fetters upon my ankles had become quite galling; My tongue was swollen in my month and cracking open from thirst. I had not gotten far from the tree when a hound, which had been lapping the blood of the bear, sprang toward me with open month. A well-directed blow from a club, which I took the precaution to secure, sent him howling away. All the hounds within hearing howled in concert, and a more frightful chorus I have never heard. I hastened onward as rapidly as possible, and there seemed to be no pursuit. I feared to deviate from my pathway to the right or left, as I had learned from my lofty point of observation, from my perch in the pinnacle of the lofty monarch of the forest, that there was a large camp to the eastward and a much less formidable one to the westward; on the one hand was Scylla, on the other Charybdis. Every hour death stared me in the face. Foes were lurking all around. There was but a step between me and death. The days of my appointed time were waning fast. Hunted like a partridge upon the mountains, by blood-hounds and bloody men, a price upon my head, escape seemed impossible. I knew that prayer, fervent prayer, was continually ascending to God in my behalf. Implicitly I believed in omnipotence of prayer—that no good thing will be denied the prayer of faith. But I had no promise to plead for longer life. It might be the will of the all-wise God to call me from earth, to suffer me to perish, as many patriotic men had done since the inauguration of rebellion, by rebel cruelty. I was never for an hour out of the hearing of howling hounds or yelping dogs. The hound ordinarily used in the pursuit of fugitive slaves is a cross between a mastiff and the bull-dog. It is very fierce, and will assault and tear to pieces the fugitive as soon as caught. A hound sometimes used is the blood-hound of the Talbot or southern breed. He has long, pendulous, drooping ears; he is tall and square-headed; has heavy, drooping lips and jowl. He has a stern expression. He is broad-chested, deep-tongued, and much slower than the cross between the mastiff and bull-dog. His powers of scenting are extraordinary. Let him smell any article of clothing that has been worn by the fugitive, and he will at once recognize his track and follow it, though it should be more than twenty-four hours old. Often one or two of these blood-hounds are kept to guide the pack. They are not so fierce as the other dogs, and any stout negro, by getting his back against a tree, so that he may not be surrounded, could defend himself with a club, and kill his assailants as fast as they approached. But the ordinary dog used to hunt the fugitive—the cross between the mastiff and the bull-dog—is so large, strong, and fierce that the fugitive stands but little chance to defend himself from the combined attack of a dozen of them. Were it not for the blood-hounds with them, he could much more readily break the trail and baffle pursuit. The blood-hound is in color tawny, with black muzzles. The former dog has some scenting powers, but it is as inferior in these to the true blood-hound as it is superior to him in blood-thirstiness and cruel, indiscriminate pugnacity. It has no utility except as a man-hunter. In hunting the fugitive slave men always accompany the hounds, and are seldom far in the rear. When the fugitive finds all his skill to baffle pursuit unavailing, he climbs a tree and awaits the arrival of the horsemen, who call off the hounds, order the slave to come down, and they then tie him up and give him one or two hundred lashes, well laid on, on his bare back. Then he is ironed and conveyed home, where he receives the remaining installments of the penalty due to his vain attempt to secure his inalienable rights—life, liberty, and the pursuit of happiness. Life, one of the inalienable rights which God ordains for man, is not servile life. Servile life is induced by the avarice and cruelty of man.

I lay down in the woods and fell asleep; visions of abundance both to eat and drink haunted me, and every unusual sound would startle me. A fly peculiar to the South, whose buzz sounded like the voice of a man in his senility, often awoke me with the fear that my enemies were near. As soon as Ursa Minor appeared I took up my line of march. The night was very dark, and I became somewhat bewildered. At length I reached a cross-roads, and as I was emerging from the woods I saw two videttes a few yards distant. As quickly and as noiselessly as possible, I made a retrograde movement. As I was retiring I heard one vidette say to his comrade, "Who is that?" He replied, "It is the corporal of the guard." "What does he want?" said the first. "O," was the reply, "I suspect he's just slipping around here to see if we are asleep."

After I had reached a safe distance in the bushes, I lay down and slept till the moon arose. To the surprise of my bewildered brain it seemed to rise in the west. Taking my bearings I hastened on, through woods, corn-fields, and swamps. Coming to a large pasture in which a number of cows were grazing, I tried to obtain some milk, but the cows would not let me approach near enough to effect my purpose. My face was not of the right color, and my costume belonged to a sex that never milked them. I traveled till day-break, when I concealed myself in a canebrake. I had scarcely fallen asleep, when I heard the sound of the reveille in a camp near by, and, listening, distinctly heard the soldiers conversing. Arising, I hastily beat a retreat, and cautiously avoiding the videttes I traveled several hours before I dared take any rest. At length I lay down amid the branches of a fallen tree and slept. Visions of home and friends flitted before me. Voices sweet and kind greeted me on all sides.

The bitter taunts of cruel officers no longer assailed my ears. The loved ones at home were present, and the joys of the past were renewed. But, alas! the falling of a limb dissipated all my fancied pleasures. The reality returned. I was still a fugitive escaping for life, and in the midst of a hostile country. I fancied the woful disappointment of the rebel officers when they learned that the bird had flown and that they could no longer wreak their vengeance upon me, nor have the pleasure of witnessing my execution. I thanked God and took courage. During this night I traveled steadily, crossing corn-fields, woods, and pastures. I crossed but one cotton-field. I suspected every bush a secessionist, though I felt much more secure at night than in daylight. I avoided roads as much as possible, traveling on none except to cross them, and this I did walking backward, so that if the hounds found my track the cavalry would be deceived when the plain tracks in the road indicated a false direction. Every possible deception was practiced by Unionists to avoid detection.

The rising sun still found me pressing onward. Hunger and thirst were now consuming me. My tongue was swollen and cracking open from thirst. I thought of opening a vein in my arm and drinking the blood. When I had almost despaired of getting water, a presentiment—I may call it an assurance as if an inspiration front heaven, took possession of my whole soul that soon I would be supplied with water. The sky was clear. No clouds indicated rain. I quietly walked along, as consciously sure of water as if I were being refreshed by it. I came to a road and crossed it. A gin house was visible a few hundred yards distant, and there was a grove near it. I knew that embowered within its sylvan shade was a plantation house. After crossing the road I came to a gorge surrounded by converging hills, from which issued a copious fountain of crystal water. Near it there was no trace of human foot, nor hoof of cattle. I seemed to be the discoverer. On beholding it I wept for joy. I knelt down and in words of thanksgiving expressed my gratitude to Almighty God for this great deliverance, this sparkling, life-giving liquid brewed amid the forest shades by the hand of Jehovah, merciful and gracious. I then stooped down and quaffed the living water, the first pure water I had tasted since my imprisonment. Oh! that men would praise the Lord for his goodness and feel truly grateful for his common benefits. Were water to become scarce men would realize its worth. Blessings brighten as they take their flight. I remained at this spring four hours, quaffing its cool, refreshing waters. I removed my clothing and performed my first ablution since I fell into rebel hands, yet the irons prevented a thorough ablution. I named this spring Fons Vitæ. I rejoiced when I discovered this spring, but not surprised, for I felt as fully assured of finding water as if an angel had spoken to me from heaven indicating its location. It came into my mind with the force of a revelation. My regret was sincere when I was compelled to leave this spring and continue my wearisome journey.

Three o'clock P. M. arrived. I felt bewildered. I knew not where I was. I might be near friends, I might be near blood-thirsty foes. I could scarcely walk. My iron bands had become very irksome. I felt that I was becoming childish. I could tell all my bones. I tried to pray, but could only utter, "God, be merciful to me a sinner." The sky became overcast with clouds. I could not distinguish the cardinal points. I therefore concealed myself and slept. It was night when I awoke, and the clouds still covered the face of the sky threateningly, concealing my guides, the stars of heaven, and rendering it impossible for me to proceed. Thus when I wished most to advance, my progress was arrested and my distressing suspense prolonged. During the night I was asleep and awake alternately, but could not at any time discern either moon or stars. I slept behind a fallen tree by a roadside. A horseman passed by at midnight. His dog, a large, ferocious animal, came running along by the side of the tree by which I was lying. When he reached me I rose suddenly, and brandishing a club menacingly, the alarmed and bowling dog incontinently and ingloriously leaving me master of the field. The horseman stopped and listened. I lay silent as the grave. After a time, which my suspense and alarm doubtless magnified, he rode onward, when I changed my hiding place for safer quarters farther in the dark forest. The next morning the sun was obscured until nine o'clock. I guess at the time, as I had not my watch. I was then sick. There was a ringing in my ears, and I was afflicted by vertigo, a dimness of vision, and faintness, which rendered me absolutely unfit for travel. It required an hour to walk a quarter of a mile. Before me was a hill, the top of which I reached after two hours laborious ascent. I despaired of getting much farther. Feeling confident that I must be near the point where intersect the counties of Tippah, Pontotoc, Itawamba, and Tishomingo, and knowing that there were many Unionists in that district, I resolved to call at the first house I came to whose appearance indicated that its inmates were not slave-holders. Slave-holders were almost invariably secessionists. If I remained in the woods I must perish, as a great storm was impending. If I met with a Unionist family I would be saved, if with a rebel family I could but perish, and I felt that I could not survive the night and approaching storm.

Soon I came to a cabin by the side of a road, two miles north of New Albany, Tippah county. The storm had reached me. The wind was blowing a gale, and the rain began to fall in torrents—just such a storm visits the gulf states after a protracted drought. I went up to the door of the cabin and rapped. "Come," was the laconic response. I pulled the latch-string. The door blew open and I staggered in. When the lady present looked upon me she threw up her hands in terror, and said:

"Are you from Tupelo?"

"I am."

"What is your name?"

"John Hill."

I suppressed my surname. I was not much surprised at the lady's alarm. My hair, long and unkempt, covered with mud, my clothes nearly torn from my body by the thorns and briars in the ditches which bisected the fields that I was compelled necessarily to cross, my face pallid, the iron bands upon my limbs, made me present a frightful apparition to her startled gaze. And coming as the harbinger of a fierce storm, added doubtless to her terror. She, scrutinizing me closely, was about to proceed with her catechising. I forestalled her by turning to her husband, a man of Herculean proportions, sitting near by saying:

"Sir, the Yankees are overrunning all our country. Why are you not in the army trying to drive them away?"

The lady replied tartly, "He's not there, and he's not goin' there, either." She then animadverted upon Jeff Davis, the Southern Confederacy, and the conscript law, in terms that pleased me much. I never before delighted so much in hearing Jeff Davis abused. I felt safe, and pointing to the iron bands, told this couple — Mr. and Mrs. Chism — of my escape from the prison at Tupelo and the death preordained by General Bragg.

Their house had been searched for Malone and me, and they were cognizant of our escape. Both husband and wife promised to render all possible aid.

Mrs. Chism immediately began to prepare supper. I told her that I could not await the slow process of cooking, that I was too near starvation for that. She turned down the table-cloth which covered the fragments remaining from dinner, and disclosed some corn bread and Irish potatoes. I thought this was the sweetest morsel I had ever tasted. After eating a little I became quite sick, and was compelled to desist. It was so long since I had partaken of any substantial food that my stomach rebelled against it. Soon Mrs. Chism prepared supper, consisting of broiled chicken and other delicacies. The fowl was small, and I ate nearly the whole of it, much to the chagrin of a little daughter of mine hostess, whom I heard complaining to her me in an adjoining room, saying, "Ma, all I could get of that chicken was a tiny piece of a wing, and wasent that gentleman a hoss to eat," with other remarks not very complimentary to my voracious appetite. I ate too heartily after so long a fast, and it caused nausea and vomiting. My stomach was too weak to bear it. After supper mine host endeavored to remove the heavy iron bands with which my ankles were encircled. Fortunately he was a blacksmith by vocation, and with the use of the implements of his trade he succeeded. I keep these as sacred relics. The good lady furnished me with water and a suit of her husband's clothes. After performing a thorough ablution I donned the suit, and was completely metamorphosed and thoroughly disguised, as my new suit was made for a man of vastly larger physical proportions. I spent the night with my new friends, during which a heavy storm passed over, accompanied by vivid lightning and loud, reverberating thunder. Had I been out in the drenching rain in my wretched and enfeebled condition I must certainly have perished.

A rebel camp was within a mile and a half, and horsemen clad in gray passed constantly. In the morning my host informed me of a Unionist who knew the country in the direction of Rienzi, the point which I now determined to reach. This gentleman was a near neighbor, Mr. Sanford by name. Mr. Chism accompanied me to a thicket near his house, in which I concealed myself. Before leaving I handed Mrs. Chism, a double eagle. She refused to take it. Said I, "You have saved my life." "I charge you nothing for that," was her laconic reply. I threw the money down upon the table and left with her husband. As we were departing, she said, "Well, if you get to the Federal lines you won't begrudge it, and if you don't you won't need it."

Mr. Chism went to the shop of Mr. Sanford, who was a hatter by trade. There were two rebel soldiers talking with him, so Mr. C. had to wait till they went away of their own accord. As he staid more than two hours I feared treachery—that he might have gone to the rebel camp and given information. I therefore left my place of concealment and ascended an adjacent hill and climbed a eucalyptus tree. When I saw Mr. Chism coming, accompanied by but one man, I descended. The reason for delay was given. Mr. Sanford said, "I am not familiar with the route to Rienzi, but will accompany you to my brother-in-law's, Mr. John Downing's, who I know is well acquainted with the road. He can take you through the woods so as to avoid the Confederate cavalry. As I undertake this at the risk of life, we must use all possible precaution. You will have to spend the day concealed in my barn. I would gladly entertain you at my house, but I have a large family and many of them are girls, and you know that girls will talk, and might say something that would lead to suspicion and search, for these rebels are lynx-eyed and are on the alert. There are many notices affixed to trees and shops and posts in the most public places describing you and offering a large reward for your capture. I will carry you provisions during the day, and at midnight we will start to Mr. Downing's. We will be compelled to make a large circuit to avoid the rebel camp, and to go around a spur of the mountain. We will have to travel forty-five miles of a circuit, while it is only nine miles as the raven flies."

At one time Mr. Sanford's twin daughters came into the barn in search of eggs. They approached near my place of concealment, but did not discover me. When Mr. S. came with delicacies his wife had prepared, I informed him of it. He said, "I will send all my girls to their uncle's on a visit, so that there may be no danger of their suspicions being aroused. We are in daily, imminent peril. I do hope that the Federal troops will make haste to occupy the country and save us from our bitter and malignant foes, who will soon attempt to force all Unionists into their army; then it will be necessary to leave home and escape to the Union lines." He brought his wife up to see me, and we sat sadly discussing the perils and troubles surrounding the loyal people of the South. At length night came, and I slept. At midnight Mr. S. awoke me. He told me to mount the horse he held by the bridle. Said he, "That is a blooded animal of high mettle and good bottom, one of the swiftest horses in Tippah Co. He runs like a streak of lightning." I provided a good whip, resolving in case of danger to put my horse to his utmost speed. We traveled rapidly till nine o'clock in the morning, having to make a detour on account of discovering an unexpected camp. We must have traveled over fifty miles. When we reached Mr. Downing's we partook of an excellent breakfast. The guerrillas had a few nights before they murdered a Unionist—a Mr. Newsom. His sentiments had become known to the rebels. They watched his house till they knew of his presence at home. He had been in concealment, but run the risk of going home to see a sick daughter. They offered him the oath of allegiance to the Confederate states. He refused to take it. In their anger they resolved upon his immediate death. Some proposed hanging, some shooting, but the majority prevailed, and these fiends in human form, these devils incarnate, then deliberately heated water, and in the presence of his weeping, pleading wife and helpless children they scalded to death their chained and defenceless victim. They then suspended the corpse from a tree, with a label attached threatening a similar death to any who should remove the corpse or bury it. Thus perished a patriot of whom the state was not worthy. These, my friends, cut down the corpse by night and buried it in the forest. May God reward them. Oh, the inhumanity of man to his fellow-man.

The mother-in-law of Mr. Newsom was a daughter of Gen. Nathaniel Green of revolutionary fame. She was very aged. I asked her, for we stopped at her house, if she remembered much about the war of the revolution. She kept repeating, "Oh, it was dreadful times. The British before, the Indians behind, and the tories in the middle."

Ere I left Mr. Downing's there were more than fifty Unionists called to see me. They held a council, and Mr. Downing was deputed to convey me to the Federal lines. We immediately set out upon our perilous journey.

Mr. John Downing, my guide, thought it best to travel by day, as the recent rains had raised the waters of the Hatchie and Tallahatchie rivers, both of which we must cross. Fording would be quite dangerous at night. We must follow trails, and thus avoid, if possible, the rebel cavalry and camps. There was one point of special danger at a place where stood a mill, at the base of converging lofty hills. We were traveling in a semi-mountainous country. We at length reached the summit of a very high bill. Far below us, winding around the base of this hill, which might not inappropriately be termed a mountain, ran the clear waters of a considerable creek. This was the dangerous point. Here was a large grist mill. We hitched our horses in copse and reconnoitered. Believing the coast to be clear, we warily descended the steep declivities, till at length we reached the mill. The miller appeared at the door and poured forth a torrent of interrogatories, to all of which my guide answered warily and discreetly, and I thought measurably allayed his suspicions. Presently we espied a covered wagon drawn by Sumpter mules approaching. The saddle marks were visible. It halted at the mill, and eleven Confederate soldiers emerged from underneath the low, dingy covering. We were about to ride on, when they halted us, and the following dialogue ensued between my guide and the soldiers, who had been out on sick furlough ever since the battle of Shiloh, and were now returning to camp at Ripley, Miss.:

"Hello! strangers, whar are ye from?"

"From New Albany, Tippah county."

"Whar ye gwine?"

"On the hunt of stray oxen. Hev ye seen nothin' of a black ox and a pided (pied) ox nowhar in yer travels?"

"No, we hain't."

"Is ther any danger of meeting any Yanks on that road over yender?"

"No, ther ain't. But ther's a road turns offen it 'bout three mile from here, to ther right, that is a mighty dangerous road. The Yankee cavalry's on it most every day. Say, who's that feller with ye? He jes' looks like death on a pale hoss."

"He's my brother-in-law from Alabam. He's hed the aiger for more'n a year, an' ther ain't no quinine in the country an' he can't git it stopt. Some of 'em thinks he's purty well gone with quick consumption."

"Golly, he looks like it. But what's that air notis up thar on the mill?"

The miller replies, "It's a notis of a reward fer a prisoner that broke jail at Tupelo. Jes' read it. I can't."

"Nun of us kin read. Jim Colquitt stopped back a piece thar to see his sister, Missis Curlee. He'll be along dreckly. We is to wait for him hyar. He kin read an' rite too."

The miller replied, "The officer that axed me to stick this notis up said a prisoner that hed escaped before wuz follered with blood-hounds an' tuck back an' put in irons, but he'd broke jail agin the day before he wuz to be hung. That old Bragg wuz all-fired mad about it, and offers a big reward to whomsomever brings him back dead or alive. His name is Mohave or suthin like that. He is a parson an' lives in Rienzi, an' it's thought he's makin' fer that point."

We were about to start, when one of the soldiers said, "Stranger, what mout your name be?"

"My name is Jim Chalmette, and my brother-in-law's name is Oliver Folsom Brownlee, from Florence, Alabam," said my guide.

The soldier then said, "Can't one of you fellers read that air notis?"

We rode up in front of it and Mr. Downing read it thus:

"Ten thousand dollars reward will be paid for the return, dead or alive, of a prisoner who escaped from the military prison at Tupelo, Miss. His name is John Mohave. He is over six feet high, of dark complexion, heavy beard, black eyes, high cheek bones, and was dressed in broadcloth, somewhat the worse for prison wear. Any soldier who captures him will, in addition to the cash reward, receive suitable promotion.

"BRAXTON BRAGG,

"Major General Commanding."

I thought Downing had read it correctly, till I rode up and read it. I felt some tremor when I recognized an exact description of myself. Even the missing molar had been noticed.

One of the soldiers said, "Well, stranger, that settles it. I thought afore yer read that notis as how yer brother-in-law mought a ben the feller what broke jail, but he don't fill the bill, by odds. But he's got on awful fine boots an' hat. They don't suit them cloze, an' his cloze don't nigh fit him. They wuz made fer a long sight bigger man."

"Them's a suit of my cloze he put on this mornin' so my wife could wash an' mend hizzen."

"Well, I s'pose yer all right, but ther's a camp about three mile from hyar. You an' yer brother-in-law hed better let them oxen go fer awhile an' come with us to camp. Chalmers or Baxter will be thar, or mebbe old Forrest hisself. He'll be mighty glad to see ye, I reckon. Then ye kin explain some things about ye that we don't zackly understand."

At this time we were surrounded by them, and Downing thought it best to express his acquiescence. One of the soldiers presently went to the wagon, and producing a jug, asked us to drink with him. We rode to the further side of the wagon. The soldier then said, "Here's to Jeff Davis and the Southern Confederacy, wishin' 'em success and that we may kill a hundred Yankees apiece an' all git home safe."

At this moment Downing said, "We must go on," and putting spurs to our horses we soon put considerable space between us and these soldiers. They called after us to halt. Downing said, "We haven't time, howsomever we're all right." We rode on rapidly, thankful that we had escaped imminent peril. We soon came to a turn in the road. Just as we made the turn, we saw two men, with guns in their hands, on a knoll covered with a heavy growth of walnut trees. We were not sure whether they were hunters or guerrillas. They called to us to halt. We did so and asked them what they wanted. They replied that they would come to the road and tell us, and said, "Wait till we come to you." Downing said, in a low tone, "We are in danger, as we are in range, and they can bring us down with their guns. We will wait till they get to the bottom of the hill, among the chaparral which will intercept the shot if they fire." He then called to them to come on. They started toward us, and when they had reached the dense chaparral, we put spurs to our horses and galloped rapidly away. When we started, the men ran back up the knoll and taking aim fired at us. The shot from one of the guns whistled harmlessly through the branches of a mulberry tree under which we were passing. The shot from the other gun was more effective. One shot struck my horse in the flank. He reared and plunged wildly. I managed, however, to keep my seat. A shot struck Downing's saddle, and glancing inflicted a wound in the thigh. The men then hastened through the chaparral, and upon reaching the road, both fired the two undischarged barrels of their guns. We were now so far away, and had turned a slight bend in the road, that the shot did us no injury. We, however, heard their patter and whistle as they passed through the branches of the trees in close proximity to us. Neither Downing nor I felt the least fear. The excitement of the moment and the comical and excited appearance of our would-be captors, both of whom had lost their hats in the bushes, excited our mirth. Downing said he believed the men were Porter Rucker and

Albert Braddock, guerrillas or partisan rangers, as Jeff Davis styled those who were engaged in hunting down Unionists, and capturing and returning to camp deserters.

"Perhaps," said I to Downing, "it will delight us hereafter to recall even the present things to mind." "Yes, if we outlive this terrible war and survive its horrors. But there is not much pleasure in them now."

In a short time we came to the road designated as dangerous by our would-be captors at the mill. As we reached it we saw in the distance ahead of us, on the road we were now traveling, a few straggling cavalrymen. They saw us and halted, apparently to await our overtaking them. We turned off on the road which the Yankee cavalry were said to frequent ere we reached them. A boy whom we overtook informed us that Baxter's rebel cavalry had just passed. They would have swift steeds to follow with any prospect of overtaking us. A former classmate in Richmond College, Ohio, Matthew Thompson by name, was an officer under Baxter, and would have recognized me had we been a few minutes earlier at that point, and been captured by this doughty rebel. Baxter's scouts infested this section for a long time, murdering Unionists and hunting with blood-hounds the poor conscripts who, having been forced into the Confederate service, endeavored to escape to the Federal lines. Baxter concocted a plot to capture Gen. U.S. Grant, but failed to accomplish his nefarious purpose.

Having traveled several hours after escaping Baxter's cavalry, we rode into the woods, dismounted, and sat down to rest and take an inventory of our injuries. Downing's boot had some blood in it and his thigh was beginning to be quite painful. The left leg of his pantaloons was completely saturated. I examined his wound, and used Downing's knife as a probe, but I could not find the shot. I cut off a piece of cloth from one of my under garments and bandaged the wound to stop the hemorrhage. My horse had bled considerably from the wound in his flank, but did not show any perceptible sign of weakness or flagging gait. We remounted and rode on Antioch or Hinkle. I think we passed through both these hamlets. Here Downing left me to return home. He must travel by a different route in returning. He would lodge that night at the house of a stalwart Unionist, Elihu Noble, who had recently moved from Ingomar, Issaquena county, to Molino Del Rey. I gave him a double eagle, and we parted with fervent adieus and good wishes for each other's welfare. I again assumed the role of a pedestrian, and ere long reached Rienzi.

When I gazed on the star spangled banner, emblem of my country's glory and power, beneath whose ample folds there was safety and protection for the poor, pursued, panting, perishing Unionist, and saw around me the loyal hosts of brave men, eager to subvert rebellion and afford protection to the wronged and persecuted southern patriot, I shed tears of joy. I felt that I was safe, my perils o'er, and from the depths of a grateful heart I returned thanks to Almighty God, who had given me my life in answer to importunate prayer, preserving me amid peculiar dangers, seen and unseen, till now I had reached the desired haven and was safe amid hosts of friends. When I reached the picket line, a horse was furnished me, and I was taken to the head-quarters of Col. Mizener. My brother, David H. Aughey, and brother-in-law, Prof. Robert K. Knight, residents of Rienzi, heard of my arrival and came at once to see and convey me to their homes. Col. M. had sent an orderly to report my presence. Col. Mizener requested me to report all that would be of service to Gen. Rosecrans, who was ten miles south at Booneville, which I did, he copying my report as I gave it. I reported the particulars of my escape, the probable number of Confederate troops in and around Tupelo, the topography of the country, the probable intentions of the rebels, the putative number of troops sent to Richmond to re-inforce Gen. Lee, the harsh, cruel, and vindictive treatment of the southern Unionists incarcerated in the bastile in Tupelo, etc. The Colonel requested me to go with him to visit Gen. Rosecrans at his head-quarters in Booneville the next morning, but at the hour specified reaction had taken place, and I was very sick. My report was carried up to Gen. Rosecrans by Col. Mizener, who immediately forwarded it to Gen. Grant at Memphis, who noted it and placed it on file. It has been published in official Records of the War of the Rebellion, Union and Confederate, Vol. 17, page 107.

Gen. W. S. Rosecrans, upon hearing that I was sick, sent Surgeon Berridge Lucas, of an Illinois brigade, raised in Peoria, Ill., and Dr. Hawley, of the 36th Ill. Infantry, to attend me during my illness. Under their skillful and efficient treatment I measurably regained health, though for some time I was apparently upon the border land, and it was feared that I would be a mental and physical wreck. My sufferings at the hands of the rebels produced a lesion from which I will never fully recover. Two of my soldier comrades have recently succumbed to a similar malady, and I cannot hope to resist it much longer. The citadel of life must eventually yield to its force, and death supervene. Skillful medical treatment and extremely temperate habits alone have thus far held it in abeyance. Hardships incurred afterward in the service, as chaplain, aggravated the malady.

But why should I repine since my country's integrity and permanence has been secured, never more to be imperiled by traitors to their government and their God? The salutary lesson they have learned will prevent a repetition of their folly.

When I recovered sufficiently to leave my room I was honored with a serenade by a brigade brass band, through the politeness of Col. Bryner and Lieut. Col. Thrush, of the 47th Ill. regiment. At the close they called for a speech, to which call I thus responded:

GENTLEMEN—I desire to express my sincere thanks for the honor conferred. In the language of the last tune played by your band, I truly feel at home again, and it fills my soul with joy to meet my friends once more. What a vast difference between Tupelo and Rienzi. There I was regarded as a base ingrate, as a despicable traitor, an enemy to the country, chained as a felon, doomed to die, and before the execution of the sentence subjected to every species of insult and contumely. Here I meet with the kindest expressions of sympathy from officers of all ranks, from the subaltern to the general, and there is not a private soldier who has heard my tale of woe that does not manifest a kindly sympathy. I hope you will speedily pass south of Tupelo, but in your victorious march to the gulf I wish you to fare better than I did in my journey from Tupelo to Rienzi. Traveling day after day without food or water would cause you to present the emaciated appearance that I do. On your route, call upon the secession sympathizers and compel them to furnish you with all the viands that you need. My good horse, Bucephalus, I left at Tupelo. He is an animal of pure blood and high mettle. The rebel general Hardee, in the true spirit of secession, appropriated—that is, stole him. He often insolently rode him by our prison, surrounded by his staff. He did not return him to me when I left. However, I did not call to demand him upon leaving. Being in haste I did not choose to spare the time, as I am a great economist of time, and leaving in the night I did not wish to disturb the slumbers of the Tupelonians. He is a bright bay. If you find him you may have him gratis. I would much prefer that he serve the Federal army. I bought him of Gen. Lionel Colquitt, at West Point, Miss., for three hundred and fifty dollars.

If you take Gen. Jordan prisoner, send me word, and I will furnish you with the irons with which he bound me, by which you may secure him till he meets the just penalty of his crimes, even death, which he richly deserves for the murder of many Unionists.

When I became convalescent I rode to Jacinto, the Federal outpost nearest to my family. I called upon Gen. Jefferson C. Davis, who at once ordered eight regiments of cavalry, accompanied by a section of artillery, to bring them into Jacinto. I soon had the pleasure of beholding my wife and child, whose faces I recently had given up all hope of ever seeing upon earth. The meeting was mutually a joyful one. Gen. Davis ushered them into his office, where I was awaiting them, and then considerately retired. My little daughter, during my ominous absence, would often try to comfort her ma by telling her, when she was weeping, "Ma, I think they will let pa loose, 'cause we pray so much for him. Don't cry, I think God will send him to us soon. He has said He will hear us when we pray."

Richard Malone lived in Jacinto. Gen. Davis and I called to see him. He rejoiced greatly upon seeing me. He had informed Gen. Davis of my capture and re-arrest. Gen. Davis had ordered the arrest of four prominent citizens of Jacinto, to be held as hostages for my safety. The officer was just about to start to execute the order when I arrived at his headquarters. The citizens were named John G. Barton, Col. Runnels, Barton Key, and Calvin Taylor.

When Malone reached the point where we agreed to meet he awaited my arrival. He gave the preconcerted signals, but I came not. We agreed to meet at a point where a garment was suspended from a post of the corn-field fence. But as there may have been more than one garment suspended from the posts, as many rebel soldiers, after washing, hung their clothes out to dry, we mistook the place, and reached the corn-field at different points, and so were compelled to set out alone on the hazardous journey. At one time Malone resolved upon the risk of walking upon a road a few hundred yards to reach a forest. A company of cavalry came suddenly upon him and ordered him to go before them, declaring that they would gladly return him to prison. They made him go on the double-quick. He said, presently, "I am very thirsty; will you give me some water?" They replied that they were going to that house on the distant hill to get water. When they reached the house and drew the water, Malone noticed that there was no dipper at the well with which to lift the water from the bucket. He said, "I will go into the house and ask for a dipper." Two cavalry men followed him, and stationed themselves at the door. Malone went into the house, shut the door, and the back door being open, he ran through the house, opened the garden gate, ran through the garden, leaped over the palings at the farther end into a corn-field. Two women who were in the house ran to the door clapping their hands and exclaiming, "O! your Yankee is gone, your prisoner has escaped." The cavalry men ran round the house, and seeing Malone running through the corn-field called to him to halt. Malone, not heeding the order, ran onward. They fired. Malone ran zigzag to avoid the bullets which whistled uncomfortably close to his ears. They failed to bring him down. They followed, but Malone outran them to a swamp, and after many other narrow risks reached his home in Jacinto.

I returned to Rienzi. I reached Rienzi from prison on the day that the 2d Michigan regiment made a present of a fine black cavalry horse to Gen. Philip Sheridan. As the presentation was made in Rienzi, the general named the horse after the town, calling him Rienzi. This was the horse he rode in his famous ride from Winchester, Va., to Cedar creek, when he turned the tide of battle, changing an inglorious rout into a glorious victory over Jubal Early. We soon left Rienzi for the North. When we reached the home of my parents the rejoicing was as if one who was dead had been restored to life. They had heard through war correspondents with the army of my imprisonment, escape, re-arrest, and re-incarceration. They had not heard of my second escape. Thirteen days after our arrival at my father's house a son was born to us, August 20th, 1862, whom we named John Knox. Our third child, Gertrude Evangeline, was born February 12, 1867. Our first child, Anna Katharine, now Mrs. Ferguson, of Congress, O., was born September 3, 1858.

As soon as I felt able to do so, I accepted the position of chaplain, first in the army of the Potomac, afterwards in the western army. The officers of the 6th Ill. calvary, of which I was chaplain, asked me at one time to give them an address on the subject of my arrest, imprisonment, and escapes. I complied with their invitation. At the close of the address, a soldier who had deserted from the rebel army and was now a member of a company in our regiment, came to Col. Lynch, who at this time commanded the 6th Ill. calvary (Col. Benjamin Grierson was the 1st colonel), and informed him that he was one of the guards on duty at the prison in Tupelo on the night of my escape. He said that I was missed in the morning, very early. One of the guards noticed my chain, which I had coiled up and left by the side of a little stump, inadvertently placing it on the side next the guards. He called the officer of the guard and showed him the chain. Soon many officers came into the prison. All the guards who had been on duty during the night were brought into the prison in irons. They thought that some of them must have been in collusion with the prisoner, or he could not have escaped. The prisoners were strictly questioned as to whether they knew anything in regard to the escape, or if any of them had rendered any assistance. They denied all knowledge of or complication in the matter. One of the officers said,"God Almighty alone must have known and helped him. He could not have gotten away without assistance, and you all deny having rendered any." Col. Lynch said, "If you had known of his intention to escape, would you have helped him?" "No," said the soldier, "I was a rebel in sentiment then, and would have done my duty and taken stringent measures to prevent his escape, had I known of his intention to do so. Two companies of cavalry were sent in pursuit, with strict orders to shoot him on sight and not bring him back alive." But providentially they never got the sight. One went in sight of the Federal pickets near Rienzi. The other visited my father-in-law's, at Paden's mills, south-east of Iuka. They again, as upon their first visit, searched the house, mills, negro quarters, and every crevice capable of secreting a hare.

A Unionist, Washington Gortney, whose name I have mentioned, was murdered by a band of guerrillas under the lead of his nearest neighbor, one Bill Robinson. Gortney and Reece had enlisted in the Union army. Gortney desired to visit his family, one mile from Paden's mills. Reece accompanied him. Robinson heard of it, and gathering a few partisan rangers, murdered Gortney in the midst of his family. Reece was left for dead, but recovered. In retaliation, a company of Federal soldiers were sent out to burn Paden's, Vawter's, and Robinson's mills and ten houses. This they accomplished, and returned. This salutary proceeding had the effect of checking guerrilla murders and predatory raids by them for a time.

How terrible for a family to see and hear the howling hounds in search of one of their number, and to hear the horrid and blasphemous oaths of the fierce dragoons, swearing what terrible vengeance they will wreak upon their victim when caught and in their power.

> "Oh! the inhumanity of man to his fellow-man
> Makes countless millions mourn."—
> "Oh! Freedom! How we love thy name,
> We who thy choicest blessings claim.
> No servile hordes now sweat and toil
> Upon our consecrated soil;
> No bondman's cries fall on our ears,
> No master's lash wrings scalding tears
> From women's eyes; none wildly flee
> From threatened scourge of a Legree.
> Exempt from slavery's fearful thrall,
> Sweet Freedom's gifts now bless us all.
> And those who once did meekly bow
> Beneath the yoke are voters now."

Chapter Six

MEMPHIS, TENNESSEE, February 12, 1888.

Rev. John H. Aughey, Chariton, Ia.:

DEAR SIR—I take the National Tribune, that most excellent soldiers' paper. In it I noticed your request for the address of Leslie Barksdale and others who were your fellow-prisoners in the South. I am now known as Melvin Estill, having changed my name for reasons which will be hereinafter given. I was a fellow-prisoner with you in that miserable den at Tupelo, Miss. Delevan Morgan, John Truesdale, Byron Porter, Ulysses Chenault, and I were conscripted, and because of our refusal to take the oath and enlist we were immured in prison. We were tried by court-martial, and condemned to death, with the proviso that if we took the oath and entered the army the sentence would be suspended. We were given twelve hours for deliberation. You will remember we consulted you, and you advised us to take the oath, enter the army, and desert the first favorable opportunity and escape to the Federal lines. We accordingly took the oath. I think our motive was suspected. We were taken to Saltillo and placed under guard in an old rickety building, with a number of other prisoners.

That same night we evaded the guards and escaped. Guided by the north star, we hastened northward with all possible speed. Soon after daylight we heard the baying of the blood-hounds; nearer and nearer they came. When they came in sight three of our number climbed a tree. Delevan Morgan and I essayed to climb a large tree that stood near. Morgan caught hold of a withered branch. It broke in his grasp and he fell to the ground. He arose and ran. I jumped down and followed him. The hounds and cavalry appeared upon the scene. Our three companions were shot, and as they fell the hounds tore them limb from limb. Morgan had sprained his ankle, and his progress was quite slow. I made a detour and concealed myself behind the huge trunk of a fallen tree. Soon the hounds overtook my friend and tore him to pieces. These hounds were under the care of a miscreant named Jasper Cain, who was assisted by one Laverty Grier, John Graham, and others.

I thought that death was inevitable. Cain and his men held a council of war.

Cain enquired, "How many prisoners did old Bragg say there wuz?" "Four," replied Grier. "Well we've got 'em all," replied Cain. Someone said he believed General Bragg said, "there wuz five," but it was decided that "it wuz only four." Cain said, "Our orders wuz, to take 'em dead or alive. Now how will we prove to old Bragg that we killed 'em all, an' git the reward?" "Take their scalps," suggested Grier. "Good, that is a bright idea," said Cain. "Now, Laverty, you scalp 'em with that 'ere knife that's in your belt." The order was obeyed, the scalps stuck in Grier's belt, and the cavalcade returned to camp.

I now hastened onward. After traveling about four miles I came to a cabin in a clearing. I knew that pursuit would not long be delayed. I went to the cabin and knocked. A lady came and opened the door. She bade me enter. I asked her if she Union or Secesh. She assumed an air of great ignorance and stupidity, and replied, "I ain't neither, I'm a Baptist." That was enough for me. I felt sure she was all right. I at once revealed my condition, and told her of my imminent peril. She and her daughter and her sick husband at once set about devising a plan of escape. There was a cave in the hillside about a half a mile distant. This lady, who was of Amazonian proportions, and her daughter, carried me to this cave. I found a cot within it and a little table. This lady, Mrs. Cameron, gave me a pair of her daughter's shoes in exchange for mine. Her daughter, Miss Alverna Cameron, put on my shoes and traveled five miles northward to a swamp. She then took off my shoes and put on a pair of her mother's, which she had carried in her apron, and returned.

Jasper Cain, after considerable delay reported to General Braxton Bragg, and told him of the fate of the prisoners, whom he had left unburied, to be devoured by wild hogs and buzzards. He then displayed exultingly the scalps which he bore as a trophy and as a proof of having carried out the orders of his commanding general. "But there are only four scalps," said the general, "where is the fifth?" "You said there wuz four prisoners what escaped," said Cain. Gen. Bragg ordered Cain to start in pursuit of the fifth at once and to bring in his scalp or consequences might follow not pleasant for Cain to contemplate. This infuriate demon obeyed with alacrity, and ere long the domicile of the Camerons was surrounded by howling hounds and blaspheming rebels. Soon, however, they seemed to have discovered the track, and off they went pell-mell on the route which Miss Alverna had taken to mislead them.

Miss Alverna and her mother visited me in the cave, bringing with them hoe cake, butter, and milk. The rebel soldiers had robbed them of all other provisions. I feasted upon the regale these kind ladies furnished me. They were delicious viands indeed to one who brought the sauce of hunger to the repast. Starvation in the rebel camp and prison had so improved my appetite that it required all they brought to appease it. Miss Alverna told me of the pursuit by Cain with his blood-hounds, and how she had misled them. They then prepared to take their departure. Mrs. Cameron and her daughter sang "Jesus, lover of my soul," and a hymn, one stanza of which I shall forever remember.

> "Savior, I look to thee,
> Be thou not far from me
> Mid storms that lower;
> On me thy care bestow,
> Thy loving kindness show,
> Thine arms around me throw
> This trying hour."

Miss Alverna then read the 31st Psalm. Two verses, the 35–6, seemed very pertinent. "My times are in thy hand; deliver me from the hands of mine enemies and from them that persecute me. Make thy face to shine upon thy servant and save me for thy mercy's sake." Also the 13th verse, etc., "Fear was on every side, while they took counsel together against me, they devised to take away my life. But I trusted in thee, O Lord, I said thou art my God. Have mercy upon me, O Lord, for I am in trouble. Thou art my rock and my fortress, therefore for thy name's sake lead me and guide me." Mrs. Cameron then led in prayer, asking the Lord to deliver me from surrounding foes, the bears, venomous serpents, and still more venomous Confederates. They then bade me goodbye and returned home. When night came I feared to stay longer in my cave. I started off on my perilous journey toward the Federal lines. I lay concealed by day and traveled by night, guided by the polar star.

One night I felt that I must run a great risk to procure some food, as I was in a starving condition. I found a cabin inhabited by slaves. I went to the door and rapped. Soon a venerable aunty appeared at the door. I asked her for something to eat. She appeared alarmed, and calling a little colored boy she bade him guide me to a place where I should be fed. When I reached the terminus of my journey under this boy's guidance, I found a man about my own age, who was, like me, a fugitive bound for the Union army. Soon a number of kind colored people appeared, and in this swamp we were fed with all the luxuries procurable by these kind friends who bore the image of God carved in ebony. My fugitive friend said his name was Johnny Peterson, and that he lived on the Taccaleeche in North Mississippi. After many thrilling adventures we reached the Union lines and were joyfully welcomed. A minister of your church informs me that, by examining the year book or minutes of your general assembly, he learns that you are pastor of the Presbyterian church in the city of Chariton, Iowa. My address will be Memphis, Tenn., for a few months. Write me at your earliest convenience.

After reaching the Federal lines both Peterson and I enlisted and fought through the war. Through fear that I might be taken prisoner and recognized, I changed my name, and found it almost impossible to resume my old name after the war.

I am glad to know that you made your escape. Tell me all about it at your earliest convenience.

Your friend,
MELVIN ESTILL.

In the years of grace, 1881–2, I was pastor of the churches of Ebenezer and Good Will, in Sumter Co., S.C. While I was conversing with Mr. Williamson, a merchant in Mayesville, a gentleman in front of his store said to another, who spoke of Judge S. McGowen: "The Judge has a national reputation as far as South Carolina is concerned." This man was evidently still laboring under the delusion that South Carolina was a sovereign, independent nation, and that the United States was a mere confederacy of nations to be dissolved at will by the states individually. The war had taught him nothing.

In conversation with prominent citizens of Sumter and Mayesville I found that there was no concealment of the frauds practiced at elections. They declared that the negroes and scalawags should not rule over them. They divulged to me the fraudulent methods by which the dominant party, though greatly in the minority numerically, retained their political power. Said I, "Suppose that congress should send a committee to inquire into the matter, what would you do?" "We would testify upon oath that there had been a free ballot and fair count." "Would that be morally right?" said I. "Of two evils choose the less," was the reply.

Sam. Lee, had there been a free ballot and fair count, would have been elected over his competitor, Richardson, by more than three to one. Yet Richardson received the governor's certificate of election, and represented the district in congress.

The Century magazine, in the April, 1885, No., publishes articles by Henry W. Grady, of Atlanta, Ga., and Edward P. Clarke, from which we quote. Mr. Clarke describes the revolution by which the minority overcame the majority who ruled in the period of reconstruction in the Carolinas, Florida, Mississippi, Louisiana, etc.

"It became evident that there must be a revolution, and it was carried through. The negroes were intimidated from going to the polls, so far as possible, and when violence did not suffice to keep them away, their ballots were tampered with and neutralized after they had been cast. By force or by fraud the race, which in several states possessed an actual numerical majority, was reduced into an apparent minority. The negro vote was practically suppressed and the majority ceased to rule. This result was inevitable. Reconstruction had sought 'to put the bottom rail on top,' to reverse the highest and lowest strata of society, to place ignorance and poverty in authority over intelligence and property. Such an attempt had never before succeeded in the world's history; it could not have succeeded permanently in the South without destroying civilization. It was from the first only a question how soon and in what way it should be defeated."

Mr. Grady's opinion is plainly inferred from the following, quoted from his article discussing the status of the freedmen:

"As a matter of course this implies the clear and unmistakable domination of the white race in the South. The assertion of that is simply the assertion of the right of character, intelligence, and property to rule. It is simply saying that the responsible and steadfast element in the community shall control, rather than the irresponsible and the migratory. It is the reassertion of the moral power that overthrew the reconstruction governments."

Thus in many southern states the minority represents in Congress the suppressed majority. This is in direct conflict with an explicit article in the Constitution of the United States adopted for the express purpose of preventing this flagrant wrong. To good men in the southern states, to all true and loyal Americans, how humiliating is this oft-repeated slander upon the fair fame of the southern states, that only by violence practiced upon a weaker race, or by fraud in tampering with the ballot-box, which necessarily includes deliberate perjury, can the cause of good government be maintained in the South. We do not believe any such libel, but what else can be meant by the language quoted above.

We cannot do better than append here an extract of a very different kind —one that does honor to the hand that wrote it and the courage that pronounced it. We take it from the inaugural address of President Cleveland.

"In the administration of a government pledged to do equal and exact justice to all men, there should be no pretext for anxiety touching the protection of the freedmen in their rights or their security in the enjoyment of their privileges under the Constitution and its amendments. All discussion as to their fitness for the place accorded to them as American citizens is idle and unprofitable, except as it suggests the necessity for their improvement. The fact that they are citizens entitles them to all the rights due to that relation and charges them with all its duties, obligations, and responsibilities."

The legislature was in session in Columbia. I visited the halls of legislation. There was a bill pending upon which there was much discussion. The bill proposed to require eight separate ballot-boxes and that but one voter at a time should enter the polling place; that no one should speak to him while in the polling place; and that if he failed to deposit his ballots in the boxes properly, his vote would be lost. Though the boxes were labeled, this would leave the illiterate voter to the almost absolute certainty of losing his vote. The fraudulent intent of the bill was patent. The Charleston News and Courier, commenting on this bill, says: "We have great confidence in the wisdom and foresight of the present General Assembly of South Carolina, and believe that in their hands the state will be safe. They will not fail to remember and to act on the knowledge that the colored voters outnumbered the white voters in South Carolina, and that while the prosperity, nay! the existence of the state in its present condition, depends on the supremacy of the civilization which the whites represent, the people of the United States (who have already proved themselves more than a match for South Carolina) will not continue to acquiesce in revolutionary processes, and will not consent to have us represented in Congress by modes which have been hitherto indispensable in the conduct of our state affairs. But were they?"

It will be observed from the above quotation that the Charleston News and Courier admits the revolutionary processes, that is, fraudulent methods used in controlling the elections in South Carolina. I found no one who denied that fraud was resorted to defeat the scalawags and colored voters. I found three colored men representing sea island districts. In those districts the colored population so greatly preponderated that they found means to prevent election frauds being practiced upon them. This may be the ultimate solution of this vexed question. The whites in the southern states increase decennially twenty per cent and the negroes thirty-five per cent. The blacks will ultimately greatly outnumber the whites in that region. In the seven Atlantic and Gulf states, the two Carolinas, Georgia, Florida, Alabama, Mississippi, and Louisiana, the whites numbered in 1880, 3,814,395, and the blacks, 3,721,481. There will be, at these proportionate rates of increase, in 1985, about 30,000,000 whites and about 125,000,000 blacks. This ratio of increase holding, the negroes will be, in one hundred years from this year of grace, 1885, quadruple the number of whites in the southern Atlantic and Gulf states. Long ere that date they will suppress with iron hand all attempts to defraud them of the right to exercise the elective franchise and to have a fair count of the ballots cast.

I found peon slavery in full force in the Carolinas, through the labor contract system. Men hire the colored people to labor for them, taking as security a lien on the prospective crop, for supplies furnished in advance. At the settlement at the close of the year the negroes are found to be in debt, and each annual settlement only increases the indebtedness. The colored people may labor hard from dawn to dusk, live sparingly, wear the coarsest clothing, and yet end the year in debt. They cannot enforce their rights, though well assured of the frauds practiced upon them.

I enquired if the Southern Presbyterian Church had made any provision for the education of the colored people, their former slaves. I learned that there was a theological seminary established at Tuskaloosa, Ala., for the education of young colored men who desired to enter the ministry. I could not learn that there was any institution under the control of the southern church for the education of the colored people in the common or higher branches. The northern church have established many good schools in the South, in which all the branches of a good common school education are taught. They have also a number of schools of a high order, in which the classics and higher mathematics are very successfully taught. I visited the Mayesville School. Misses Kate H. Moorhead and Jennie S. Hemphill, of Bridgewater, Beaver Co., Pa., were the very efficient teachers. There were enrolled 150 scholars, in every grade of progress. These young ladies labored from dawn until dusk, and seemed never to weary of their arduous duties, which they doubtless entered upon con amore. Many sable children have they enlightened and evangelized. Many other schools and seminaries and colleges under the control of the northern church are doing a noble, a grand work among the children of freedmen and poor whites.

The public school system of South Carolina and many other states was organized by the reconstruction governments, and since these have been overthrown, the powers that be have not abrogated it, though there is much opposition to this relic of "Yankee, negro, and scalawag rule." Revolutions seldom go backward, and it is probable that the public school system may survive, and by its beneficent effects overcome the prejudice of the ex-slaveholders against the education of all classes. Strange that any should oppose universal education—that glory and cheap defense of states and nations.

I attended the meeting of the synod of Atlantic, which was held in Columbia, S.C., in December, 1881. I saw there a large number of educated colored men, who, as Presbyterian ministers, were conducting the business of synod in a very creditable manner. I heard some of them preach. Their sermons were earnest, lucid expositions of practical duties, enforced by pertinent quotations from the word of God.

The moderator, Rev. Moses Aaron Hopkins, presided with dignity and ability. On points of order his rulings were admirable. He afterward received the appointment from President Cleveland of minister to Liberia, where he died of acclimating fever, lamented by the whole synod of Atlantic. Many colored men were present as ruling elders, representing churches in the bounds of the synod, which embraces the states of North and South Carolina and Georgia. When I was a citizen of the South, in the ante bellum days, these men were all illiterate slaves, whom to teach the alphabet was made a crime punishable by incarceration in the penitentiary.

It is not wise to say that the former times were better than these. The change for the better seemed to me to indicate the millennial dawn.

Before the war these men were helpless slaves, with no rights that white men felt bound to respect, scourged to their tasks by the lash of the cruel, brutal overseer, many of whom delighted in every refinement of cruelty, universally denied legal marriage, even by masters who were professedly christians, not suffered to learn to read the word of God, affirmed by a decision of the supreme court of the U.S. to be chattels personal, possessed of no rights above that of the ox or ass. Now the key of knowledge is placed in the hands of this chattel, by which he opens the door which gives his eager, anxious mind access to all the stores of intellectual wisdom and spiritual lore. His disabilities are yet many, through peon bondage and fraudulent disfranchisement, but they are no greater than those of the poor whites of the South, but he is rising in the scale of intelligence; he is improving his opportunities, he is increasing and waxing strong in numbers and power, and the day is not distant when, rising to the full dignity of full-fledged manhood, he will assert and maintain his God-given rights, if need be at the cannon's mouth and at the point of the bayonet. *He who would be free, himself must strike the blow*. The government has enfranchised him, and bestowed upon him all civil rights, but they are in part kept back by fraud, but he will ere long, we trust, burst the shackles by which he is illegally bound and become a freeman, in deed, as well as in name, possessed of and enjoying all the rights, immunities, and franchises of an American citizen with which our national constitution endows him, and which he, knowing and prizing even above life itself, will dare maintain as his birthright forever.

In 1883 I had an invitation to a field of labor in Kentucky. I went down to look at the lay of the land. At Bowling Green I met Col. George M. Edgar, who was president of a female seminary. I remarked to the colonel, who was a Presbyterian, that it was unfortunate that there were two branches of the Presbyterian church in that state. In many towns each branch has a feeble organization struggling for existence. United, their success would be assured, and their aggressive power quadrupled. The colonel replied that union could be effected in no other way than by the northern branch coming over to them with their property. They could never unite with a church that intermeddled with politics by making political deliverances, as the Northern General Assembly had done during the late civil war. They had declared slavery to be heresy, and secession treason and rebellion, and that as a church the southern branch was guilty of schism in separating from the northern assembly.

I replied, "Did the southern assembly ever make any political deliverances?" The colonel responded, "No, sir. I challenge you to point to a single one."

I replied, "The southern assembly of 1862 took action, of which this is part, 'The assembly desires to record with its solemn approval this fact of the unanimity of our people in supporting a contest to which religion as well as patriotism now summons the citizens of this country, and to implore for them the blessing of God in the course which they are now pursuing. The long continued agitations of our adversaries have wrought within us a deeper conviction of the divine appointment of domestic servitude, and have led to a clearer comprehension of the duties we owe to the African race. We hesitate not to affirm that it is the peculiar mission of the southern church to conserve the institution of slavery and make it a blessing to both master and slave.' Now, colonel, if that be the peculiar mission of the southern church, her mission has terminated, and it might be well to return to the bosom of the church whence you departed. It may be, however, that the following deliverance made after slavery had been abolished prevents it. In 1865 the southern assembly adopted a long paper, in which this occurs: 'While the existence of slavery in its civil aspects may be regarded as a settled question, an issue now gone, yet the lawfulness of the relation as a question of social morality and of scriptural truth has lost nothing of its importance.' This from the assembly of 1862: 'From all our churches we hear the report that the ranks of the armies of our national independence are crowded with the noblest of our brethren and the choicest of our youth, who have rushed to the rescue of the republic, driven by the impulses of patriotism in obedience to the call of God and our country. We sympathize with you as you consecrate everything dear on earth on the altar of patriotic duty.' Again: 'The antagonism of northern and southern sentiment on the subject of slavery lies at the root of all the difficulties which have resulted in the dismemberment of the Federal Union, and have involved us in the horrors of an unnatural war.' In 1861 the southern assembly resolved to spend half an hour in prayer to Almighty God for his blessing on these Confederate States. 'The assembly met and spent the first half hour in special prayer for the blessing of God upon the cause of the Confederate States, according to previous order.' After many other deliverances, both political and martial, in 1865, the southern general assembly, with most remarkable self-complacency, made this utterance: 'Upon no one subject is the mind of this assembly more clearly ascertained, upon no one doctrine is there a more solid or perfect agreement among those whom this assembly represents, than the non-secular and non-political character of the church of Jesus Christ.' It would have been a glorious thing for your religion if you had not mingled politics with it, for your politics are of such a character as to impair the worth of any religion with which they are mixed. Now, colonel, please to be silent forever hereafter as to the non-political character of the southern church. How could a Southerner, sentimentally opposed to human slavery, and who was a loyal citizen of the United States of America, remain a member of a church which declared slavery to be a divine institution, and declared resistance to the government to be true patriotism?"

"Well," said the colonel, "I am willing to argue the question of secession."

To which I replied, "Colonel, I had hoped that that issue had been buried beyond the possibility of resurrection."

"Sir," said the colonel, "It is mere twaddle for a man to declare that a state has no right to secede."

"Col.," I replied, "Henry Clay, Daniel Webster, Gen. Jackson, and many other eminent statesmen, both northern and southern, believed that a state had not the right to secede."

"I admit that," said the Col.

"Well," replied I, "I prefer their twaddle to that of less lights."

The Col. returned to the charge by saying that Virginia and some of the other states had framed a proviso granting the right of secession at will before they agreed to adopt the Federal constitution.

Said I, "Did the other states agree to the proviso?"

"Yes," said the Col., "they did."

"Well, sir," I answered, "is the proviso you speak of inserted in the constitution of the United States?"

"No, I believe not," admitted the Col.

"Well, sir," I said, "if it is not written in the constitution of the United States, it is not of any binding force. But if, as you admit, it is not in the constitution of the United States, where is it?"

The Col. replied that he did not know.

"No, nor does anyone else know," said I. "Your statement is a mere figment of the imagination. But when," I continued, "will you try to exercise this right of secession again."

Col. Edgar answered, "I am as far as anyone from ever wishing to try it again."

"Col.," said I, "it may not do much harm to hold the sentiments you entertain, merely as abstract theories, but the moment you attempt to carry them out in action and give them a practical bearing, there will be ten million bayonets ready to prevent your rebellious designs against our national integrity."

"Sir," said the Col., "one who entertains and expresses the sentiments you do would not be welcomed as a resident of this section."

"Sir," said I, "I have no intention of settling here. I suffered once, for the expression of loyal sentiments, the loss of all things temporal except life, and saved that only by the skin of my teeth."

I said, "Goodbye, Col.," and started to leave. To my surprise the colonel then cordially invited me to visit the female seminary, at 9 o'clock the next morning, and to take part in the opening exercises. I accepted his invitation. At the close of the opening exercises, which I conducted, the colonel asked me to address the young ladies. I complied with his request. I then accepted an invitation to dine with the colonel, who, as long as I remained in Bowling Green, treated me with marked courtesy. I think that he regretted his brusqueness. He met me on Saturday, and told me that on tomorrow he must hear his old friend and former pastor preach, Rev. Dr. R. K. Smoot, of the state of Texas, but that if I should preach on the succeeding Sabbath he would hear me. In the bellum and ante bellum days the expression of sentiments such as I expressed would have met with dire punishment. Now the penalty is comparatively light. The world moves. I visited the graded public schools of Bowling Green. Prof. Wylie, of Danville, Ind., was the very efficient principal. This school was conducted as successfully as our best northern schools, but the public school system of the state I found to be as yet quite inefficient. Progress, however, is being made. Educational interests move slowly in the South. A few years ago there were no public schools, and it requires time to create a popular sentiment that will give them a high degree of efficiency.

The question of reunion is before the general assemblies of both the northern and southern Presbyterian churches. That reunion is a consummation devoutly to be wished, is patent to all who have made this subject a matter of investigation. The southern church was born of rebellion. Her prominent ministers entered the arena of politics, and in sermons, magazine articles, and stump speeches urged the states to secede in order to the strengthening and perpetuation of the institution of slavery. After their success in inducing many states to plunge madly into the maelstrom of secession and treason, they effected the organization of the general assembly of the Presbyterian church in the Confederate States of America, thus linking with their church the name of the rebellious usurpation, recognizing it as a government to which allegiance was due, praying for its success in overcoming the Federal authority and in establishing a permanent slave-holding confederacy founded upon the total subversion of the rights of man. Rev. Dr. J. H. Thornwell, of S. C., was a leader in the secession movement. I have heard Rev. Dr. B. M. Palmer, Revs. Carothers and Gaston, of Mississippi, Mitchell, of Alabama, J. N. Waddell, of Tenn., and many other Presbyterian ministers, all from the pulpit, and some of them from the platform, discuss all the phases of the secession movement, urging the people to favor secession, as the institution of slavery could not otherwise be extended and perpetuated. This church, in its origin, history, ecclesiastical deliverances, and affiliations, is so associated with and allied to slavery and secession that nothing but union with the northern church can give her proper confidence and standing with the loyal people of the United States of America. The southern church would, by reunion, be made national. It is now territorially confined to the former slave states. By union many weak churches would become strong and able for self-support, through the coalescing of contiguous congregations. We would no longer hear of the northern branch and the southern branch of the Presbyterian church. The schism would be at an end, and our glorious church would no longer be sectional but national, her boundaries being coterminous with the republic, and her evangelizing influences would speedily be quadrupled in their efficiency. The majority of the southern branch would not, if they could, re-establish slavery, and they regard the secession idea as no longer tenable, and in every way they give their adhesion to principles made the supreme law of the land by the stern legislation of war.

There are a few bourbons in the southern branch who are unable to forget anything or to learn anything. These bitterly oppose reunion. Did the majority of the southern ministers hold the sentiments of this factious minority, reunion would be the height of folly and madness. "How could two walk together unless they are agreed?" at least as far as essentials are concerned. A committee appointed by the minority of the Southern General Assembly dissenting from reunion have published an "open letter," purporting to be the views of the protestants against reunion. Those who hold the opinions couched in the open letter have not been reconstructed, and would be a discordant element in the reunited church. They hold views that could not be tolerated by the northern branch, principles, both political and scientific, so contrary to reason, truth, and justice, that were they, as citizens, to attempt to give them a practical bearing, another civil war would speedily ensue. Dr. W. C. Gray, editor of The Interior, says: "Rev. Dr. R. L. Dabney (one of the committee) is constantly howling, 'They have robbed us of our lawful bondmen.' He doubtless desires the return of the stolen property. Nothing but full restitution and a humble apology would satisfy him. This would restore human slavery to the South." The Presbyterian Banner thus speaks of this unreconstructed rebel: "Rev. Dr. Dabney seems unable to accept the new situation in the South, and is not in good temper with the dispensations of Providence. He does not believe that the southern people have any direct responsibility in the education of the colored people. For a man of Dr. Dabney's gifts and attainments to write such stuff as this is most strange. 'The northern people have everywhere proclaimed that the bible teaches the abolition dogma, and advised them not to listen to any bible which does not. But we know that our bible condemns the abolition dogma. We cannot, we dare not falsify God's truth, even for the amiable purpose of getting access to the negro minds. Those who have obstructed us by falsifying and misrepresenting God's word, must bear the responsibility.' This accords with the view adopted by the Southern General Assembly in 1865, just after the suppression of armed rebellion and the enfranchisement of the slaves, which was as follows: 'The lawfulness of the relation' of slavery, 'as a question of social morality and of scriptural truth, has lost nothing of its importance.' While the war was progressing the southern branch declared it to be the peculiar mission of their church to conserve the institution of slavery." As this cannot be done till the South becomes strong enough to re-enslave her "lawful bondmen," taken violently from her by "robbers," it seems to be her duty to perpetuate the doctrine of slavery as one of "social morality and scriptural truth," till it can be restored to its pristine vigor.

This committee has decided that the question, "whether the allegiance of the citizen is primarily due to the state or to the central authority," was not determined by our forefathers.

There is probably not a minister in the northern church who believes that political deliverance. All regard it as a political heresy fraught with danger, and as a treasonable view necessary to be suppressed vi et armis, if any practical bearing should be given it in the interests of state sovereignty and secession.

We believe that our fathers who framed the Federal Constitution spoke with no uncertain sound, and that they formed a "perpetual union," which it was treason to attempt to dissever. Rev. Dr. R.K. Smoot, one of the committeemen, was pastor of the church at Bowling Green, Ky., at the commencement of the war. He was a virulent and violent secessionist, and did all he could to harass and annoy the members of his church who were loyal to the government. One of whom, in his rebellious wrath, challenged to mortal combat in the duel, according to the southern code of honor. Save the mark! At last he sent all of them letters of dismission, for which they had not applied, and thus drove them out of the church. While Mr. Smoot was a student at Hanover College, Indiana, he was repeatedly guilty of the infraction of the college laws. The faculty often found it necessary to admonish and reprove him, but he remained obdurate and incorrigible. At length, Rev. Drs. Edwards and Crowe, the president and vice president of the college, summoned Mr. Smoot into their presence and advised him to send in his declinature longer to receive aid as a beneficiary of the education fund, as they deemed him unworthy of it. Mr. Smoot wished to know if this course were compulsory upon him. They replied that in case he declined to accept their advice, compulsory measures would be enforced. Mr. Smoot became quite angry, and affirmed that this was persecution on account of his southern birth, and in his wrath he declared that he hoped that the time would speedily come when, in civil war, he would be able with his own hands to discharge a cannon loaded with grape and canister for the destruction of his northern enemies, and for securing southern independence and freedom from northern domination. Circumstances pointed very strongly to Mr. Smoot as the assassin of a Federal picket at Bowling Green, Ky., while that city was in the occupancy of the Federal army in the civil war.

A young man was robbed of $2,000 at a hotel in Louisville, Ky. Dr. Smoot roomed with him at the time, and many believed that the reverend Dr. was the robber, as circumstances very strongly implicated him in the robbery. The minority brethren should have chosen a man of less unsavory reputation to serve on their committee. The committee state that, "It cannot be denied that God has divided the human race into several distinct groups, for the sake of keeping them apart." They also affirm that the "differentiation through color and other physical characteristics are fixed by the hand of God, since science fails to trace the natural causes by which it could be produced and history is silent as to the time when these changes. occurred." Thus making their own ignorance the basis and proof of a false, odious, and indefensible theory.

Do they really believe in the unity of the human race?

Again, the committee inform us that wherever the people belonging to different groups have practiced amalgamation, the result has been a stock inferior in quality to both the factors which sunk their superior virtues in an emasculated progeny. That in Mexico and South America, where the people of different groups have intermingled and thus enfeebled their offspring, we see slipping from their hands the reins of power.

These last two propositions are presented as arguments to establish the first.

Many believe that science does trace the causes of difference in the races of men. They regard it as due to climate, food, and mode of life. They would be loth to accept without argument the ipse dixit of the committee that it is due to the miraculous interposition of Almighty God, in order to create, propagate, and perpetuate superior and inferior races of men. Rev. David Livingstone, who spent many years in the heart of Africa, and whose subjection to climatic influence and food and mode of life were not different from that of the natives, though a Scotchman of fair complexion when he entered the Dark Continent, had become, when found by Stanley, as bronzed and dark as the Makololos whom he had rescued from the degradation of heathenism. Had he taken his wife and children with him to the land of Ham, after a few generations they would have become veritable negroes. There are many black Jews in Africa. Climate, food, and mode of life have rendered them undistinguishable from the negro.

As to the Mexicans and South Americans losing power because of their mixed blood, the committee is at fault, not knowing the facts of history. The Spanish people are of unmixed blood. Their colonial possessions, one after another, in Mexico and South America, were, after fierce and bloody struggles on the ensanguined plains of battle, wrested from the Spaniards by the mixed races. Does this prove their inferiority?

Many southern people pride themselves on being lineal descendants of Pocahontas. Are her descendants inferior in virtue or intelligence? The Randolphs, the Bakers, the Oswalds, the Castlemans prove their superiority. Are the mulattoes, the quadroons, and the octoroons, who are found by millions in the South, an emasculated progeny inferior to their mothers (their fathers are supposed to be unknown)? Their superior intelligence disproves the theory of the committee. Must we receive as truth all those political and scientific fallacies in order to induce them to unite with us? The southern church united with the new school body in the South on the same basis of union as that which served as the basis of union—the standards pure and simple—between the old and new school Presbyterians in the North, and yet this latter union is mentioned, by this committee, as an argument against reunion with the northern church.

When I lived in the South, in the ante bellum days, the fact that the races of men were marked by diversities of color and physical characteristics was not made an objection to miscegenation, as that was, and still is, practiced to a fearful extent in the South, but it was advanced by the southern people as an unanswerable and irrefragable argument in favor of the right and duty of the superior to reduce to slavery the inferior race. The committee declare: "At the first we hoped to hold him (the negro) in connection with us in our churches, as in the old time we were accustomed to worship together in the house of God. We were slow in coming to his ground, when under the race instinct he demanded a church and ministry of his own." Just prior to this they have said, or rather asked the question: "How can two races be brought together in nearly equal numbers in those confidential and sacred relations which belong to the ministry of the Word without entailing that personal intimacy between ministry and people which must end in the general amalgamation of discordant races."

Yes, there may be something of excellent reasoning in this. In the old time you were accustomed to worship together in the house of God, and if that "personal intimacy in those confidential and sacred relations" was the true cause of that amalgamation which has resulted in changing the hue of more than half of your former slaves, it is well to let them have churches and a ministry of their own.

The committee speak as if they were in extreme peril, and as if, were the colored people to worship with the white people in nearly equal numbers, general amalgamation could not be avoided and would be the result in the near future. Your danger seems imminent, and we would not urge you to unite with the northern church if the result would be a general stampede of your daughters into the arms of the negro. It is your strong argument, your sheet anchor to keep your barque from drifting out upon the stormy ocean of reunion. Your wayward sons and daughters must be restrained. At least, there must be no temptation thrown in their way to induce them to gratify their perverted tastes and prurient desires. It might be well to elaborate additional arguments so that this impending calamity may be averted. Our northern missionaries and teachers who are laboring among the colored people of the South, though outnumbered by them twenty to one, are in no peril. No case of amalgamation has ever occurred among them. Their tastes and instincts will ever prevent a calamity so deplorable. I think it possible that the "race instinct," which has led the colored people to go out from you, will interpose a barrier to amalgamation, and were you to woo them, I think you would not succeed in winning them back to worship with you as in the old time, therefore your children will be measurably safe.

Re-union, desirable as it may be in certain aspects, could not be entertained for a moment were the majority of the southern people found to hold the political, scientific, and absurd theories of the committee.

The northern branch has not made a deliverance in regard to evolution. The southern branch has decided, at least in part, this vexed scientific question. Though they will doubtless admit that the body of Eve, the mother of all living, was made of ossified dust, yet they have decided ecclesiastically that the body of Adam was made of dust inorganic. They may deem it their duty in the near future to decide the mooted question whether the wife of Moses was an Ethiopian of the negro race, or the question, "If the northern people will not restore to us our 'lawful bondmen,' what means would we be justifiable in using to compel them to restore to us those human chattels of which they have robbed us, that we may hold them in bondage as we did in the old time." It is true, as the Master teaches, that Christians are the light of the world and the salt of the earth. The truth of the gospel is to work like leaven until the whole structure of society is changed. But there is need of earnest hearts and strong hands to accomplish this result. The purpose is to permeate every department of human life, and men are the agency. Wherever there is iniquity the church is summoned to cry aloud and spare not. When there is a sword in the land the danger must be exposed. Who, if not the church, shall dissect and denounce corruption? Who, if not the church, shall expound to the state the principles of righteousness, and emphasize the importance of morality in law? The function of the state is comparatively limited, but the sphere of the church covers the whole domain of morals and religion. The Bible is dogmatic against iniquity. It is the duty of the church to reprove sin wherever found, and strive for its eradication, whether in the domain of science or politics, whether in the state, the family, or the individual. The claim of the southern church is, that it is within its province "to conclude nothing but that which is ecclesiastical." Its theory and practice are diametrically opposed to each other. Its purely political deliverances are numerous, and they were all made in the interests of slavery and secession.

Rev. Dr. R. L. Dabney was a member and prominent leader of the synod of Virginia, which, in October, 1861, made this deliverance: "Resolved, That the assertion of their rights and separate independence by the Confederate States is necessary and righteous. . . . The question of civil allegiance has been properly determined as to us by the commonwealth of which we are citizens."

Now he joins in condemning the northern church for "a palpable invasion of the province of the state," in deciding a political question. O, consistency, thou art a jewel!

The Philadelphia Presbyterian, of April 21, 1888, noticing the southern digest, among other things, says: "It is somewhat amusing to see that the southern assembly in 1861 approved a clause in the constitution of the Confederate States."

From the synod of North Carolina, in 1861, we have this deliverance: "Resolved, That the synod sits appointed by her Divine Head as a witness for the right and for truth, truly sympathizes with the state and with the Confederate States in their present righteous struggle, and cordially approves their action in asserting and maintaining their sovereignty and severing the ties that bound us to the late United States of America."

From the presbytery of Charleston, July 24,1861, we have this deliverance: "We do most heartily, with the full approval of our conscience before our Lord God, unanimously approve the action of the state and people of the Confederate States of America."

When the southern general assembly, which were holding their sessions in Baltimore in 1888, adjourned to Philadelphia to unite with the northern general assembly in the centennial celebration of the organization of the general assembly in 1788, Rev. Dr. Bullock, the moderator of the southern assembly, repeatedly alluded to the southern church by the appellation of the Presbyterian church of North America. He thus seemed to ignore the United States of America. Was this designed or accidental? Is it true that the name of the southern church has been changed so as no longer to recognize the United States? Has the southern branch ever made a loyal deliverance since their secession and slavery deliverances, or during their existence as a separate organization?

The Northern General Assembly of 1888, adopted the following resolution, *nemine contradicente*:

Resolved, On the near approach of Decoration Day, the day set apart in memory of those, who, during the civil war, gave their lives that the union and the country should not die, this General Assembly desires to put on record its grateful recognition of the inestimable services, the devotion unto death, of these heroic patriot soldiers, and our undying attachment to the great principle for which they fought and died, and with the great multitude of our fellow-citizens to extend our prayerful sympathy to those throughout our whole country to whom this day brings still the memory of immeasurable bereavement.

It is probable that a few leaders in the southern church, if reunion were consummated, would continue a ceaseless agitation which would embroil the church in a perpetual turmoil. Many in the South blindly and implicitly follow the lead of those whom they esteem as "big men." A few southern politicians (not statesmen), ambitious as Lucifer, inflamed that very excitable thing, the southern heart, and precipitated the rebellion in opposition to the wishes and warnings of the conservative and loyal majority. A few ecclesiastical leaders are endeavoring to prevent reunion by threats of secession from the church if it be approved by the majority, and by a resort to tactics, subterfuges, and stratagems, which they will persistently practice in order to compel the majority to yield to them and make an unconditional surrender for the sake of peace.

For these reasons it is probably best to postpone reunion, at least for another decade, when it is to be hoped that sentiments and theories and practices so repugnant and abhorrent to Christians and friends of stable government and human rights, shall have disappeared from the southern church. Then they will be welcomed with open arms and joyful acclamations by the whole membership of the northern church. For this blessed consummation let all true Christians ever devoutly pray. Then will there be indeed a new and regenerated South, relegating into the gulf of oblivion the grim, absurd, and barbarous traditions of the past era, and rising, phoenix-like from her ashes, she will join with the North and the East and the West with glad acclaim in the angel's song "Glory to God in the highest, peace on earth, good will to men." This will be indeed the golden age, the harbinger of millennial glory, which we trust is soon to be ushered in all its fullness and blessedness, to gladden the hearts of all men everywhere, and to unite in bonds of sympathy and love all races and kindreds and tongues and nations to earth's remotest bounds, and to make them one in Christ Jesus.

Since the war I have been very kindly and hospitably received by the southern people while a sojourner among them. They say, "We will gladly welcome northern people as citizens, if they will only let politics alone." I enquired if that meant that northern people who emigrate South must refrain from voting and from holding office. They replied, "That is just what we mean." Said I, "You wish us to purchase citizenship at too great a cost. The exercise of the elective franchise, that badge of freemen, will not be basely bartered for a 'mess of pottage' by the descendants of revolutionary sires who shed their blood on many an ensanguined battle field to secure this priceless boon for themselves and their posterity, to be enjoyed and exercised till the last moment of recorded time."

The reason assigned for this course is, that if a "free ballot and fair count" were tolerated it would change the political complexion of many of the southern states, notably the states of South Carolina, Mississippi, Lousiana, and Florida. The colored people and "scalawags" in these states outnumber the party in power, and the majority of the northern immigrants would doubtless join with them and bring about a political revolution, which, they say, "we must prevent by all the means that God and nature have placed in our power." This is the reason that they contravene the idea of allowing residents among them of northern birth to vote or hold office.

I have found a spirit of intolerance prevailing among the colored people. If one of their number should vote with the dominant party he immediately lost caste and was virtually ostracised. I enquired what punishment would be inflicted upon a renegade colored man. The reply I received, which was vociferously applauded, was, "The women would drive him from the settlement with switches." A missionary sent them, who was not of their party, would not be received as a religious teacher or minister of the gospel. They are very bitter against the white people who defraud them and keep them in peon bondage through the infamous labor contract system, and who defraud them of the exercise of the elective franchise, guaranteed them by constitutional amendment. They are earnestly hoping and praying for deliverance to come. Every American should resent every insult offered to humanity, for if the rights of the lowliest are trampled upon the rights of the highest are not safe.

The day of vengeance and wrath will come perhaps much sooner than the southern people are aware. Many feel as I did, when residing in the Carolinas in 1881 and 1882, that I would be willing, if there were any hope of ultimate success, to shoulder my musket, and throwing down the gage of battle, contend to the bitter end for my God-given and constitutional rights of which I was fraudulently deprived, for I had no more privilege than the darkest African to vote and have my vote counted if I chose to cast my ballot against the dominant party.

Coming events cast their shadows before. This great crime against the genius of free institutions and the republican form of government will not long be tolerated. This stain upon our nation's fair escutcheon will, we opine, be speedily washed away, and, if necessary, in the blood of the offenders.

Before the war I felt certain that slavery was doomed and near its extinction. The insolence of the slave-holders, the increasing rigors and barbarities of slavery, led to the conviction that if God were just and merciful he would not longer tolerate in his providence an institution whose victims, numbered by millions, were subjected to every refinement of cruelty that base men could devise.

There was an additional evidence that redemption was drawing nigh in the fact that the prayers of the oppressed slave for deliverance were daily ascending to the throne of a prayer hearing and prayer answering God, and in the knowledge that millions of humane Christian people, North and South, were fervently imploring God to hasten the time when Ethiopia should stretch out her hands to God, when every yoke should be broken and the oppressed become free, God thus pouring out the spirit of grace and of supplication upon his people, putting it into their hearts to pray mightily for the deliverance of the bondmen, the benign spirit of the age, the quickened conscience of the wise and good, the increase of an enlightened public opinion, the wide dissemination of Gospel truth, the signs of the times, and the fulfillment of prophecy, indicating the probably speedy approach of the millennium—all, all conspiring to the overthrow of this horrid, murderous Moloch; and these elements of its destruction were observable by even the least acute observer.

It is now evident that the moral sense of the nation is aroused to a true view of the enormity of the crime against civil liberty, practiced with bold effrontery, and thus far with impunity, by the southern people, in preventing, by fraud, intimidation, and violence, a free expression of political opinion at the polls by those who have a constitutional right to exercise the elective franchise. The end is near of this great wickedness. Thousands have been murdered at the polls when endeavoring to exercise the rights of American freemen. Had an American citizen who had committed no crime lost his life at the hands of Austrians or Mexicans our government would have speedily instituted a court of inquiry, or have sent a minister plenipotentiary with full powers to investigate the outrage, and see to it that the perpetrators of the crime were brought to speedy and condign punishment; or, failing in this, through the escape of the criminals, the nation whose citizens were the guilty parties would be held responsible for the act which could only be atoned for by an humble apology and ample reparation.

In the South many, very many, of our best and truest men, true to moral principle and loyal to the government, have fallen by the hands of ex-Confederates for this reason and no other, that they were loyal and patriotic—and the government has been silent. Occasionally congress has gone so far as to appoint a committee of investigation. The murderers were proven guilty, but they were not brought to justice, and when the committee returned to make their report to congress these southern murderers slew all who had as witnesses testified against them. What impotence on the part of congress. Can they expect any more witnesses to criminate themselves (in Southern estimation), by testifying against the murderers of loyal men? Many thousands of loyal men have been murdered since the war. Congress has discovered the murderers in numerous instances, but not one of them has been punished, and with impunity they have been suffered to continue their murders by putting to death all who testified against them before the congressional committee. What the object of the congressional investigation was is a mystery difficult of solution. Sometime, "in the course of human events," congressional investigation may be undertaken with some object in view worthy of the great nation whose interests they have been chosen to subserve, and of the citizens of the republic, whose lives and property they should protect by the exercise of all the powers vested in them, whether the endangered persons are citizens of South Carolina or Massachusetts, and without regard to their "race, color, or previous condition of servitude."

Land of great fertility can be purchased in the Gulf states at from two to ten dollars per acre. In the near future the attention of northern people will be attracted to this cheap and productive land, when an exodus from the North to this genial clime, of gigantic proportions, will be inaugurated. Within five years after its commencement ten million robust, energetic Yankees, with all the vim and perseverance of that people will be precipitated upon the South. They will come with their churches, their free schools, and their higher educational institutions. They will come with their innate ideas in regard to civil liberty and human rights. And as iconoclasts they will, with irresistible might, destroy the idols of the southern oligarchs, and establish and cherish civil and religious liberty in its true and highest sense. They will coalesce with the loyal element of the South, thus making it at once dominant politically and ecclesiastically. Then, portraits of the arch traitors, Jeff Davis, and Gen. R.E. Lee, and Stonewall Jackson, et alii., will no longer be found adorning the walls of southern parlors. The portraits of patriots will supersede them. Histories of the war, lauding treason and arguing in favor of the treasonable principles underlying the "lost cause," will be driven from circulation, and thus the minds of the rising generation of southern youth will no longer be poisoned by them. Monuments erected to commemorate the perfidious acts of hostility against the government by perjured rebels will be suffered to fall into decay, or will be removed and destroyed. The southern papers would then be compelled to be loyal, and in their utterances give no uncertain sound.

Chapter Seven

The notorious Col. Smith, under the nom de plume of "Bill Arp," thus writes in the weekly Atlanta Constitution of Jan. 3, 1888: "The northern man ought to say: 'Oh! well, those people down south thought they were right, and they are just as patriotic as we are. . . . Let us begin to pension their soldiers, just as we pension ours. In fact we ought to pay them something for their slaves. England paid for hers when they were set free, and Gladstone, that great and good man, got three hundred thousand dollars for his, and our southern brethren are just as good as Gladstone. The South is looming up, and she will come to the front in a few years. She is solid and always will be," etc. Pension the soldiers of the defunct Southern Confederacy, that military usurpation which marshaled its millions to subvert the government purchased for us at infinite cost by our revolutionary sires! Forbid it, Almighty God! Forbid it, heaven! The servants of the devil might as well make this demand of the judge in the great judgment day: "Reward us as well as those upon the right hand. We served your enemy, the devil. We promoted his interest with fidelity, but heaven has triumphed over us and we found the devil, our lord, a bad paymaster. In his service we have lost all. We staked all we possessed upon the issue of the contest, the supernal powers have triumphed over the infernal, and all is lost. Do thou pay us, even as thou payest thy loyal servants, many of whom at the bidding of our master, the devil, we put to death, and we would have destroyed them all if it had been possible for us to compass their destruction. It is true we have never repented nor confessed that we erred in choosing the service of the devil, and in aiding and abetting his warfare against heaven. But we are in a sad plight. Do thou compensate us for the losses we have incurred in our attempt to subvert thy throne."

Yes, Bill Arp, you ought to be paid. You fought against the government in the interest of human bondage. You strove to sever the Union cemented with the blood of our patriot fathers. In mistaken clemency the government spared the lives of the whole rebellious horde, who strove to raze it to its foundations. Yes, you ought to have been paid long ago, and if you had received your

just deserts you would not now be on terra firma to make a demand so insolent, and with such brazen-faced effrontery.

"If all are pardoned, and pardoned as a mere act of clemency, the very
substance of government is made nugatory," says Isaac Taylor, and, I fear,
with truth. Treason should have been made odious by the death penalty being
visited upon many of the arch conspirators. Now they demand the reward of
loyalty, and compensation for their slaves. Would Gladstone have received
compensation for his emancipated slaves if he had rebelled against his government and inaugurated a civil war to perpetuate slavery? No. When overcome
he would have been blown to pieces from the mouth of a cannon, as were the
leaders of the Sepoy rebellion, and his property would have been confiscated,
including his slaves.

If the penalty due to treason had been inflicted upon many of the chief
conspirators in the South, the survivors would have a more salutary respect
for the government whose mistaken clemency spares their forfeited lives. Now
they live to make the most insolent demands. Now they have reached the
sublime height of arrogance and presumption, by asking for the reward of
loyalty and the same compensation as that nobly earned by those who imperiled their lives in defense of the government assailed by those minions of
treason. What will be their next demand?

Let there be more legislation by congress in the interests of the loyal majority in the South. At least let congress emancipate this loyal majority from their
disabilities imposed by the disloyal and semi-loyal elements who bear rule and
repress all opposition to their peculiar modes and acts against the true principles of civil liberty and human rights. Oh! that God would in His providence
hasten the time when some irenicon may be found, and it can be truly said
of our country,

"Land of happy union, where the East
Smiles on the West in love, and northern snows
Melt in the ardor of the genial South."

Wilkes-Barre, Luzerne Co., Pa., July 4, 1888.
THE SOUTHERN LOYALISTS.

Col. Benj. H. Grierson, of the 6th Illinois cavalry, with his regiment, together with the 7th Ill. and the 2d Iowa, by order of Gen. U.S. Grant, made his
famous raid in April, 1863, from LaGrange, Tennessee, through Mississippi to
Baton Rouge, La. As a result of his operation Gen. Grierson writes: "The
strength of the rebels has been overestimated. They have neither the arms

nor the resources we have given them credit for. Passing through their country I found thousands of good Union men who were ready and anxious to rally round the old flag whenever it was possible. I could have brought away a thousand with me who were anxious to come—men whom I found fugitives from their homes, hid in swamps and forests where they were hunted like wild beasts by conscripting officers with blood-hounds."

Pollard says: In the last periods of the war the demoralization of the Confederacy was painfully apparent. Rich and powerful citizens managed to escape the conscription—it was said in Richmond that it was easier for a camel to go through the eye of a needle than for a rich man to enter Camp Lee. But the rigor of the law did not spare the poor and helpless, and the complaint was made in the Confederate Congress that even destitute cripples had been taken from their homes and confined in the conscription camps without reference to physical disability so conspicuous and pitiful. It was not unusual to see at the railroad stations long lines of squalid men with scraps of blankets in their hands, or small pine boxes of provisions, or whatever else they might snatch in their hurried departure from their homes, whence they had been taken almost without a moment's notice and ticketed for the various camps of instruction in the Confederacy. In armies thus recruited desertions were the events of every day. The conscript, constantly on short rations, sometimes without a scrap of meat, and frequently in a condition bordering on absolute starvation, hearing constantly of destitution at home, and being distressed with the sufferings of his family, was constantly devising plans of escape that he might go to their relief. It was estimated in 1864 that the conscription would put more than 400,000 men in the field. Scarcely one-fourth of this number were found under arms when the close of the war tore the veil from the thin lines of Confederate defence. Thousands of Confederate soldiers were sent by the Confederate government to engage with packs of blood-hounds in the hunt for deserters and conscripts, who, when caught, would desert again at the first favorable opportunity. Thus the army was depleted. The great majority of these conscripts and deserters were Unionists. They hated the Confederate cause with a perfect hatred. Pollard writes in his history: Much has been said of the sufferings, persecutions, humiliations, and spoliations inflicted upon Union men in the South, but when the period arrives for a dispassionate examination of the real facts, the reader of history will be amazed at the moderation of the southern people, more especially of the Confederate government toward a class of persons capable of so much mischief in a society threatened by imminent and fearful peril from within and without. He states as an offset that a system of terror was established in the

North, where public sentiment was unanimous as against the South; opinions only differing as to the best means of reducing the distant rebellion. This system of terror he asserts could only be warranted in the South. The following letter is a specimen of the truculent hatred of the southern secessionist toward the Unionist:

ABINGDON, VA., Oct. 2, 1861.
My Dear Wife:
I have left you and our children in the land of the despot, but God grant that I may soon be able to make the Union men of Kentucky feel the edge of my knife. From this day I hold every Union traitor as my enemy, and from him I scorn to receive quarter, and to him I will never grant any, for they are cowards and villains enough. Brother Henry and I arrived here without hindrance. I have had chills all the way, but I hope to live to kill forty Yankees for every chill I have ever had. I learn that Hardee is still in the Arkansas lines, inactive, and if this proves true I will tender my resignation and go immediately to Kentucky. I hope that I will do my duty as a rebel and a free man. Since I hate the Union men of Kentucky, I hope to begin the work of murder in earnest, and if I ever spare one of them, may hell be my portion. I want to see Union blood deep enough to swim my horse in.
Your husband,
JAMES BLACKBURN.
(Brother of Gov. Blackburn.)

The white Unionists suffered the loss of all things, and for them there is no redress. The Government will not pay for their property destroyed or confiscated by the rebels, nor will they grant them a pension for loss of health caused by their incarceration in rebel prisons, and although many have lost their lives at rebel hands, their families receive no pension. They do not complain of this neglect, but the survivors rejoice in the subversion of rebellion, and feel themselves more than compensated for all their losses by its overthrow. In one settlement in North Carolina there lived a large number of unconditional Union men. Twelve of these men were forced into the army by the conscripting officers. Muskets were given them, but every man of them refused to touch the weapons. Every conceivable insult and outrage were heaped upon them. They were starved, tied up and whipped; still they remained firm to their conscientious convictions. Finally the muskets were strapped to their bodies. One of these men was singled out as especially obnoxious, and whipped unmercifully. The officer in charge was lawless and brutal, and on one occasion ordered him to be shot as an example to others. He called out a file of men to shoot him. While his executioners were drawn up before him, standing within twelve feet of their victim, the latter, raising his eyes to heaven and elevating his hands, cried out in a loud voice: "Father, forgive them, they know not what they do." Instantly came the order to fire. But instead of obeying it the men dropped their muskets and refused, declaring that they could not kill such a man. This refusal so enraged the officer that he knocked the victim down and then strove repeatedly to trample him to death under his horse's feet. But the animal persistently refused to step over his prostrate body.

In the end they were marched with the rebel army to Gettysburg. In that battle they remained entirely passive, fired no shot, and trusted in God for preservation. Very early in the action the officer referred to was killed. These men, all unhurt, were taken prisoners and sent to Fort Delaware. Here, by accident, it became known in Philadelphia that a number of Friends were among the captured, and two members of the society went down to inquire into the circumstances, but they were refused permission to see them. They went immediately to Washington, and there obtained an order for their discharge, conditioned upon their taking an affirmation of their allegiance. This opened their prison door. The affirmation made, these martyrs for conscience's sake were released, and coming to Philadelphia were cared for by the Friends of that hospitable city.

In a memorial addressed to President Lincoln by Union officers who were prisoners, occurs this statement in regard to the prisoners of war at Andersonville: "They are fast losing hope and becoming utterly reckless of life. Numbers, crazed by their sufferings, wander about in a state of idiocy. Others deliberately cross the dead line and are remorselessly shot down."

The following is an extract from an official report by Col. D. T. Chandler, formerly an inspector general in the Confederate service, addressed to Col. Chilton, at Richmond, Va., under date of Aug. 5, 1864:

"My duty requires me respectfully to recommend a change in the officer in command of the post, Brigadier General J. H. Winder, and the substitution in his place of someone who unites both energy and good judgment with some feelings of humanity and consideration for the welfare and comfort (so far as is consistent with their safe keeping) of the vast number of unfortunates placed under his control; someone who at least does not advocate, deliberately and in cold blood, the propriety of leaving them in their present condition until their number has been sufficiently reduced by death to make the present arrangements suffice for their accommodation, who will not consider it a

matter of self-laudation, boasting that he has never been inside the stockade
—a place of horrors which it is difficult to describe, and which is a disgrace
to civilization—the condition of which he might, by the exercise of a little
energy and judgment, even with the limited means at his command, have
considerably improved."

The Confederate authorities at Richmond were thus officially notified of
these atrocities, and yet took no action. The conclusion seems inevitable that
they fully approved the measures adopted by the commanding officers at
Andersonville, and also at Belle Isle, which was so immediately under their
eyes that ignorance could not possibly be pleaded.

In the southern prison pens where our soldiers and Unionists were incarcerated, diarrhoea ground out their bowels, scurvy cut off their extremities,
rheumatism racked their bones, the sun parched their skin, the nights chilled
their blood, the storms beat upon them until their garments looked like the
clothing of a scarecrow, and the silent frost stole upon many a one and held
his eyes closed so tightly that the morning sun could not warm to life.

John Beman, a watchman employed on a southern steamboat, who had a
family in Boston, Mass., was arrested by a vigilance committee for the expression of opinions loyal to the United States government. The committee proposed to forgive him if he took an oath to support the southern states. He
indignantly repelled the proposition and said that he would die first, when
they immediately hanged him.

The congressional committee on the conduct of the war report that Major
Bradford, who was captain at Fort Pillow, while being conveyed from
Brownsville to Jackson was taken by five rebels, one an officer, led about fifty
yards from the line of march and deliberately murdered, in view of all those
assembled. He fell instantly, pierced by three musket balls, even while asking
that his life might be spared, as he had fought them manfully and deserved
a better fate. The motive assigned for the murder of Major Bradford was the
fact that, although a native of the South, he remained loyal to his government.
Major Bradford had witnessed the murder in cold blood of three hundred of
his fellow-prisoners after their surrender at Fort Pillow.

Gen. Wm. T. Sherman to the mayor of Atlanta: "I myself have seen, in
Missouri, Kentucky, Tennessee, and Mississippi, hundreds and thousands of
women and children fleeing from your armies and desperadoes, hungry and
with bleeding feet. Now that war comes home to you you feel very differently.
You deprecate its horrors, but did not feel them when you sent car loads of
soldiers and ammunition and moulded shell and shot to carry war into Kentucky and Tennessee and Mississippi, to desolate the homes of hundreds of

thousands of good loyal people, who only ask to live in peace at their old homes and under the government of their inheritance."

Captain Phillips, who captured Florence, Alabama, says, in his official report: "We have met the most gratifying proofs of loyalty everywhere, across the Tennessee, and in North Mississippi and North Alabama, where we visited. Most affecting instances greeted us hourly. Men, women, and children gathered in crowds, shouted their welcome, and hailed their national flag with an enthusiasm there was no mistaking. It was genuine and heart-felt. They have experienced, as they related, every possible form of persecution. Tears flowed down the cheeks of the men as well as of the women."

A British officer, Lieutenant Col. Fremantle, of the Cold Stream Guards, who made a tour of inspection during the war, says: "I met Capt.—, of Duff's Cavalry. The captain was rather a boaster. Some Unionists had crossed the river to Matamoras, Mexico. This captain had made a raid across the river and had carried off some of these 'renegadoes,' one of whom, Montgomery, he had left on the road to Brownsville. General Bee, a brother of General Bee who was killed at Manassas, told me that the Montgomery affair was against his sanction and he was sorry for it. He said that Davis, another renegado, would also have been put to death had it not been for the intercession of his wife. Gen. Bee had restored Davis to the Mexicans. Half an hour after we left Gen. Bee we came to the spot where Montgomery had been 'left,' and sure enough, about two hundred yards to the left of the road, we found him. He had been slightly buried, but his head and arms were above the ground, his arms tied together, the rope still round his neck, but part of it still dangling from a small mosquite tree. Dogs or wolves had probably scraped the earth from the body, and there was no flesh on the bones. I obtained this, my first observation of lynch law, within three hours after landing in America. About three miles beyond this we came to Col. Duff's encampment. He is a fine looking, handsome Scotchman. He received me with much hospitality. Col. Duff confessed that the Montgomery affair was all wrong, but he added that his boys meant well. I was presented to—, rather a sinister-looking party, with long yellow hair down to his shoulders. This is the man who hanged Montgomery. We were treated by all the officers with much consideration. Col. Luckett gave me a letter to Gen. Van Dorn, whom they consider the beau ideal of a cavalry soldier. They said from time immemorial the Yankees had been despised by the Southerners as a race inferior to themselves in courage and in honorable sentiments. Duff's regiment is called the Partisan Rangers. They are armed with carbines and six-shooters. I saw them come in from a scouting expedition against the Indians, 300 miles off. They told me that they were in the habit of scalping an Indian when they caught him, and that they never spared one, because the only good Indian was a dead Indian. This regiment had been employed in quelling a counter-revolution of Unionists in Texas. Nothing could exceed the rancor with which they spoke of these renegadoes, as they called them. When I suggested to some of the Texans that they might as well bury the body of Montgomery a little better, they did not at all agree with me, but said it ought not to have been buried at all, but left hanging as a warning to others. Col. Duff comes from Perth. He was one of the leading characters in the secession of Texas. He said his brother was a banker at Dunkeld. At the consulate, —— , a Texas Unionist, confided his sentiments to me. On the next evening he came to me and said he hoped I would not compromise his safety by revealing to anyone the sentiments he expressed the day before.

"I attended the evening parade and saw Gen. Bee, Cols. Luckett, Buchel, Duff, and —— . The latter, who hanged Montgomery, actually improves upon acquaintance.

"Gen. Bee took me for a drive in his ambulance, and introduced me to Major Leon Smith, who captured the Harriet Lane. After the Harriet Lane had been captured she was fired into by the other ships, and Major Smith told me that his blood being up he sent the ex-master of the Harriet Lane to Commodore Renshaw, with a message that, unless the firing was stopped, he would massacre the captured crew. After hearing this, Commodore Renshaw blew up his ship with himself in her. I met Gen. Bankhead Magruder. He speaks of the Puritans with intense disgust, and of the first importation of them as 'that pestiferous crew of the May Flower!' . . . Mr. Sargent and the judge finished the gin, and the former being rather drunk entertained us with a detailed description of his treatment of a refractory negro girl, which, by his own account must have been very severe. The distance from Brownsville to San Antonio is 330 miles. San Antonio is prettily situated on both banks of the river of the same name. It contains about 10,000 inhabitants, and is the largest place in Texas, except Galveston. The houses are well built of stone, generally one or two stories high. All have verandas in front. In the neighborhood of San Antonio one-third of the population is German, and many of them by no means loyal to the Confederate cause. They resisted by force of arms, but were settled by Duff's regiment. I heard a dispute between—and a German militia general. The latter spoke strongly in disapproval of 'secret or night lynching.' In spite of their hanging, shooting, etc., there is much to like in the southern chivalry.

"An able-bodied male negro in Texas brings $2,500, while a well skilled seamstress is worth $3,500. In the cars I was introduced to General Samuel

Houston, the founder of Texan independence. He told me he was born in Virginia seventy years ago, that he was United States senator at thirty, and governor of Tennessee at thirty-six. He emigrated into Texas in 1832; headed the revolt of Texas, and defeated the Mexicans at San Jacinto in 1836. He then became President of the Republic of Texas, which he annexed to the United States in 1845. As governor of the state in 1860, he had opposed the secession movement and was deposed. He is evidently a remarkable and clever man, and much disappointed at having to subside from his former grandeur. I was introduced to Col. Chubb, who served as coxswain to the United States ship Java. He was guilty of hiring a colored crew at Boston and then coolly selling them at Galveston. I was introduced to Major—, a brother-in-law to the man who had hanged the Unionist, Montgomery. He spoke with some pride of the exploit of his relative. An indignant drayman came to complain of a military outrage. A semi-drunken Texan, of Pyron's regiment, had ordered him to halt; the latter declining to do so, the Texan fired five shots at him from his six shooter. Capt. Foster said that the regiment would probably hang the soldier for being such a disgracefully bad shot.

"We breakfasted a Huntsville. The Federal officers captured in the Harriet Lane are confined in the penitentiary, and are not treated as prisoners of war. This seems to be the system now with regard to officers, since the enlistment of negroes by northerners. My fellow-travelers of all classes are much given to talk about their 'peculiar institution.' They do not attempt to deny that there are many instances of cruelty, and all seem to be perfectly aware that slavery, which they did not invent but which they inherited from us (English), is and always will be the great bar to the sympathy of the civilized world. I have heard these words used over and over again.

I started again by stage for Monroe, La. My companions were a Mississippi planter, a mad dentist from New Orleans (called by courtesy doctor), an old man from Matagorda, buying slaves cheap in Louisiana, a wounded officer, and a soldier. The soldier was a very intelligent Missourian, who told me (as others have) that at the commencement of the troubles both he and his family were strong Unionists, but the Lincolnites by using coercion had forced them to take one side or the other and now there were no more bitter secessionists. This soldier (Mr. Douglas) was on his way to join Bragg's army. A Confederate soldier when wounded is not given his discharge, but is employed at such work as he is competent to perform. Mr. Douglas is quite lame, but will be employed at mounted duties or at writing.

"At a charming little town called Minden, I met an Englishman, who deplored to me that he had been such a fool as to naturalize himself, as he was in hourly dread of conscription. Nearly every man in this part of the country has a military title. Remarking upon the prevalence of military titles, Gen. Johnson said, 'You must be astonished to find how fond we are of titles, though we are all republicans, and as we can't get any other sort, we all take military ones.' I find the soldiers sober from necessity, as there is literally no liquor to be got. There is great indisposition upon the part of the Confederates to take prisoners, particularly among these wild Mississippians. One of Henderson's scouts apologized for bringing in a Yankee prisoner by saying that he surrendered so quick he couldn't kill him. Gen. Johnston told me this evening that he had been wounded ten times. He was the senior officer of the old army who joined the Confederates, and he commanded the Virginia army till he was severely wounded at Seven Pines, called Fair Oaks, by the Federals. News arrived this evening of the hanging of a negro regiment with forty Yankee officers. I attended a review by Gen. Hardee. After the review the troops were harangued by Bishop Elliott, in an excellent address, partly religious, partly patriotic. Col. Richmond gave me the particulars of Gen. VanDorn's death. He had ravished the wife of Dr. Peters, and was shot by the aggrieved husband."

This, from a southern newspaper indicates the temper of the times in 1861: "We unhesitatingly say that the cause of justice and the cause of humanity itself demands that the black flag shall be unfurled on every field—that extermination and death shall be proclaimed against the hellish miscreants who persist in polluting our soil with their crimes. We will stop the effusion of blood, we will arrest the horrors of war, by terrific slaughter of the foe, by examples of overwhelming and unsparing vengeance. When Oliver Cromwell massacred the garrison of Drogheda, suffering not a man to escape, he justified it on the ground that his object was to bring the war to a close, to stop the effusion of blood, and that it was, therefore, a merciful act on his part. The South cannot afford longer to trifle. She must strike the most fearful blows—the war cry of extermination must be raised."

The Nashville (Tenn.) Courier published this news item:

"We learn that a squad of twelve men were sent to Franklin yesterday to arrest some Lincolnites. They had collected to the number of fifteen at the house of one of their number, one Bell, and defying the party, fired at them, killing one man by the name of Lee, and wounding one or two more. Our men then charged the house and set fire to it, and all the men in it, it is believed, but two, who escaped, perished in the conflagration."

The act of the Confederate congress for the suppression of the slave trade was couched in the usual terms, but contained a provision for dealing with the negroes found on board the captured vessels, which is somewhat amusing. "If the vessel is cleared from any port in the United States, the president shall communicate with any governor of that state, and shall offer to deliver such negroes to the said state on receiving a guarantee that the said negroes shall enjoy the rights and privileges of freemen in such state, or in any other state of the United States, or that they shall be transported to Africa and there be set at liberty, without expense to the government." The notion of the Confederate states bargaining with Massachusetts or Ohio that a negro shall have all the rights and privileges of a freeman might imply a doubt as to the sincerity of their professions in behalf of the negro. In default of the foreign state accepting this offer, the president was empowered to receive any propositions made for the transportation of the negroes to Africa by private persons; should no such philanthropist offer himself, the president shall cause the said negroes to be sold at public auction to the highest bidder. This is a sad declension from the lofty morality of the earlier part of the clause. This act was passed with entire unanimity by the Confederate congress.

Near the close of the war the Confederate congress called upon the negro for help, offering him his freedom and a quarter section of government land for his services as a soldier. But the offer came too late, the rebellion soon after collapsed. The South, before this, professed to regard freedom as a curse to the negro and slavery as a blessing. O! consistency, thou art a jewel.

The southern leaders had been preparing for years to destroy the Union. Mr. Keitt, of South Carolina, in the convention which met to carry the state out of the Union, said: "I have been engaged in this movement ever since I entered political life." Mr. Inglis said, "Most of us have had this subject under consideration for twenty years." Mr. Rhett said, "It is nothing produced by Mr. Lincoln's election or the non-execution of the fugitive slave law. It is a matter that has been gathering head for thirty years."

Preamble to the Florida ordinance of secession:

WHEREAS, All hope of preserving the Union upon terms consistent with the safety and honor of the slave-holding states has been finally dissipated by the recent indications of the strength of the antislavery sentiment of the free states. This compels Florida to secede from the Union, and to become a sovereign and independent nation, and that all ordinances heretofore adopted, in so far as they create or recognize the confederacy of states called the United States of America are rescinded.

Stephen A. Douglas said: "The question is, are we to maintain the country of our fathers or allow it to be stricken down by those who, when they can no longer govern, threaten to destroy? What cause, what excuse do disunionists give us for breaking up the best government on which the sun of heaven ever shed its rays? They are dissatisfied with the result of the presidential election. Did they never get beaten before? Are we to resort to the sword when we get defeated at the ballot-box? I understand it that the voice of the people expressed in the mode appointed by the constitution must command the obedience of every citizen. They assume, on the election of a particular candidate, that their rights are not safe in the Union. What evidence do they present of this? I defy any man to show any act upon which it is based. What act was omitted to be done? I appeal to these assembled thousands, that so far as the constitutional rights of slave-holders are concerned, nothing has been done and nothing omitted, of which they can complain. There has never been a time from the day that Washington was inaugurated first president of the United States, when the rights of the southern states stood firmer under the laws of the land than they do now; there never was a time when they had not as good cause for disunion as they have today. What good cause have they now that has not existed under every administration. If they say the territorial question—now, for the first time, there is no act of congress prohibiting slavery anywhere. If it be the enforcement of the laws, the only complaints that I have heard have been of the too vigorous and too faithful fulfillment of the fugitive slave law. Then what reason have they? The slavery question is a mere excuse. The election of Lincoln is a mere pretext. The present secession movement is the result of an enormous conspiracy formed more than a year since, formed by the leaders in the Southern Confederacy more than twelve months ago. But this is no time for the detail of causes. The conspiracy is now known. Armies have been raised, war is levied to accomplish it. There are only two sides to this question. Every man must be for the Union or against it. There can be no more neutrals in this war, only patriots or traitors.

"Thank God, Illinois is not divided upon the question. I know they expected to present a united South against a divided North. They hoped that in the northern states party questions would bring civil war between democrats and republicans, when the South would step in with her cohorts, aid one party to conquer the other, and then make easy prey of the victors. Their scheme was carnage and civil war in the North. There is but one way to defeat this. In Illinois it is being so defeated by closing up the ranks. I express it as my conviction before God that it is the duty of every American citizen to rally around the flag of his country."

Gen. Grant says: "In the South no opposition was allowed to the government which had been set up. The Union sentiment was thoroughly subdued."

In Kentucky Valley, Ala., ten Unionists were arrested at their homes, taken to a Primitive Baptist church and tried by the vigilantes, and condemned as submissionists and as traitors to the Southern Confederacy, and immediately shot. Their names were: G. W. Castleman, Eli Paul Manning, Geo. Pentecost, Emory Paden, Rodman Tankersley, Sydney Smith, John Bunyan, Verner Kaiser Knight, Clay Bonar, and David Crockett, Jr.

Like the ferocious tiger when he tastes blood, they started to arrest Louis Saterthwaite, a noted Unionist. Upon reaching his cabin they found it barricaded. They ordered Saterthwaite to open the door. He refused. Going to the woods they procured a large log to be used as a battering-ram to break down the door. As they came within range a well directed volley from the cabin leveled ten of these miscreants in the dust. This unexpected defense caused the assailants to drop their battering-ram and beat a hasty retreat to an adjoining forest. Four of their number were killed outright: Joe Hines, Sam Kendall, Bill Gaddy, and Josh Blue. The others managed to crawl into the woods, but Jo Bardwell, through whose head a buckshot had passed, died the next day. Saterthwaite had with him five friends, staunch Unionists, who resolved to sell their lives as dearly as possible. Their names were Middleton Walker, John Franklin, Alonzo Winston, Morris Jefferson, and Pelham Shelby. Upon the retreat of their enemies they held a council of war and decided that as soon as the twilight deepened into night they would make their escape, and abandoning their homes and families for a time, would follow the polar star till they reached some Union outpost. They well knew that the discomfited vigilantes would soon return with large reinforcements, and they had no hope that mercy would be shown them by these infuriate demons incarnate. Two days elapsed before the vigilantes returned. They came five hundred strong, led by Aaron Bloch, a virulent secessionist, but such was their dread that they did not dare leave the woods. At length, the cannon which they had sent for arrived, and they, with this engine of war, demolished the cabin without demanding a surrender. But the birds had flown and were far on their way toward the Federal lines. A large company for pursuit was organized. Fifty hounds were secured and put on the trail. For four days they followed fast. Saterthwaite and his little band of compatriots had reached the Union lines. The general in command, kindly granting his request, sent out a large force of cavalry to bring in the families of these men and of the ten that were murdered. Six hours after they had left the camp they heard the loud baying of the blood-hounds, indicating the near approach of their foes. Concealing themselves they awaited their advent. Soon they came in full view and in good range. A well directed volley emptied many a saddle. They turned and fled. Pursuit was rapid. Twenty-five prisoners were captured, and many vigilantes were slain. The families were reached and brought into the Federal lines and sent north. As to the twenty-five prisoners, Rufus Curlee, their leader, was compelled to witness the death by hanging of twenty-three of the number. Curlee then met the fate of his confederates in guilt. Gideon Brevoort was recognized by Saterthwaite as a Unionist who was compelled to join this band of pursuers as a guide, in order to save his life. He was brought in with them and at once enlisted in the service of the government in a company of sappers and miners. He was a man of fine physique, and of great physical strength. He proved an invaluable addition to the service. Near the close of the war he was instantly killed by a rebel sharp-shooter, while engaged with others in the construction of a pontoon bridge, and was buried with the honors of war. His comrades erected a monument to his memory. They confiscated a number of monuments found in a marble works in a town near their encampment. Two of their number, marble cutters, engraved on the monument the following: "In Memoriam. Died on the field of honor, March 1st, 1865, Gideon Brevoort, aged 32 yrs. 4 mos. and 15 days."

If we had not removed our encampment, his friends, Seymour Carpenter and Marquis Glover, would have covered the whole monument with laudatory inscriptions and epitaphs.

A letter from his brother, Prof. Franklin Brevoort, found in Gideon's tent after his burial, may be interesting:

MEMPHIS, TENN., Dec. 16, 1864,

Dear Brother:

I have just learned your address. I, too, made my escape to the Federal lines. When the tocsin of war sounded I was teaching in Pensacola, Florida. Teachers and ministers employed in their vocation were by Confederate law exempt from service in the army. When the summer vacation of 1861 came I felt that body, soul, and spirit with united voice demanded rest—a period of absolute freedom from all secular cares and avocations. The duties of the class-room had been peculiarly severe and exacting during the academic year just closed. But the trying ordeal was passed, and vacation had come. Homer and Horace, Virgil and Xenophon, Legendre and Bourdon, Watts and Whately, and all the tomes of ancient and modern lore were consigned for the time to the gloomy alcoves of the library, there to rest in silent companionship till vacation ended and scholastic duties were resumed.

The young men have donned their hunting apparel and hied away to the forest, where the red deer wander, and to the rivers, where the finny tribes abound, and I, whither shall I go? The bow that is kept continually in a high state of tension, and the mind that is never relaxed, lose elasticity and become permanently impaired. The environment has a tendency to recall the duties performed in it, which one wishes wholly to throw off for a time, and thus the benefits of recreation are diminished. It is better, therefore, that needful rest be taken at some place remote from the scenes of labor. New scenes, new faces, new employments divert the mind, and call into action other faculties, and give those that have been overburdened the desired rest. With this end in view I prepared to leave our classic shades and hie away to the home of one of my students, whose warm invitation I felt happy in accepting. On a beautiful morning, just as the auroral brightness was assuming a vermilion hue, sure harbinger of coming day, the colored coachman drove to my door and I was soon outward bound for the home of Jasper Pettigru, whose hospitable residence I was never to reach. The oriole, the mocking-bird, the paroquet flitted from tree to tree, and a great variety of feathered songsters made the forests vocal with their harmony, and by the brilliancy of their plumage encircled our pathway with a halo of glory. One could readily imagine himself in the enchanted land. The balmy air, the fragrant flowers, the silvery sparkling waters, the odor-laden breeze, all contributed to the highest happiness, the most ecstatic delight of the votaries of pleasure—a crowd of whom were with me in the diligence. But ever and anon there came borne upon the unwilling breeze an agonizing sigh, proceeding from the inmost recesses of a bleeding, broken heart—a heart crushed by some sorrow too great to be sustained long and the victim live. I thought perhaps it is a fugitive slave on the top of the diligence who is being returned to his master. When we arrived at Daphne, Ala., where I intended lodging for the night with an old friend, Joe Poindexter, an officer got out of the diligence, ordered a carriage from the livery stable, and obtaining assistance, took a white man from the top of the stage and placed him on the rear seat of the carriage. He said this was a state prisoner whom he was conveying into the presence of Col. Bonham, at Tensas, to be dealt with as he was accustomed to deal with all tories. As my friend lived near Tensas, I mentioned this fact to this man, whose name was Major Samuel Rodney. Major Rodney said he would be glad to have me go with him for company. I at once accepted the proffered favor, having a desire to assist, if possible, this suffering Unionist. When within two miles of Tensas we came to the residence of a gentleman, a friend of Major Rodney, Col. Wardlaw by name (if my memory is correct). A dance was in progress at his house, and he insisted upon Major Rodney's attending the dance. The major said this tory must be delivered tonight to Col. Bonham. "Can't your friend take him in?"

replied the colonel. "Yes, or I can drive in and return," said the major. "You'd miss oceans of fun if you were to do that. Just send him in and let your friend put the team in the livery stable at Tensas. I'll send for it in the morning." I cordially assented to this arrangement.

After driving a few hundred yards I asked my prisoner to give me his story. He replied that his name was Isaac Simpson, that he was a Unionist, and supposed that this would be the last night of his life, as Col. Bonham spared the lives of no Unionists, and that he would not recant his opinions to save his life. I replied, "I, too, am a Unionist." "Glory to God," said the prisoner, "then there is yet hope for me." "Yes, we will survive or perish together." Col. Rodney had given me the key of the prisoner's manacles. I had no difficulty in liberating him. There was no road by which to turn off, so we were compelled to go into Tensas, then bear north, and trust in God for divine guidance. We drove rapidly, and were far, very far from Tensas by daylight. Near Shongalo, Smith Co., Miss., we sold our horses and carriage to a planter for $500, Confederate money. At Tougaloo, Hinds Co., we bought suits of clothes in order to conceal our identity. At Brandon, Miss., we bought tickets for Grand Junction, Tenn., and without any further special adventures reached Cairo, Ill., where we both enlisted in the Federal service. At Brandon I bought a newspaper which gave a description of us, and offered a large reward for our capture.

Prof. Simpson has never yet been able to correspond with his family, nor has he heard what may have befallen them since his arrest; nor have I been able to visit my student friend for whose hospitable mansion I started in what appears, because of the thronging events and various vicissitudes of the past years, to be the "auld lang syne." We hope that soon the bottom will fall out of that rotten old hulk—the Southern Confederacy.

Please write to me at your very earliest convenience and tell me all about yourself.

Your affectionate brother,
FRANKLIN BREVOORT.

On April 29, 1877, occurred the cold-blooded assassination of Judge Chisholm, of Kemper Co., Miss., and the killing of his little son and the wounding of his brave young daughter, aged eighteen, who died of her wounds soon after. This tragedy, and the fact that every physician in the place refused to attend upon her dying father and herself, reveal the state of terrorism which prevailed under the reign of the "White League" in the South.

An armed band of two hundred chivalrous white men attacked this family, and after the brave young girl had, with her right arm, parried the guns of several of those defenders of their rights, which were placed almost against her father's breast, while with the other arm around her wounded father's neck, she received a wound which shattered her right hand and was six times wounded in one of her legs. Her father at last fell, pierced by eleven balls. He still lived, and this heroic girl, though fatally wounded herself, assisted her dying father to their home, a distance of over one hundred yards. Her younger brother of thirteen years of age was shot dead while clinging to his father. Gov. Stone, of Mississippi, refused to send aid and protection to this distressed family. The great crime of which Judge Chisholm was guilty was his staunch adherence to the government, and his attempt to enforce the laws as sheriff of the county.

Near this, Rev. James Pelan, my dear friend and co-presbyter, was murdered because of his avowed Union sentiments, though he was a non-combatant, and only desired to live in quietness and retirement till the contest was decided. We were both members of the Presbytery of Tombeckbee. I was by far less discreet than my friend Pelan. I could not conceal my sentiments by a judicious reticence when in the presence of avowed secessionists. My friend Pelan warned me again and again against rashness and ill-timed expression of opinions which would be sure to bring down upon my devoted head the murderous wrath of the devotees of treason. I still live, but my dear friend Pelan died a martyr to the truth, at the hands of those atrociously cruel men.

When the southern people hate, it is with great intensity; if they love their love is intense. In the war times the secessionists would destroy Unionists as they would vipers or rattlesnakes or water moccasins or cotton-mouths. They had no spark of sympathy or compassion for them. They loved their friends, and would promote their interests in every possible way. They took delight in serving their friends, and I personally owe them a debt of gratitude for much kindness shown me by the southern people during my sojourn among them in the ante bellum days. Any favor I desired was accorded gladly. I never found them deceitful. If they manifested friendship it was genuine, if they did not like anyone they made no pretense of friendship. I found them generous and truthful. A minister in traveling always went directly to a brother minister's house, and invariably met a glad welcome and munificent entertainment. I knew of one exception. The Rev. Mr. Bland, of Memphis Presbytery, visited the city of Memphis, accompanied by his wife. They went directly to the residence of the pastor of the 1st Presbyterian church of that city. They were received in the parlor. It was cold weather and there was no fire in the parlor. After remaining awhile, and receiving no invitation to stay, they left, quite indignant at their uncivil treatment. At the next session of presbytery the attention of presbytery was called to this incivility. The minister guilty of this breach of the rules of hospitality prevailing in the South found it necessary to make a humble apology for his rudeness. He, however, never regained the confidence of his brethren and ere long found it necessary to seek another and distant field of labor.

Mr. Woolley wished to borrow money from a Mr. Goodloe. Mr. John H. Brown, at the request of Mr. Woolley, agreed to become his security. Upon reflection, Mr. Brown changed his opinion in regard to becoming surety for Mr. Woolley, and instead of going to Mr. Woolley and informing him that he had reconsidered the matter and had reversed his decision, he went to Mr. Goodloe and said to him, "When Mr. Woolley comes to you and asks to borrow money, I wish you would tell him that you have no money to lend." Mr. Goodloe replied "I have the money to lend, and, sir, if a d——d lie has to be told you must tell it yourself." This affair becoming known, Mr. Brown lost caste at once in the community.

I knew of four grave elders in a northern church who wished to accomplish a certain purpose which they knew could only be attained by clandestine means. They held a private meeting, and after a full discussion of the matter, agreed upon a false statement, to the principle underlying which at least two of their number were sentimentally opposed.

At the next regular meeting of session, the one designated as spokesman, in solemn tones and with a sanctimonious air, made the statement agreed upon. Upon the presumption of the truth of the statement but one result could follow, and they secured the end desired. Upon the discovery of the falsehood, one of its perpetrators called upon the minister and said he hoped that he would not take offense at what they had done, as they had, at a private meeting, decided that the course they had pursued was the best to be taken under the circumstances. The minister replied that they should have told the truth and have given the real reasons which had led them to desire the end they had secured by falsehood.

"Yes," he replied, "it would have been better. I was opposed to the principle upon which the statement was based. Yes, it would have been better to have told the truth."

"Certainly it would, for you have led your minister to make unwittingly a false statement to the other congregation in his pastoral charge, which, to establish his own veracity, he must publicly correct, and must give his reasons for having been misled. This will necessarily criminate you, and expose your duplicity. It was a sin of no small magnitude to fabricate a falsehood, and, in your official capacity as office-bearers in the church of Jesus Christ, deliberately, and in accordance with your preconcerted scheme announce it as the truth in order to accomplish an end really beyond the realm of your jurisdiction, and thus determine a matter by no means within your province to decide. It would have been the part of true wisdom, even after you had taken your seats as members of session, to have followed the dictates of an enlightened conscience, and the teachings of God's word, and to have uttered nothing but truth, though with the certainty of failure to accomplish your wicked and unhallowed purpose. The end, even though right, which it was not in this case, does not justify the use of such base, craven, cowardly means."

This probably could not have occurred in the South. Lying is not one of their vices. It is regarded as the act of a coward, who has not the principles of a brave and true man. Their sins are open before going to judgment. This probably could not occur again in the North. It was probably an anomalous case, without precedent or parallel. Four church officers, who have been elected as overseers of their brethren in spiritual things, conspiring together to fabricate a falsehood and to palm it off upon their unsuspecting minister as truth, is doubtless an act unparalleled in and unknown to the annals of any other church North or South.

It might be well to state that the spokesman, and probably the chief fabricator of the false statement, was neither born nor bred in America, nor was he brought up within the pale of the Presbyterian church.

Chapter Eight

Gen L. Q. C. Lamar, of the rebel army, once said to me, "The ten commandments are suspended during the prevalence of war." This seemed to be a true statement; at all events the Southern Confederacy ignored them all during its whole wicked existence. "Inter arma leges silent" was its motto and practice, both in regard to Divine and human laws, till God in his providence and wrath blotted out its name as a nation from under heaven—a justly merited doom.

The heroism of the loyal women of the South, in their patient, uncomplaining endurance of persecution, often unto death, is deserving of lasting remembrance. They concealed their husbands, sons, brothers, and lovers from the rage and malice of the secessionists, in swamps, caverns, and mountain fastnesses, and at the risk of life carried them provisions while in hiding. They toiled with their own hands in the field to procure a support for themselves and those dependent upon them. Many sleepless vigils were endured by them while they and those dear to them were every hour environed by fearful peril. They possessed intense convictions. They were women of faith and prayer, and they abounded in good works. The remembrances of those righteous, holy, and loyal women is blessed.

THE NORTH AND SOUTH CONTRASTED.

In the year of our Lord, 1856, I listened to an address pronounced by Col. Jefferson Davis, in Holly Springs, Mississippi, in which he strongly and unequivocally avowed secession sentiments, and urged his auditors to make due preparation for it, as it was an event greatly to be desired and would be an accomplished fact in the near future, as sure as fate. He thus spoke:

"The people of the North and South are not homogeneous and they never have been. From the first the Union was an alliance between two peoples as diverse in habits, manners and customs, and modes of thought as in their climates and productions. The South has always been restive under this bond. There are strong contrasts between the characteristics and idiosyncrasies of the people of each section. These existed in the mother country. The chivalric

Norman Cavaliers settled the South. The Puritans of Saxon origin, exiled and poverty stricken, settled on the cold, rugged, bleak, and inhospitable shores of New England. When I contemplate the hostility of their descendants to our peculiar, patriarchal, popular, and truly beneficent institution—an institution so essential to southern prosperity, and the conservation and development of a high type of civilization, I can look with great leniency upon the persecution and banishment by our ancestors of a people so superstitious, hypocritical, inappreciative, meddlesome, and refractory. They brought the same spirit with them to the new world. They envy us our superior civilization and many advantages. The Norman and the Saxon can never coalesce. They can never live under the same government on terms of equality. The Norman, by his ancestral traditions, by his intellectual superiority and restless ambition, aspires to bear rule and hold the reins of government. And this consummation of his hopes and aims he eventually secures. All history proves this. The Cavaliers have always been the rulers. The Puritans the ruled. There is no common bond of sympathy, no affinity by which to cement the heterogeneous elements into homogeneity. Slavery gives us superiority so patent that the world readily recognizes it. When our citizens travel abroad they are accorded honors never bestowed upon Yankee travelers. Labor to wring by the sweat of the face a bare subsistence out of a barren glebe, leaves upon the features the ineffaceable marks of their plebeian condition and origin. I have seen them abroad aping the manners of the refined and cultured Southron, and northern mudsills is the whispered comment of the courtly European, who cannot be deceived by the exhibition of the stolen livery. The ass's ears protrude from the lion's skin.

"They threaten war if we secede. We would have secession, peaceably if we can, forcibly if we must. If they force war upon us because we spurn with contempt governmental association with them, let them come. We will welcome them with bloody hands to hospitable graves. There is, however, no necessity for any fear that the Yankees will attempt to retain us by force in a Union which we will sever whatever may be the consequences. I will volunteer to shed all the blood from my own veins that will be necessary to be shed because of the secession of Mississippi from the Union. We have submitted too long to Yankee insolence and domination. I long to enjoy the sweets of liberty, and to see my fellow-citizens of Mississippi in the enjoyment of them. I was educated in the North and I regard it as the greatest misfortune my life. I fear that during my sojourn there I adopted insensibly some of their brusque manners and imbibed some of the modes of thought of an inferior people. I think, however, I have gotten quit of them, but it required extraordinary and persistent effort to do so. I would advise our people to patronize no longer teachers and ministers from the North. They insidiously instill sentiments hostile to southern interests. Their students and parishioners are in peril so long as they are under the mental and moral instruction of men born and bred in the abolition states. Our slave-holding population not subject to the necessity of manual labor have all their time to devote to literary pursuits, to the rites of hospitality, and to social and convivial pleasures and recreations. This is impossible among a people toiling for a livelihood, their minds engrossed with the problems connected with the daily supply of their physical necessities, taking thought in regard to what they shall eat, what they shall drink, and wherewithal they shall be clothed. Physical drudgery is their predestined lot, and concomitant mental anxiety attending it precludes the possibility of a high degree of culture and refinement. The otium cum dignitate is found alone in southern society. Slavery removes us far from the untoward condition that militates against advanced thought.

"The slave, the serf, the peasant, the mudsills of society, will always exist to toil and perform necessary physical drudgery. Providence has so ordained it, and has so constituted society. There are the ruler and the ruled, the noble and the peasant, the slave and his master, the employé and the employer. Those who toil and moil, and those who enjoy the fruit of their labor. And we do not wish to rebel at the allotments of Divine Providence. Providence has been kind to us, and we must not surrender our birthright. Cotton is king, and we must see to it that he is not dethroned. We can rule the North better out of the Union than in it. New England avarice will bow the supple knee to our king. They must have cotton. Subvert their manufacturing interests and they perish. They will perforce become tributary to us, and it will be a happy sight to behold the Yankee cringing at our feet, supplicating us for permission to live—his insolence all gone, his moral ideas radically changed, and his hostility to slavery merged into professed love for our peculiar institution. I am not a prophet, nor a prophet's son, but I will venture the prediction that another decade will not pass until all these things will be fulfilled. Heaven speed the day of their complete consummation. Coming events cast their shadows before."

Pollard, the historian of The Lost Cause, thus speaks of an address of President Davis upon the return of the peace commissioners, Hunter, Campbell, and Stevens: "He made a powerful and eloquent address, but in parts of it he fell into weak and bombastic speech, and betrayed that boastful characteristic of almost all his oral utterances in the war. As a writer, Mr. Davis is careful, meditative, and full of dignity; but as a speaker he is imprudent, and in moments of passion he frequently blurts out what first comes into his mind. On this occasion he was boastful, almost to the point of grotesqueness. He declared that the march which Sherman was then making would be his last, and would conduct him to ruin. He predicted that before the summer solstice fell upon the country it would be the North that would be soliciting peace. He affirmed that the military situation of the Confederacy was all that he could desire, and drawing up his figure, and in tones of scornful defiance heard to the remotest parts of the building, he remarked that the Federal authorities who had so complacently conferred with the commissioners of the Confederacy little knew that they were talking to their masters."

A quotation from the same history will be pertinent: "Slavery is the most prominent cause of distinction between the civilizations or social autonomies of North and South. In the ante-revolutionary period the differences between the populations of the northern and southern colonies had already been strongly marked. The early colonists did not bear with them, from the mother country to the shores of the New World, any greater degree of congeniality than existed among them at home. They had come, not only from different stocks of population, but from different feuds, in religion and politics. There could be no congeniality between the Puritan exiles who established themselves upon the cold, rugged, and cheerless soil of New England, and the Cavaliers who sought the brighter climate of the South, and drank in their baronial halls in Virginia confusion to round-heads and regicides. The intolerance of the Puritan, the painful thrift of the northern colonists, their external forms of piety, their lack of the sentimentalism which makes up the half of modern civilization, are traits of character visible in their descendants. On the other hand, the colonists of Virginia and the Carolinas were from the first distinguished for their polite manners, their fine sentiments, their attachment to a sort of feudal life, their landed gentry, their love of field sports and dangerous adventure, and the prodigal and improvident aristocracy that dispensed its stores in constant rounds of hospitality and gaiety. Slavery established in the South a peculiar and noble type of civilization. It was not without attendant vices, but the virtues which followed in its train were numerous and peculiar, and asserted the general good effect of the institution on the ideas and manners of the South. If habits of command sometimes degenerated into cruelty and insolence, yet in numerous instances they inculcated notions of chivalry, polished the manners, and produced many noble and generous virtues. If the relief of a large class of whites from the demands of physical labor gave occasion in some instances for idle and dissolute lives, yet at the same time it afforded opportunity for extraordinary culture, elevated the standards of scholarship in the South, enlarged and emancipated social inter-course, and established schools of individual refinement. The South had an element in its society—a landed gentry—which the North envied, and for which its substitute was a coarse, ostentatious aristocracy, that smelt of the trade, and that, however it cleansed itself and aped the elegance of the South, could never entirely subdue a sneaking sense of its own inferiority. The civili-zation of the North was coarse and materialistic. That of the South was scant of shows, but highly refined and sentimental. The South was a vast agricul-tural country, waste lands, forest, and swamps often gave to the eye dreary picture; there were no thick and intricate nets of internal improvement to astonish and bewilder the traveler, no country picturesque with towns and villages to please his vision. Northern men ridiculed the apparent scantiness of the South, and took it as an evidence of inferiority. But this was the coarse judgment of the surface of things. The agricultural pursuits of the South fixed its features, and however it might decline in the scale of gross prosperity, its people were trained in the highest civilization, were models of manners for the whole country, rivaled the sentimentalism of the oldest countries of Europe, established the only schools of honor in America, and presented a striking contrast in their well-balanced character to the conceit and giddiness of the Northern people. There is a singularly bitter hate which is inseparable from a sense of inferiority, and every close observer of northern society has discovered how there lurked in every form of hostility to the South, the con-viction that the northern man, however disguised with ostentation, was coarse and inferior in comparison with the aristocracy and chivalry of the South."

Pollard states, at the close of his history, that "the Confederates have gone out of the war with the consciousness that they were the better men."

Pollard also states that the people of the South were reduced to terrible straits during the war. He thinks the lowest degree of humiliation was reached when delicate and refined ladies were compelled to perform the drudgery of cooking for themselves and their children to avoid starvation. The whole tenor of southern teaching led to the prevalent belief that manual or mental labor for pecuniary remuneration was degrading. The degradation of labor was dreaded by all classes and conditions of the whites. The colored people were driven to it by the lash.

Manual labor was associated in the southern mind with slavery. In the eleven seceded states forming the Southern Confederacy there were but two hundred and fifty thousand slave-holders. The great majority of the white population were non-slave-holders. Social ostracism was rigorously enforced.

The poor whites were less esteemed by the rich than the slaves. Many of the slaves were more intelligent than they. Notably the house servants, who, by their intimate association with their masters' families, had gained a surprising amount of general information. Many of them were mulattoes, quadroons, and octoroons. They entertained a very low estimate of the poor white, regarding him as much lower in the scale of intelligence than themselves. The cracker and the sandhiller were the objects of their derision. They scorned association with them, and often spoke of them and treated them with scorn and contempt.

The cause of the poverty and illiteracy of the poor whites of the South is easily accounted for by their history and disabilities. Bancroft, the historian, thus speaks of this class:

"A class of people dwell in the southern states whose history and character have received less attention than they deserve. These people have been properly called the poor whites of the South. The original charter of King James, extending from Florida to the present northern boundary of the United States, was divided into two departments, named North and South Virginia. They have ultimately become the North and the South. The South was originally colonized by the Norman element, then esteemed the English aristocracy, while the North was chiefly peopled by the race termed the Saxon, an equality and liberty loving people. The South from the first sought to maintain high and low classes; the North equality. At a certain time the English Government opened its prisons and poured forth a flood of convicts upon the southern colonies. At this period the aristocratic party, both in England and America, was hostile to educating the lower classes.

"Sir William Berkley, an early governor of Virginia, said, 'Every man instructs his children according to his ability;' a method which left the ignorant in hopeless blindness. The instinct of aristocracy dreaded the general diffusion of intelligence, and even the enfranchising influence of the ministers. 'The ministers,' continued Sir William, 'should pray oftener and preach less. But I thank God there are no free schools, no printing, and I hope we shall not have them these hundred years, for learning has brought disobedience, heresy, and sects into the world, and printing has divulged them and libels against the best government. God keep us from both.'" (Bancroft's History, Vol. II.)

The people of the South now became permanently divided into an aristocracy and the convict race of poor whites. The latter, for the want of education, were disqualified to rise, and sank deeper and deeper into wickedness and degradation, lost all spirit of enterprise and self-respect, and became too indolent to seek fortunes or better their condition. In the east they habited along the coasts of North and South Carolina, and near large rivers, as the Great Pedee, Yadkin, and Cape Fear, a climate that favored their indolence. They lived on oysters, crabs, and periwinkles, and had a strange habit of eating clay, hence they were known by the name of clay-eaters. A more substantial subsistence, however, was furnished from half wild hogs and cattle. The former of these subsisted in the woods upon roots and mast, the latter upon browse and range. To these may be added the opossum, fattened upon wild grapes. About the same time with the convicts, the negro race was introduced into this country, which, from the first, was held to be more respectable than the convict race. The traveler, passing up the Pedee on the early steamboats which navigated it, would be surprised to see at night-fall fires lighted up along the banks and on the neighboring hills. Upon enquiring he would be told that these were the encampments of the poor whites for the sake of shad fishing. If he were a European, it would lead him to think of the gypsies of his native country; indeed they resemble the gypsies. Their habits are migratory, they own no real estate, and might, not inappropriately, be called American gypsies. Their want of enterprise and energy has been mentioned. To this, however, there were exceptions. Many picked up courage and beat back to the mountains. The famous county of Buncombe was largely settled by poor whites. Some of these were descendants of depredators and murderers who possessed great energy. The spirit of violence continuing in the veins of some, would reappear in future generations by the law of heredity. Hence from the notorious Buncombe were known to come many notorious characters, so that any violent character in the settlement of the Southwest was commonly slanged with the epithet of "Roarer from Bunkum," and in the same phraseology, a plucky deed was denominated "Bunkum." Some of the most audacious thieves and bloody highwaymen that ever infested the earth emigrated to the South-west from the Pedee and Yadkin. Such were the Puebloes of East Tennessee, and the Harpes of Kentucky. The majority of these people have not the least tendency to acknowledge God or recognize religion. In this they coincide with the gypsies, but profanity uttered in the most trite and distasteful oaths seemed to them a second nature: They practice every vice and have but few virtues. Families of the patrician order, falling into decay, are compelled by force of circumstances to migrate north or to unite their destiny with this class. And many families of poor but respectable people, being unable to educate their children because of the expense attending it, and manual labor being considered disgraceful, gradually sink till they become blended with the poor and vicious whites. Their aristocratic neighbors lend no helping hand to enable them to avoid this catastrophe, and avert a fate worse than death.

In the antebellum days there was not a single free school for the education of youth in the seven states which afterward seceded and organized the Southern Confederacy. The dominant class, the slave-holders, numbered but a quarter of a million. This class ignored the existence of the poor whites, except so far as it was possible to use them, and they ruled with rigor over the blacks, and wishing to extend their domination they determined to rule or ruin the whole United States of America. According to state laws, it was a criminal act to teach a slave to read. Although there was no statutory enactment to prevent the children of the poor whites from receiving instruction, they were debarred from even a rudimentary education by their environment. Free schools were unknown, the slave-holders controlled the schools and rigorously excluded the children of the poor. It seemed an utter impossibility for a child belonging to the lower class to secure an education. Senator McDuffie, of South Carolina, became the patron of a poor white child, and gave him the benefit of the schools. He learned rapidly and became an eminent minister, known to the world as Rev. Jas. H.. Thornwell, D. D. Some ladies educated a poor white boy who is known to fame as Hon. Alexander Stephens. It is not for want of intellectuality, but for lack of opportunity that the children of the poor whites are ignorant. It seems strange that Dr. Thornwell and Alexander Stephens should have become champions of slavery, the institution guilty of oppressing beyond measure the class to which they belonged, and in which they would have remained had it not been for the charity of individuals whose benevolence in this line was a glorious exception to the prevalent sentiment of the southern aristocracy.

I was principal of the high school connected with the Princeton, Ind., graded schools. A number of refugee children belonging to the poor white class of the South attended these schools. They fully equaled the other children in progress in their studies. Afterward I was superintendent of the Cambridge City and Leavenworth graded schools, in the same state, and found many children of refugee families in attendance. These children showed no intellectual inferiority, but kept equal pace with the other children in all their studies. The masses of the people in the South were deprived of every privilege. They were kept in ignorance, that they might not know their wrongs, and they were reduced to and kept in extreme poverty by every possible device, that they might not be able to rise superior to the degradation which their environment had forced upon them. To contemplate this bestial wretchedness, hopeless ignorance, and forlorn condition, filled with joy the souls of the aristocratic slave-holding oligarchy—if it be conceded that they were possessed of souls.

Slave-holders were bitterly opposed to the education of the masses, and used every possible means to prevent their acquiring even the ability to read and write. They desired for their own caste a monopoly of wealth, culture, and everything that rendered life worth living. There were some glorious exceptions to this view. Tishomingo county, in the north-eastern corner of Mississippi, contained many Scotch and Scotch-Irish people. These people were anxious to give their children a good education. There were but few slaves in the county and the majority of the people could not be induced to favor secession.

A Presbyterian minister, who became president of Corona Female College, located in Corinth, Miss., strove by tongue and pen to rouse the people of the state to adopt measures looking to the education of the masses. He delivered an address before the legislature at Jackson, urging upon the legislators the necessity of adopting a free school system for the state, but his efforts were looked upon with disfavor by the slave-holders; some of his utterances had the true ring and were well-nigh prophetic. This divine, Rev. L. B. Gaston, published an article in the Corona Wreath, a monthly periodical, edited by his wife, Mrs. Susan B. Gaston, which I will copy. Its earnest plea for the general diffusion of knowledge among the people only rendered Mr. Gaston unpopular, and failed of convincing men joined to their idol—slavery, that popular education was desirable. This article was published in the July number in the year 1858:

"The idea of universal education is the grand central idea of the age. But in this country no system, however perfect, no enactments, however enlightened, and no authority, however constituted, can attain to the full accomplishment of their object, however praiseworthy and laudable, without the hearty and efficient co-operation of public sentiment. These extracts are taken from Randall's Common School System of New York, and are placed at the head of our speculations on the subject of education, as indicative of our feelings and purposes in adopting it as a standing theme for discussion and remark. It is even now apparent that the current century will be noted in the pages of history for the educational progress made by human family, for the expansion given to the idea that knowledge is power; and for the device and establishment of a comprehensive system of popular instruction. In committing to record its memorable events, it will be the future historian's task to trace the rise of national dominion and grandeur to the introduction of schools for the instruction of the masses, and to contrast the conditions of those states and kingdoms that adopted or rejected the policy. With almost prophetic pen we can predict the attainment of empire to the little kingdom of Prussia, simply from a consideration of the vast moral and intellectual power that is now growing up through the medium of her common school system, which was perfected in 1819. As the past history of the world furnishes no parallel to such a case—a people universally educated in the best literature, science, art, and religion that time has ever produced—we know not how to estimate the force, or calculate the action of her power; but this generation will not pass away before the national policy of Prussia will tell upon the destinies of Europe. We have the light of all past ages to show that a people trained or educated to be of one mind and feeling are irresistible to all surrounding nations not so taught or disciplined. Numbers in this comparison are of minor consequence. Mind has always governed matter, or mere brute force, and so it ever will govern. Regarding this as the order of nature, and looking to the condition and prospects of our own country, our feelings are profoundly stirred with mingled emotion. In one portion of it we find that education is fully appreciated, and the means of dispensing it to all are judiciously applied. The North has always been distinguished for its attention to this great social interest, but within the last thirty years it has made advances that seem to border on perfection. By means of public meetings, addresses, and lectures, teachers' associations and institutes, governors' messages and superinten-dents' reports, the public mind has become thoroughly imbued with the spirit of education. The cities, towns, and populated country have been meted out and districted for schools, within a convenient distance from every man's dwelling, and in some states the school-house door, like that of the church, is thrown open and made free to all of a schoolable age. These measures and appliances that constitute the most powerful machinery for intellectual elabo-ration and development are almost unknown in the South. The work of educa-tion with them is the movement of a spirit, with us it is the operation of a simple sense of expediency. They have accumulated means of knowledge, we are dependent.

"There you may see the evolution of the steam engine in its thousand protean forms, of the steam threshers, and diggers, and reapers, of the Cyclopean gnomes that mould iron like wax, of the machines that sew, weld, stamp, dovetail, bevel, shear, turn, weigh, weave, spin, saw, veneer. We are comparatively destitute of all these mechanical appliances and powers. They have type foundries, book-printing presses, authors, writers, publishers, and other instrumentalities for producing and dispensing knowledge of which we have scarcely any. They furnish our school-books, our center table and library

books, and most of our current and periodical literature. They provide, prepare, and administer the larger portion of our intellectual food, and God never
made a man, much less a people, to receive sustenance without being subject
to the sustainer. While we, therefore, take pride in the North, as a portion of
our country, for the eminence to which it has attained in the world of letters,
and the glory to which it is advancing, we cannot but view with sensations
of alarm the adverse bearing and threatening tendency of its social organism
upon the state and well-being of the South.

"The difference of attention paid to the single matter of education by the
two sections of the Union, North and South, leads directly to the generation
of a strife between them, the most bitter and destructive contests for power
will inevitably grow out of unequal association. The wiser and more crafty
portion will strive to rule its less cultivated and capable associate. To those
who have the discernment to perceive it, this is no longer a philosophical
speculation; it is stubborn and grating fact. The North already holds three of
the four great reins of national control—commerce, manufactures, and legislation. It would soon have the fourth, religion, had not our southern politicians had sense enough (and just about sense enough) to discover what was
going on, and by a sort of wild, vehement clamor, rouse the whole nation to
a feeling of the wrong meditated against our political rights. It remained only
for our pulpit and religious press to become thoroughly abolitionized for the
North to have consummated its purpose—absolute ascendency. But the
resistance of the South, through its politicians, has brought a healthier religious sentiment, and a reaction favorable to it is taking place in our own
country and throughout the world. But this advantage is of small moment,
and will soon pass away, if not husbanded and vigorously improved by a
direct resort to fundamental considerations.

Our stumping politicians as a class are very ordinary men, and as public
teachers are exceedingly unreliable. Generally the braggart and buffoon is
more than a match for the sober, earnest, sound reasoner before the people.
The rank of competition for office is deteriorating and becoming less gifted
in almost every canvass. The great lights of former days have expired, and we
have no successors to Hayne, Crawford, Calhoun, Randolph, Clay, Benton, and
Jackson to lift up and bear onward the banner of the South. In legislation and
governmental policy we can no longer cope with the North. Unrestrained by
constitutions and unchecked by master minds, they will use us at discretion,
and our wisdom will be to bear it. Revolt, secession, or revolution will be
worse than madness; for we can build no Chinese wall high and strong
enough to bar the intercourse or intrusion of neighbors wiser than we are.

We are doomed to degradation low, if we do not change materially the present aspect of things.

"And let us pause to consider what there is innate in man or people to produce such disparity of progress and power. Why are they our masters? Why can they control our labor, dictate our opinions, agitate our passions, and lull us into quiescence as they choose?

"Is it because they are naturally our superiors in whatever advances man over his fellow-man? Has our Yankee brother a clearer head, a sounder heart, and a bigger soul than a southern born? Does he grow up on a more fruitful soil, under a more genial sun, or in a wider field for the expansion of mind and the cultivation of genius? Can we believe that the people who generate and mature such moral monstrosities as Millerism, Mormonism, Free-loveism, Spiritism, Beecherism, women's rights conventions, etc., etc., are the people that Heaven has ordained to be our rulers? Eternal Justice forbid it. And yet we are the strong man shorn and bound—the Philistines are upon us. Why is it so? What is it? We demand, what is it that makes the difference between the North and South. It is simply education. Would that we had a hundred tongues and iron voice to proclaim it till every southern ear should hear it in notes of startling thunder. We are overmatched. We are subdued, and from this thralldom there is no escape by human means, but by the redeeming process of universal education. To have the work partially done—one class taught and another neglected—is only aggravating the evils of our condition. It is quickening the body politic to feel the miseries of its situation, without imparting the ability to obtain relief. We must begin at the foundation if we would elevate the superstructure. We must make capable voters if we would have able representatives. We must be respectable at home if we would command respect abroad. And we must be powerful in intellect if we would prevail in counsel.

"We have thus opened up a subject which we expect to present in some form or other in every following number of this periodical. Its intrinsic merits are sufficient to entitle it to all the consideration we are able to bestow upon it. But we adduce directly the plain, practical reason that addresses every southern man's and every national patriot's heart—the equalization of the different parts of the Union for the integrity and well-being of the whole—that we may secure attention to the subject. We enter a field of discussion to which we see no well-defined limits. The race of man is nearly six thousand years old, and yet the question, What is education proper? has never been settled. Perhaps it cannot be arbitrarily determined, but as an appliance it must be modified and adapted to the varied characters and conditions of men.

But be that as it may be, it is with us an open question. What is education proper for us? By what scheme shall we enlist the teaching talent and subject to discipline the teachable mind of the South? To this investigation we hope to call forth many a competent assistant. We hope to see it occupy a prominent place in the newspapers of the state, and to become a common theme for discussion by candidates before the people. By so doing we hope to prepare the way for our next legislature to take hold of the subject of popular instruction and turn to good account the vast resources at our command for supporting a system of schools that may embrace all classes and conditions of society. We have the materials and means for rearing up the most cultivated, accomplished, refined, polished, and powerful population on earth, for we have a strictly laboring class in the producing and sustaining avocations of life. We could have a most capable operative and managing class, and then a class exempt from manual labor, which by proper mental culture and application would become the glory and defence of the South, and command the respect and admiration of the world. Let there be light."

The wealthy class in the South were not possessed of a high degree of culture. They were much inferior to the educated class in the North. They received their education in northern colleges and seminaries, or of teachers of northern birth and education who had gone south to pursue their vocation. Spending life in a ceaseless round of hilarious social enjoyments and pleasures, and often in dissipation and vicious associations, was not conducive of a high degree of mental culture. It was a lady of wealth and high social position who informed me that she very much feared that there would soon be a resurrection of the negroes. It was a company of aristocratic slave-holders who, upon organizing themselves into the Silver Gray Home Guards, in Jan., 1861, adopted this as one of the articles of their constitution: "Section 2, Art. 3. We will not leave the state of Mississippi unless it be invaded." It was a physician of high standing who informed me that Gen. Albert Sidney Johnson had been killed in the battle of Shiloh. He averred that the femoral artery had been severed below the knee which caused hemorrhage and resulted in death.

Servile insurrections were constantly feared, especially by the female portion of the population. I lodged a few days at the house of Dr. Dunlap, near Holly Springs. Mrs. Dunlap informed me that she noticed a large gathering of their colored people at one of the cabins. Wishing to learn the cause, she slipped round to the back window unobserved, as the night was dark, to play the role of an eavesdropper. A well-dressed burly African, in an earnest tone, was haranguing them after this manner: "I tells you, ladies an' gentlemen, we's all gwine to be free before long. We's all going to enjoy liberty, mos' right away. We won't be slaves no longer an' be whipped an' cuffed by de white folks." "How duz you know all dat?" said White Jim, an octoroon. "Why didn't I hear massa Jeff Davis say so. I done drove him out in de carriage to dat stan' where he 'dressed de people today, an' I hed to wait to bring him back. From what he said de people of de Norf is comin' down to set us free an' dey'll jes mow dese southern people down as dey mows de grass. An' he said de northern people believed in negro 'quality, dat de white folks up dar wuz willing to marry our daughters an' let us marry theirn. Jes be ready, as the hime sez, your redemption draweth nigh." Mrs. Dunlap said: "The doctor, as soon as I informed him of what was going on, went out with a whip and drove off this orator whose incendiary speech had a tendency to incite servile insurrection. He ought to have tied him up and given him five hundred lashes."

In 1856 one slave murdered another. Judge Scroggs, of Holly Springs, inserted a card in the papers asking for information, as he could not find any law to meet the case. Afterward he published a card stating that as there was no law to punish one slave for the murder of another, he had ordered that the culprit receive three hundred lashes, and had sent him home to his master. A physician in Lexington, Ky., forcibly violated the person of a female patient —an octoroon. A moot court was held by the young lawyers of the city, who tried the physician, and the jury impaneled for the occasion condemned him to pay for the oysters. This woman was married, and suffered severe mental anguish because of the crime committed against her virtue, but she could obtain no redress. A planter living in Fayette county, Ky., murdered his wife because she truthfully accused him of infidelity to his marriage vows. The murder was witnessed by forty of his slaves, two of whom were severely wounded trying to save the life of their mistress. The murderer was arrested, tried, and acquitted for lack of testimony, slaves being incompetent by southern law to give testimony in a court of justice. But retributive justice overtook this man a few months after his acquittal. He died at the hands of his brother-in-law.

In the Mississippi bottoms and in mountainous districts, in the everglades of Florida and places not easily accessible, large numbers of maroons make their homes. Here they live in comparative security and raise families. The maroons prefer death to slavery. They have bludgeons with sharp knife blades deftly inserted in the heavy end of them, and woe to the hound that comes within their reach. Those who live upon the mountains are properly called cimaroons. They are very adroit in evading capture, and should they be captured they will induce other slaves to escape with them and become dwellers and troglodytes amid the fastnesses of the mountains, or they will make their home on some hummock near a lagoon, whose shores are embowered by the evergreen cypress, the long-leafed pine, the trailing vine, and the pendent moss. By the aid of the friendly lagoon or bayou they can evade the sleuth-hound, and the fish which abound are readily taken in their skillfully woven nets. By the aid of traps they feast upon wild turkeys, opossums, wild pigeons, and every variety of game. Without the aid of guns the wild deer becomes a victim of their skillfully constructed snares. From a noxious plant indigenous to southern swamps, they manufacture a subtle poison in which they saturate meat and place it near the kennels of hounds. The poison is nearly inodorous and insipid. It is sure death to all animals born blind. The maroons call it "stagger pizen," because the poisoned animal staggers as if intoxicated till almost the last moment of its existence. When pursued by hounds, pieces of meat saturated with this poisonous decoction are thrown on his track by the fugitive as he flies; the hounds devour it with avidity. It is a very active poison. Its fatal effects are speedily developed, and as there is no known antidote the hounds soon die in convulsive agony. Thus many a poor hunted fugitive has been saved from a cruel death, or the infliction of a terrible flagellation with the loss of dear but precarious liberty, at apparently the last moment, even when the hounds were within a mile of their victim, proving the truth of the adage, "Man's extremity is God's opportunity."

Postscript

AMERICAN SLAVERY AS IT NOW STANDS
REVEALED TO THE WORLD.[1]

Whatever may be yet the issue of the American conflict, it will have done two great things, — it will have cast a flood of light upon the condition of the American slaves,—it will have given freedom to great masses of them, if not to all.

Until the secession war broke out, the means of accurately ascertaining the positive conditions of the slave in the United States were scanty, and to a great extent doubtful. On the one hand, we had the representations of masters and of their friends. These were always likely to be warped by self-interest; even when most sincerely meant, to exhibit but a portion of the truth. In all countries the best employers are the most accessible, the most willing to come forward in testimony of the condition of the employed; yet none are generally more ignorant of the worst practices used in their trade. How much more must this be the case in the slave system, where every possible malpractice in the employment of labor must be intensified a hundredfold, by the practically absolute powers of the master, and by the darkness with which he has the right to surround his proceedings. Here evidently those who come into the light of publicity will be those only who have no cause, or think they have no cause, to fear it; and who, living in comparative light themselves, have no idea of what may be passing in the dens of darkness around them. The tendency of slave-owning is, moreover, emphatically, one of insulation. The best of slave-owners as well as the worst would fain have never a neighbor, since all intercourse with other plantations tends to undermine either the slave-owner's moral or his physical authority.

Now slavery has come to be seen at once in all its breadth and in all its detail. Where formerly it could only be outlined or lightly sketched from a few points of view, it may now be photographed in its minutest features, and from every point. The mass of testimony is overwhelming, and may be checked and counterchecked from white to black and from black to white to any extent.

[1] From *Good Words*, edited by Norman McLeod, D.D., and published in Edinburgh and Glasgow, Scotland.

But an ugly picture it offers, look at it how and whence you will. For the result
of all this mass of new evidence is simply this,—that the worst that has been
hitherto said by isolated voices against American slavery, has been abundantly
confirmed; that the distant picture of it has turned out faint and pale beside
the reality; that contact with the "patriarchal institution," so far from convert-
ing one sincere abolitionist from the errors of his ways, or confounding one
dishonest one, has turned into ardent abolitionists, hundreds and thousands
of men who, when they first went down South, were avowedly strong pro-
slavery men.

The legal elements of the slave's condition have long since been known.
They are all mainly summed up in this: He is not a person, but a thing; at least
as towards his master, he or she has no signal honor, no family ties. There is
no punishment under any of the southern slave-codes for the worst outrage
by a master on a slave woman's virtue, on a slave man's marriage-tie; no legal
limit to the uses to which he may put either. The slave has no rights of property; is legally forbidden to develop his intellect by education.

Instead of saying, Because slaves are property they will be well treated, the
true reasoning is, Because slaves are property, therefore they will be ill-
treated, therefore they will surely call forth against them in many an instance
every latent capacity of absolute devilhood which lies in the master's bosom.

Are you sorry that this should be so? God forbid. As is the tree, so is its
fruit. Thank God that men do not gather grapes of thorns, or figs of thistles!
else would they allow the whole world to be over-spread of them. Let the
thorn tear, let the thistle prick, that man may know that they are there simply
to be fought with and rooted out.

Now the worst side of slavery is no doubt the moral side of it. Though it
had no evil physical side to it, it would yet be abominable. Though every slave
had plenty to eat, plenty to drink, good shelter, good clothing, moderate work,
skillful care in sickness, it is yet hideous that a man should not be a man, a
husband not a husband, a father not a father. But the war has shown that the
physical maltreatment of slaves was anything but a rare exception.

An officer, writing from Louisiana to the Boston Transcript, stated that not
one recruit "in fifteen is free from marks of severe lashing," and that "more
than one-half are rejected" (the rejections being themselves more than half
of the number that offer) "because of disability, arising from lashing of whips,
and biting of dogs on their calves and thighs;" whilst Mr. Wesley Richards,
a surgeon, writing May 25, 1863, to the Cincinnati Free Nation, after examining about 700 recruits, says that "at least one-half bore evidence of having
been severely whipped and maltreated in various ways;" some "stabbed with

a knife, others shot through the limbs, some wounded with clubs until their bones were broken," and others had their hamstrings cut to prevent their running off. And General Saxton, in command of the Department of the South (comprising South Carolina, Georgia, Florida), on being examined before the "Freedmen's Inquiry Commission," stated that there was scarcely one of the negroes whose back was not "covered with scars." East and West, it will be seen, the testimony is the same.

The Rev. William Taylor, in a pamphlet on the "Cause and probable results of the Civil War in America," relates the following, which has the advantage of showing the patriarchal institution under its "pious" aspect:

"A dear friend of mine, in my native county, in the Shenandoah Valley, Virginia, was passing the house of a neighbor, and saw in the barn-yard, suspended from a beam . . . a colored woman hung up by her hands. She was nearly naked, had been whipped until she was unable to moan aloud, and had an ear of Indian corn stuck in her mouth as a gag. In that condition she was left hanging till her master should take his breakfast, and have family prayers. My friend went in to see him, and remonstrated in vain to have her taken down, till after the family devotions were over. . . . This pious (?) family I knew well, and their three children, William, Arthur, and Adeline, were taught authority between the ages of five and ten years by being set to whip the said poor woman at will, and she was beaten and scarred up so as to present a most unnatural and hideous appearance."

But these are only the milder mercies of the eastern seaboard. We must go to the dreaded Southwest to find the lashings carried to the pitch of disabling the sufferer—the stabbings, shootings, poundings of limbs with clubs, cutting of hamstrings, of which the surgeons speak. Yet the surgeons had nothing to say but to men, and those living ones. In God's avenging hosts, which we see not, there may be other and more helpless recruits. The Rev. Mr. Aughey, who was a minister in Mississippi at the outbreak of secession, in a work called the "Iron Furnace," tells of some of these. "Mr. Pipkin, who resided near Holly Springs (Mississippi), had a negro woman whipped to death while I was at his house during a Session of Presbytery. Mr. Cole, of Waterford, Mississippi, had a woman whipped to death by his overseer. But such cruel scourgings are of daily occurrence. . . . Mrs. Frederick recently whipped a boy to death within a half a mile of my residence. Old Mr. Cole, of Waterford, Mississippi," (apparently the same patriarch as before referred to) "punished his negroes by slitting the soles of their feet with his bowie-knife. One man he put into a cotton-press, and turned the screw until life was extinct. He stated that he only intended to alarm the man, but carried the joke too far." Of course the laws which exist in every state against the murder or torturing of slaves are about as well observed as might be laws enacted by wolves against sheep-murder, and providing that between wolf and sheep no sheep could be witness. Sometimes, indeed, in this black Southwest, some peculiarly atrocious excess of patriarchalism raises the horror even of the white crowd, and the offender is lynched or his or her home burnt down. But in no single one of the instances above quoted do we find that any punishment was inflicted. When Mrs. Frederick, of Mississippi, whipped her slave boy to death, the coroner's jury returned a verdict of death by cruelty; but Mr. Aughey expressly states that "nothing more was done."

In the real South the lash is evidently a regular daily element of the institution. "I am residing," writes Mr. Aughey, "on the banks of the Yockanookany. In this vicinity there are large plantations, cultivated by hundreds of negroes. . . . Every night the negroes are brought to a judgment-seat. The overseer presides. If they have not labored to suit him, or if their task is unfulfilled, they are chained to a post and severely whipped." Of these overseers the writer has just said: "I never knew a pious overseer — never. . . . Overseers, as a class, are worse than slave-owners themselves. They are cruel, brutal, licentious, dissipated, and profane. They always carry a loaded whip, a revolver, and a bowie-knife." Such are the dispensers of the Southern slave-owners' justice. Of course the terror they excite is extreme; and the writer says he has known an instance of a woman, through fright, giving birth to a child at the whipping-post. It need hardly be said that it is at the option of the overseer to strip the slaves to any extent. "In Louisiana, women, preparatory to whipping, are often stripped to a state of perfect nudity." Black women only, some aristocrat of color may think. "There is a girl," said one Colonel Hanna, a member of Mr. Aughey's church, to the latter, "who does not look very white in the face, owing to exposure; but when I strip her to whip her, I find that she has a skin as fair as my wife." It is thus evidently the habit of these Mississippi patriarchs to strip and whip women as white of skin as their own wives. And the slaves are so fond of the system that "every night," Mr. Aughey tells us, "the Mississippi woods resound with the deep-mouthed baying of the blood-hounds."

Remember always, that, between Virginia, and even South Carolina, on the one hand, and the Southwest on the other, every intermediate stage must be supposed to exist. E. g., Mr. Taylor — a Virginian, let us recollect, of the

Shenandoah Valley, whose wife was brought up in Alabama—mentions an instance in the latter state where a master, riding home with a runaway, flogged the latter with a heavy whip "till he sunk in his tracks, and died within a few hours;" whereupon all the neighborhood sympathized deeply with the patriarch who had lost so valuable a man, and deemed the accident "a warning to niggers to stay at home and mind their own business." "One beautiful Sabbath morning," says Mr. Aughey, "I stood on the levee at Baton Rouge, Louisiana, and counted twenty-seven sugar-houses in full blast. I found that the negroes were compelled to labor eighteen hours per day, and were not permitted to rest on the Sabbath during the rolling season. The negroes on most plantations have a truck patch, which they cultivate on the Sabbath. I have pointed out the sin of thus laboring on the Sabbath, but they plead necessity; their children, they state, must suffer from hunger if they did not cultivate their truck patch, and their masters would not give them time on any other day." But even where the work is not in itself so severe, it is made oppressive by its continuousness. Thus, in the sea islands, where the hours of work were from daylight to five P. M. , there was no cessation of labor allowed for meals, and the slave must eat whatever food he could get without leaving off his hoeing or cotton picking. And those who are most overworked are of course the weakest—those least able to bear it—women and children.

In passing from the physical to the moral aspects of slavery, we are met by the great difficulty that a large portion of its daily working consists really of things such as should not be named among Christian men. It is difficult for us to realize the fact that men and women professing to be Christians should allow other men and women around them, whom they claim as their own property, to gratify their passions like brute beasts, the name of marriage representing a mere temporary relation. In the sea islands, Captain Hooper bears testimony to the fact that "many of the negro men have two or three wives, and children by each." The masters, it is distinctly stated, do not care whether the slave women are married or not, so long as they have children, nor have they, as a matter of fact, any scruple in breaking up such unions. The wife and children of Solomon Bradley, an "Uncle Tom" among the Port Royal negroes, were sold away some years ago, and he never expects to meet with them again.

Between white and colored it is a principle of law throughout the slave states that there can be no legal union. But the number of mixed bloods shows that the white man's horror of "amalgamation" only starts into vitality within the church door. On Port Royal island already the "yellow niggers" form a considerable part of the population. "In almost all the schools," says Mr.

Nordhoff, "You find children with blue eyes and light hair—oftenest yellow."
Yet the description lists found at Hilton Head of the slaves shipped thence
showed that the greater number of these were mixed bloods. Now as such
shipments are almost universally for the dreaded South, it follows that the
"patriarchs" and their overseers send their own offspring to a harsher slavery
than that around themselves. And, owing partly to these shipments of the
mixed breeds, partly to the more unbridled licentiousness of the whites themselves, it appears beyond a doubt that in the South and Southwest the propor-
tion of "white" and "yellow niggers" is far higher than in the eastern states.
Mr. Aughey speaks of preaching "to a large congregation of slaves, the third
of whom were as white as himself," some with red hair and blue eyes. We
remember that slave in Mississippi whose skin, when she was stripped for
whipping, was as white as that of her master's wife. Mr. De Camp, the surgeon above referred to, speaks of having seen standing before him three negro
recruits, in whom the "the most critical examination could not detect the
slightest trace of negro blood." General MacDow says that in the district of
Louisiana which he is writing from, there are very few slaves of unmixed
negro blood. It is notorious that many planters have families of white and
families of colored children, and perhaps give the latter to wait on the former.
Remember always that the chastity of the slave has no legal protection. I
cannot here enter into details; suffice it to say that the slave system has this
enforced incest at the will of the master. But, without descending to such
horrors, let any of my countrywomen picture to herself what must be the lot
of women (often, as we have seen, as white as herself) placed from year's end
to year's end under the absolute control of an overseer such as Mr. Aughey,
and in fact almost all witnesses, describes—"cruel, brutal, licentious," always
armed with the loaded whip, the bowie-knife, and the revolver—liable, too,
at any time, without any recourse under heaven, to be sold or hired out into
harlotry, as is practically done in every southern city—and then say whether
the system in which such things are possible has the right to insult God and
man any longer by its existence.

Treating the slave thus like a brute, none could feel surprised if he were
to become such. The colored witnesses who have been examined before the
Freedmen's Inquiry Commission are very frank on the subject of the moral
condition of their race. The slaves, says Robert Small—a bold fellow, who ran
a steamer, the "Planter," out of Charleston Harbor, past Sumter and its dangers, to join the Federal fleet, a feat which Mr. Nordhoff calls "one of the
bravest and most brilliant acts of the war"—are very envious of one another,
cannot bear to see anyone of their number advanced to any position which

all cannot reach, and will resort to any means in their power to degrade him. They are, as slaves, selfish, cowardly, untruthful, thievish. Though they have strong religious impulses, their religion is little more than sentiment. Even professedly pious slaves have often no scruple in "taking" from their masters —the term "stealing" being reserved for thefts as between themselves—the general argument being that, as their masters take everything from them, they may take back what they can. And let it always be remembered that the negro has no means of self-improvement. A father is known to have received twenty lashes for teaching his son to read. "In Mississippi," says Mr. Aughey, "a man who taught slaves to read or write would be sent to the penitentiary instanter." As a matter of fact, out of the eight thousand slaves whom the occupation of Port Royal threw upon the hands of the Federal government, only a very few had picked up the elements of book learning, and a couple of the older men were able actually to read. And whilst the means of self-instruction are forbidden by law, religious teaching is entirely subject to the discretion of the master. If the preacher does not preach sound patriarchal doctrine he is either hunted out of slavedom or lynched within it.

The jargon used by the slave is of itself sufficient proof of the degradation to which he has been reduced. It is not, like the dialects and patois of our own country, of France, Germany, Italy, a form of speech probably coeval with the language, and which had originally as good a chance of developing into the standard one. It is a mere corruption of the master's language, the fruit of estrangement and neglect.

Such, then, is southern slavery, as it now stands thoroughly revealed to the world—a system which, aiming at treating black men as brutes, not only succeeds in making them such, but generally makes two brutes for one—the white and the black. Mr. Aughey, after an experience of eleven years in eight different slave states, declares that he has "never yet seen any example of slavery" that he did not "deem sinful." He "cannot do otherwise than pronounce it an unmitigated curse" to white and black alike.

There is but one touch to add to the above picture. Bad as it was in itself, slavery was getting worse. South Carolina—the acknowledged pioneer of secession, which tried thirty years ago, by means of "nullification," to throw off the control of the Federal authority; which was the first to declare actual secession, the first to fire upon the Federal flag, the first to reduce a Federal fort by force of arms—is a state which, as one of the luminaries of secession, the Hon. L. W. Spratt, has declared, fairly exhibits "the normal nature of the institution" in a population where the slaves outnumber the freemen by 120,000. Yet in this state the Freedmen's Inquiry Commissioners emphatically declare slavery "has been darkening in its shades of inhumanity from year to year." They found "conclusive evidence that half a century since its phase was much milder than now. It is the uniform testimony of emancipated freedmen from this state, above the age of sixty, that in their youth slavery was a merciful and considerate system compared with what it has been for thirty years past. These old men are bright and intelligent compared with the younger field hands, in many of whom a stolid, sullen despondency attests the stupefying influence of slave-driving under its more recent phase."

And what is true of South Carolina is true of all the South. Within the last quarter of a century especially, slavery, from a mere practice, has grown into a system and a creed. Its economic powers have been calculated to the last figure. It has reckoned exactly what work could be got out of a man at every species of labor—how many years he should "last" at cotton-growing, how many at rice-growing, how many at sugar-growing, etc.; the relative advantages of driving him—i.e., killing him off quick—or husbanding his strength, have been discussed; and food, clothing, shelter, have been regulated with reference to the data obtained. On the other hand—since by one of the most inflexible, most awful, yet most salutary, rules of God's government, those who "set up their idols in their heart, and put the stumbling-block of their iniquity before their face," when they inquire of the Lord, shall always be answered "according to the multitude of their idols," so the South, proclaiming the evil thing slavery to be good, has thought to find its consecration even in that Book which is a message to all mankind of deliverance from every shape of bondage; and it has hardened itself in this faith, and its priests and prophets have been deceived of the Lord to speak lies in its ears, to prophesy unto it the smooth things which it loved, till at last, in its devilish pride, unable to brook the very contact of freedom, it turned away as from an accursed thing, and would fain set up its own model republic, based, said its vice president, "upon the great truth that the negro is not equal to the white man; that slavery, subordination to the superior race, is his natural and normal condition."

And then were seen upon the walls of slavery's palace fingers of a man's hand, writing "Mene, mene, Tekel." Then struck for the Southern slave an hour such as his friends afar off had scarcely hoped to see, but which, with blind God-sent instinct, he seems himself to have been long waiting for. From the moment that the secession flag was raised, slavery, as all see now, was doomed.

And while we may admire the gallantry with which the southern slaveholders have carried on the contest with the North; and may do full justice to the purity of the motives which led a Stonewall Jackson into the thick of so many a fight, we must remember that the heroic defense of Vicksburg or Sumter no more palliates southern slavery than did the heroic defense of Jerusalem by the Jews palliate the crucifixion of our Lord.

J.M. LUDLOW., December, 1863.

MASSACRE OF TEXAN UNIONISTS.

From the time when Twiggs betrayed Texas into the hands of the Confederates, the loyal people of that state suffered intensely from the cruelties of the insurgents. In Western Texas, where there were few slave-holders, and consequently more patriotism, the Union element was very strong and pertinacious, and the inhabitants were both hated and feared by the banditti of the conspirators, who moved over the country with fire and rope, to destroy property and strangle loyal citizens. The sufferings of the Texas loyalists were intensified early in the summer of 1862, after the reverses of the Confederates in Tennessee, when Texas was placed under martial law. The country was scoured by guerrilla bands, who committed the most atrocious crimes, robbing and murdering all who were suspected of being friends of their country. Great numbers of the loyalists attempted to flee from the state to Mexico, singly and in small parties. The earlier fugitives escaped, but a greater portion were captured by the guerrillas and murdered. One of the organs of the conspirators (San Antonio Herald) said exultingly, "Their bones are bleaching on the soil of every county from Red River to the Rio Grande, and in the counties of Wise and Denton their bodies are suspended by scores from the Black Jacks."

A notable and representative instance of the treatment received by the Texan loyalists at the hands of their oppressors is found in the narrative of an attempt of about sixty of them, mostly young Germans belonging to the best families in western Texas, to leave the country. They collected at Fredericksburg, on the frontier, intending to make their way to New Orleans by way of Mexico, and join the national army. On the night of the ninth of August they encamped on the edge of a cedar brake, on the Neuces river, about forty miles from the Rio Grande. They had moved with such secrecy that they scarcely felt any apprehension of danger from the guerrillas who were scouring the country, with orders to kill all Unionists. But they were betrayed and a leader named Duff sent over one hundred men to surprise and destroy them. At near daylight they approached the camp, and captured one of the party. His life was offered him as a reward, if he would lead them to the camp of his companions. He refused and was hanged. The guerrillas then fell upon the patriots, who were sleeping. A desperate struggle ensued, and at length, opposed by overwhelming numbers and superior weapons, the Unionists were conquered, but not till two-thirds of their number were killed or wounded. The survivors fled toward the Rio Grande. Some escaped, and others were captured, tortured, and hung. The wounded already in the hands of the insurgents were murdered in the most barbarous manner, by bullets, bayonets, bowie-knives, and hanging. Some who were actually dying were dragged to trees and hung by the fiends. The commander of the butchers, Lieutenant Lilley, afterward boasted that he killed several of the wounded with his own hands, emptying two revolvers in shooting them. The lives of forty of the sixty young men were sacrificed, at an expense to the murderers of eight killed and fourteen wounded in the battle. When the banner of the Republic gave protection to the loyalists of Texas, three years later, measures were taken to collect the remains of the slain, and bury them. This was accomplished, and a fine monument was erected to their memory.—

"The Civil War in America," by B.J. Lossing, Vol. II page 537.

THE KU-KLUX. —THE STORY OF CAPTAIN ROBERT W. BOONE.
Facts about the Ku-Klux and their outrageous doings startle us most when they come to us in the shape of a personal narrative. When a reliable man can say, "I have seen these things," and can give every incident of events that have only been outlined in the newspapers, his evidence becomes interesting to the people.

Perhaps no man is better qualified to speak of the secret societies of the South, their nature, their aims, and their doings than Captain Robert W. Boone, now in this city. This will appear if we glance at his career, certainly one of the most remarkable shaped by the war and by the events which followed in the South.

Capt. Boone is a native of North Carolina, and a great-grandson of Daniel Boone. He was about fifteen years of age when the Carolinas seceded, and he made his mark by tearing down a rebel flag which had been raised by his brother, a captain in the Confederate service. Encouraged by his mother, he stood firm in his course as a Union man, left the state, made his way to Kentucky, and in a few weeks entered the secret service of the United States army —a department that became so famous and so useful in the army operations in Kentucky and Tennessee.

The old Boone instinct made this boy a good scout, a good pilot, and a good spy. So efficient was he that after the siege of Knoxville he was made a captain, with head-quarters at Knoxville. He operated with his organization or command in East Tennessee, Western North Carolina, Northern Georgia, and South Carolina.

He was captured seven times, and was sentenced to be shot at Salisbury, N.C., in 1862. He scaled the walls of the prison, however, and though shot through the body, escaped. In 1863 he was captured by Wheeler, and was sentenced to be hung at Ashville, N.C. Again he escaped.

During these eight years of service he belonged to eight different Confederate regiments, serving a part of the time as a private, and part of the time as a commissioned officer, and gaining much valuable information. He, of course, had many adventures, and came out with many wounds. He was known then as Charlie Davis, and hundreds of Union officers, piloted by him to the Union lines, rescued by his command from rebel guards or prisons, have good cause to remember him with grateful feelings.

After the war Capt. Davis (Boone) came North, but went to South Carolina in 1869 to organize the detective force of the state. It becoming evident that there was a secret organization of rebel sympathizers, against which the legitimate government could make little headway, Capt. Boone disappeared from South Carolina and appeared in Georgia as a cotton buyer from North Carolina, rebel in sympathy, and violent in his talk against the tyranny of the Federal government. He joined the order then known as the White Brotherhood, whose declared object was the protection of the widows and orphans of deceased rebel soldiers, and whose platform included the banding together of all sympathizers of the Lost Cause for the advancement of personal and political interest. The society, which it was said had organized in Washington, numbered at that time 834,000 members, including all the rebel sympathizers in the South—merchants, lawyers, farmers, traders, mechanics. Hostility to negroes showed itself in violence and outrage, and even the leaders of the organization admitted that in this way only could they intimidate the blacks. Possessing himself of all the signs, passwords, etc., Capt. Boone returned to South Carolina to put the denials of such an organization in that state to the test. He traveled extensively, was recognized everywhere as a member of the order, and saw all their plans and aims from behind the scenes. The society adopted the name Ku-Klux to frighten the negroes, and the reckless men of the order perpetrated outrages that were never mentioned in print. During the years of '69 and '70, ninety-three cold blooded murders were perpetrated in South Carolina alone. Hundreds of negroes and many white men were brutally whipped and otherwise abused. At Lawrence court-house, eighteen men were killed in one day, and the struggle at Newberry was what would have been a slaughter of Union men, had not Captain Boone managed to have troops put in an opportune appearance. In all his observations he collected facts, names, dates. He thoroughly understood the animus of the order, and understood their mode of action. Finally, when his report to the state officers had caused action, the signs and passwords of the order were changed, and suspicion being directed against himself, his usefulness ceased.

His statements made under oath before the investigating committee at Washington and substantiated by the records and by the circumstances of the many cases, and by the testimony of others eminently hostile to him, is a strange chapter in the history of the Southern States. The whole thing in a nutshell is, that the outrages have not been exaggerated, but on the contrary that not one-half have been reported, and, that when reported many of the acts lost something of their brutality because of the absence of the particulars that could not be made public in a newspaper.

The Government did not act in the Ku-Klux business a moment too soon. The Government would have been criminal had it delayed longer. The Government acted with the facts as learned by scores of men like Captain Boone, and as coming in the stories of thousands of persecuted citizens, before its officers, not trusting alone to the excited narrative of refugees. And the time will come when all good men, both North and South, will commend this action of the Government as one of its best deeds.

—*Toledo Blade.*

THE UNITED STATES IN 1984.

"This is a bad world," President Dwight, of Yale, used to say to his Senior class; "but, gentlemen, it is a good world to do good in."

We were reminded of the president's remark on reading the calculations of another clergyman, Mr. F.B. Lincke, one of Queen Victoria's chaplains, who has been ciphering out the destiny of the English-speaking world. After doing a number of hard sums, he comes to the conclusion that, one hundred years from now, there will be nearly as many people speaking the English language as there are now inhabitants of the earth.

He figures it up thus: Great Britain and Ireland, seventy millions; South Africa, sixteen millions; Australia, forty-eight millions; Canada, sixty-four millions; the United States, eight hundred millions; total, nine hundred and ninety-eight millions.

Having arrived at this enormous result, Mr. Lincke enters upon conjectures as to the kind of people those thousand millions are likely to be. He has remarked, in reading the history of the past, that the dream of the philosopher comes true, and he thinks, therefore, that what the best men and women are now striving for with pen, tongue, and hand, will be realized in and by that future multitude.

They will all be in some degree educated. There will be no class deaf to the wisdom of the age, blind to its art, insensible to its aspiration. There will be no estates too large to be a good to the owners, and, as a rule, the farmer will be the owner of the acres he tills; "Landlordism," so far as the naked land is concerned, will not exist. The largest class will be farmers, living on their own land, and holding no more of it than they can utilize.

The nations will live in peace through free-trade and courts of arbitration, knowing no rivalry apart from the generous strife to excel in the arts and the virtues. Instead of contending on the field of battle for vulgar and odious mastery, the nations will, as Victor Hugo has it, give one another rendezvous at International Expositions—the "true fields of battle" for civilized men.

There will be, of course, no such thing as rank or caste, but every honest man will stand in all companies the equal brother of the rest, whether he be scavenger or statesman.

Are these but the idle thoughts of an optimist? *That depends upon us*, who have the honor to inhabit the English-speaking world at the present time. It depends much upon the youngest of us who will live in the dawn of that greater day, and some of whom will be known as all but contemporaries of the thousand millions who will speak our language in 1984.

Index

www.ingramcontent.com/pod-product-compliance
Lightning Source LLC
Chambersburg PA
CBHW020517100426
42813CB00030B/3287/J